11/16   8

D1022245

Integral Consciousness and the Future of Evolution

"This is a very thoughtful, informed and readable book. It will be of great interest to anyone interested in the future of civilization, the planet and the universe itself. It demonstrates wide familiarity with the natural sciences, developmental psychology, political thought, philosophy and spiritual traditions. It is the sort of synthesis that we can all profit from as we face the next century."

—Dr. John Haught, Professor of Theology, Georgetown University,
and author of Deeper Than Darwin

"This book is integral in the best sense: an ingenious gathering of patterns from many fields, giving us a brilliant and useful perspective on the nature of Reality. It is a kind of philosopher's stone in helping us understand emergent evolution, an alchemical vessel that takes our leaden thoughts and turns them into gold. It invites the reader to reconsider his self and his society in the light of universal analogues. Herein we have a work that can open minds as well as hearts to new ways of being and appreciation for who we are and what we yet may be. What is offered here is unique, a new ecology of self, world and soul such as only the ancients ever dared to portray."

—Jean Houston, Ph.D., Author of 25 books in human development, and Senior
Consultant to the United Nations in Human Development

"McIntosh makes a signal contribution to the debate on the direction and nature of evolution, one of the most fundamental issues of our time. He frames his ideas in the context of an integral worldview, likewise a critical aspect of the new understanding. His theory merits sustained consideration and development."

— Dr. Ervin Laszlo, Distinguished system scientist, President of the Club of
Budapest, and author of over 30 books on evolution

"McIntosh has produced quite an impressive synthesis of the leading minds that have contributed to the contours and DNA codes of the emerging "Integral Age." He portrays the work of Clare W. Graves more clearly and accurately than any other person who writes with an Integral pen. McIntosh grasps the essence of Graves's point of view and the dynamics that craft and turn the spiral, serving as a cartographer of the emergence of the integral stage of consciousness. And, his perspective on what many call "world centric" is both informed and realistic. Far too many of those who write about the spiral are naive and simplistic, believing one can simply paper over the deep cultural divides or developmental strata. This book is refreshing, indeed."

— Dr. Don Edward Beck, Co-author of Spiral Dynamics
and Founder of the Center for Human Emergence

"Reading this book is like joining hands with a brother of deep understanding and commitment to our conscious evolution. Steve McIntosh is a powerful guide to applying our integral consciousness to the actual process of self and social evolution. I recommend this book wholeheartedly."
—*Barbara Marx Hubbard*, President, *Foundation for Conscious Evolution*

"Integral consciousness is truly the philosophical and spiritual hope for the new century. It is a powerful new worldview essential for all who profess a serious interest in understanding the world and changing it for the better. McIntosh's book is an educational journey through the fundamentals of integral philosophy and a fascinating exploration of some its most important themes. Carefully researched and tightly argued, this work is an important contribution to a field destined to impact world culture and the direction of human evolution."
— *Carter Phipps*, *Executive Editor*, What Is Enlightenment? Magazine

Integral Consciousness and the Future of Evolution

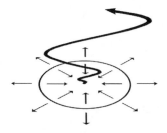

Integral Consciousness and the Future of Evolution

HOW THE INTEGRAL WORLDVIEW IS TRANSFORMING POLITICS, CULTURE AND SPIRITUALITY

Steve McIntosh

PARAGON HOUSE
St. Paul, Minnesota

First Edition 2007

Published in the United States by
Paragon House
1925 Oakcrest Ave, Suite 7
St. Paul, MN 55113
www.paragonhouse.com

Copyright © 2007 by Steve McIntosh

All rights reserved. No part of this book may be reproduced, in any form, without written permission from the publisher, unless by a reviewer who wishes to quote brief passages.

Credits for pictures used with permission in chapter 7: James Mark Baldwin: © University of Toronto; Henri Bergson: © Getty Images; Jean Gebser: © The Gebser Society; Jürgen Habermas: © Jürgen Habermas; G.W.F. Hegel: © Bildarchiv Preussischer Kulturbesitz / Art Resourse, NY; Pierre Teilhard de Chardin: © Getty Research Library; Clare W. Graves © Don Edward Beck; Alfred North Whitehead: © Getty Images; Ken Wilber: © Ken Wilber.

Library of Congress Cataloging-in-Publication Data

    McIntosh, Steve, 1960-
      Integral consciousness and the future of evolution : how the integral
    worldview is transforming politics, culture, and spirituality / Steve
    McIntosh.
      p. cm.
    Includes bibliographical references and index.
    ISBN 978-1-55778-867-2 (hardcover : alk. paper) 1. Consciousness. 2.
    Evolution. I. Title.
    BF311.M4287 2007
    149--dc22
                        2007021976

The paper used in this publication meets the minimum requirements of American National Standard for Information Sciences—Permanence of Paper for Printed Library Materials, ANSI standard Z39.48-1992.

Manufactured in the United States of America
10 9 8 7 6 5 4 3

For current information about all releases from Paragon House, visit the website
at http://www.paragonhouse.com

Dedicated to

Tehya McIntosh

who has added all things needful

Acknowledgments

I WISH TO THANK AND ACKNOWLEDGE: MY FRIEND AND EDITOR, Byron Belitsos, whose literary prowess, breadth of knowledge, and depth of insight have made invaluable contributions to this text; my agent John White; readers and advisers: Lindsay Moore, Jordan Gruber, Chuck Thurston, Carter Phipps, Frank Visser, John Hay, David Zindell, Brad Reynolds, Ben Levy, Kurt Koch, Boyd Willat, Brigitte Mars, and my loving family, Tehya, Ian and Peter, for their patience and endless support.

Contents

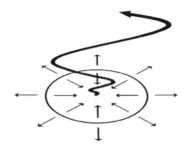

PART I
THE MAIN NARRATIVE

CHAPTER 1

Introduction to Integral Philosophy

FOR THOSE OF US WHO HAVE BEEN ON A SPIRITUAL PATH FOR A while, there often arises a strong desire to try to make a meaningful difference in the world around us. But this outwardly directed urge to service is often dampened when we remember Gandhi's famous saying that "we must *become* the change we want to see in the world," which inevitably leads back to the task of working on ourselves. Nevertheless, those who have managed to make a positive difference in the world (like Gandhi) have always intrigued me. I've always had a passionate interest in the times in history that were marked by dramatic advances. This led me to closely study these periods in which significant cultural evolution—improvement of the human condition—had occurred, searching for clues as to what had actually triggered and sustained this growth.

As I look back on it now, I can see that this interest in cultural evolution has been a major theme in my life; it has determined most of my life choices from an early age. Through my study of history, I initially concluded that *art* was one of the primary levers of social progress. Art had marked the advances of the Renaissance, and in my own lifetime, music had played a significant role in producing cultural evolution. Thus for a long time I concentrated on studying art movements and their role in changing the way people felt and thought about the world. But not only did I study the art movements of the past, I also tried to anticipate the art movements of the future. I experimented with new forms of art and tried to discern the tenets of an emerging new aesthetic; I even started a company with the intention of participating in what seemed at the time to be a significant new art movement. Although this anticipated art movement has yet to fully materialize, these efforts weren't in vain. The company is going strong. But more importantly, this search for the causes of cultural evolution led me to the discovery of a new way of seeing things best described as *integral philosophy*.

Integral philosophy is a new understanding of how the influences of evolution affect the development of consciousness and culture. Although aspects of it have been around for a long time, it's only since the late 1990s that the essential elements of integral philosophy have been coming together into a coherent whole. The power of this new philosophy becomes self-evident to those who use it because it actually raises their consciousness. It's a philosophy of evolution that literally causes evolution. This book, however, is not so much about a philosophy as it is about the results of this philosophy—the newly emerging worldview known as *integral consciousness*.

In this book I argue that a new, historically significant "level" of consciousness and culture is emerging in our time, and that the emergence of this new *integral worldview* is in many ways the evolutionary equivalent of the emergence of the *modernist worldview* during the period known as the Enlightenment of the seventeenth and eighteenth centuries. And just as the rise of modernism changed the world forever, we can expect similar (but more benign) progress from the rise of integralism. "Integral consciousness" is a new perspective on the world that expands our perception of reality and provides fresh motivation to make a positive difference. This new way of seeing and living arises from an enlarged set of values framed by an expanded understanding of cultural evolution.

As we will come to see, when we participate in integral consciousness, when we make meaning from the perspective of the integral worldview and adopt its values, we become endowed with the power to make significant progress in the improvement of both our selves and conditions in our world. Integral consciousness thus promises to produce exactly the kind of evolution that the world needs most. As we consider what form a successful future might take, we begin to realize that without some kind of positive cultural evolution, the future of humanity looks pretty bleak. However, as I will argue in the pages ahead, history shows that cultural evolution has indeed occurred in the past, and the same forces that caused evolution then can thus be reasonably expected to continue into the future. And now with integral philosophy, we are provided with a clearer view of how future cultural evolution is likely to unfold and how we can participate in it directly.

Integral philosophy has emerged out of the various efforts of twentieth-century thinkers to fashion a new philosophy that comes to terms with the staggering facts of evolution itself. Among these philosophers of evolution, two of the most significant are Pierre Teilhard de Chardin (1881–1955) and Alfred North Whitehead (1861–1947). However, despite the enduring contributions of Teilhard and Whitehead, integral philosophy is much more than just a contemporary understanding of these great thinkers. Because these philosophers worked in the first half of the twentieth-century, they were not informed by the more recent insights of systems science and developmental psychology (nor were they informed by each other). Moreover, although the work of Teilhard and Whitehead was far ahead of its time, it came before the significant cultural evolution produced by the emergence of *postmodernism*. The word "postmodern," of course, is a battleground of meaning. But I use this term to describe the overall stage of cultural evolution that has arisen in the last fifty years as an alternative to modernism (which I also define and describe in the pages ahead). As we will see, integral philosophy could not have appeared in its current form before now; its power rests on a host of important insights and developments that have only recently emerged. Today, the most significant proponent of integral philosophy is Ken Wilber, but important contributions are also being made by others, including Don Beck. A summary of the ideas of these writers, together with an overview of the broader lineage of integral philosophy, is found in chapter 7, entitled "The Founders of Integral Philosophy."

Since I began in 2001, I have entirely rewritten this book three times. Part of the problem has been that every time I tried to describe this worldview—to teach the subject of integral consciousness—it has taught me. That is, integral consciousness seems to be a kind of self-organizing dynamic system with a life of its own. Sometimes it seems as though it won't stand still long enough to actually be explained. The growing and emerging nature of the integral world-view is testimony to its status, not as a philosophy in the conventional sense, but as a new vantage point, a new stage of awareness that is just now becoming available.

Integral consciousness is emerging throughout the developed world. And since I began writing five years ago, the integral movement has grown immensely. In the course of writing this book I've corresponded with integral practitioners on five continents; given presentations to sizable audiences; consulted with numerous organizations; read hundreds of related books; attended conferences; and thought and felt about this subject to the maximum extent of my ability. It seems to me that I've been living in integral consciousness for over ten years now, and I can testify that it is what it appears to be: a new, historically significant level of human civilization.

Although I have respectable academic credentials, I'm not a professional philosopher. But as American author Robert Pirsig has observed, most professional philosophers relate to philosophy as art historians relate to art. Professional philosophers are excellent at refining and consolidating existing philosophical systems, but not always as good at creating new philosophy. I use the word "philosophy" very loosely, but in general accord with the dictionary definition of philosophy as "the investigation of causes and laws underlying reality." So my approach to this new philosophy will thus be more pragmatic than academic.

As we will discover in this book, integral consciousness arises from lived values, and when we begin to make meaning from within the integral worldview, this inevitably improves both our inner life and our external circumstances. The enlarged perspectives and clarified values of integral consciousness provide the power to achieve transcendent goals. In fact, this book is the direct result of the increased energy and new ability I have received from this emerging new *structure of history* that is appearing in our time. Yet despite my passion for the power of this new understanding of evolution, my intention is to keep it in objective perspective. While I'm certainly not a "neutral journalist" merely reporting on this interesting development—while I am certainly an advocate of the integral worldview—I also want to ensure that the integral philosophy I'm describing remains in strict agreement with scientific and historical facts.

Critical to my approach is the need to maintain the ethic that keeps integral philosophy free from religious bias. Although integral philosophy has a strong spiritual component, its spirituality is broad enough to include a wide diversity of spiritual beliefs because it is careful to minimize its reliance on metaphysics. Like the three legs of a stool, science, philosophy, and religion each have an important role to play in supporting higher levels of civilization. These different approaches to truth each address distinct and irreducible aspects of human experience that must be accounted for in any integral understanding of reality. And while these diverse fields do well to inform and support each other, like the legs of a stool they must be kept apart; if they come too close together the stool falls over. That is, philosophy must not be limited to only what can be proved by science, nor should it be extended to encompass matters of faith or propositions that must be taken on the authority of a spiritual teacher or a religious text. Integral philosophy is thus informed by science and religion, but it remains respectfully independent of both.

This account of integral philosophy draws on the work of hundreds of other writers and thinkers, yet many of the insights in the pages ahead are original. But as I trust you will come to see for yourself, integral consciousness provides abundant opportunities for original discoveries. As has happened time and again in the history of the emergence of new stages of culture, ordinary people serve to bring forward the new truth, new beauty, and new ideals of morality that always accompany the birth of a new historical level. And if you adopt the integral worldview and begin using it for yourself, I believe you will undoubtedly discover original insights of your own. Just as during the original Enlightenment, when aristocratic amateurs armed with the scientific method were able to make significant new discoveries about the natural world, we can expect that in this *Second Enlightenment* similar discoveries can now be made within the newly understood realm of evolving human culture.

In fact, the most remarkable aspect of integral philosophy is just how practically useful it is. Integral philosophy is increasingly being employed by regular thinking people who are using it to make significant progress in family life, in business, in education, in politics, and in many other areas where evolution is sorely needed. But ultimately, the most useful aspect of the integral way of seeing things is how it actually increases the scope of our awareness. As this book will demonstrate, the integral worldview delivers the power of elevated stages of consciousness. Thus, the "cash value" of integral philosophy is found in its method and practice for permanently raising our own consciousness as well as the consciousness of those around us. The rise of the integral worldview provides a way for us to literally *become the change* we want to see in the world.

While integral philosophy is highly practical and immediately useful, it can also be fairly conceptual and intellectually demanding. So in order to do the subject justice, I've written the book in two parts. Part I, "The Main Narrative," provides an introduction and overview of usable integral philosophy and the new worldview it enacts. If all you read of this book are the 147 pages of the Main Narrative, you'll have a taste of the power of integral philosophy and you'll be able to begin using it. But once you begin to see the world through the illuminating lens of integral consciousness, you'll likely be motivated to explore its deeper aspects, which are described in Part II, entitled "A Deeper Discussion." Part II explores the foundations of integral philosophy and describes the leading edge of its ongoing development. It also justifies and defends the integral worldview by providing answers to the questions of those who may be understandably skeptical about some of integral philosophy's claims.

The Main Narrative begins by exploring the subject of human consciousness. This leads to a broader discussion of what Teilhard called the "within of things"—the *internal universe* wherein the evolution of both consciousness and culture take place. Our discussion of evolution then turns to a brief examination of the important contributions that systems science has made to integral philosophy. With this background in place, we next explore the heart of integral consciousness: the *expanded vertical perspective* that comes from knowledge of the naturally arising stages of consciousness and their dynamic metabolism of values. We'll examine each stage of consciousness that has emerged in human history, including each stage's enduring contributions and debilitating pathologies. Once we have achieved a working understanding of the existing stages of consciousness, we'll then be ready to examine the next significant level of awareness that is now emerging on the horizon of history—the integral stage of consciousness and culture. After spending some time discussing the nature of integral consciousness, we'll explore what it means to live and practice an integral lifestyle. Then in the last two chapters of the Main Narrative we'll discuss the implications of integral consciousness for both politics and spirituality. I focus on these two topics because I believe it is in these areas that integral philosophy will have the greatest impact on our civilization. Following the six chapters of Part I are the four chapters of Part II's Deeper Discussion. However, we'll save the introduction of these chapters until the beginning of Part II, which starts on page 149.

Reading a new book is a large investment, and to be induced to make any investment we must be promised a return. So my promise to you is that if you read and consider the ideas in this book, they will literally raise your consciousness. As we'll explore throughout our discussion, adopting the worldview of integral consciousness actually "wires up" new parts of your brain, and this increase in consciousness is actually a very palpable experience. Of course, because each person's individual experience is unique, I can't tell you exactly how you'll be benefited by this higher state of consciousness—but I can say how it has benefited me: Adopting the integral worldview has caused my experiential awareness to become larger and more complex; I see things now that I couldn't see before. Integral consciousness has endowed me with more energy for life, more compassion for others, more personal power and strategic wisdom, and perhaps most important, integral philosophy has shown me how to participate in what promises to be the most exciting developmental opportunity that will occur during our lives on this planet. And while this may sound hyperbolic, from my perspective this description is an understatement. So I trust that once you have tried on the integral worldview, you too will be unashamedly passionate about its tremendous potential.

CHAPTER 2

The Internal Universe

THE SUBJECT OF CONSCIOUSNESS HAS BEEN THE FOCUS OF INTENSE investigation by philosophers since at least the seventeenth century. Until recently, however, scientists have largely avoided the subject because of the way it tended to undermine their "quasi-religious commitment to the metaphysical principles of scientific materialism." Consciousness doesn't fit into the conventional scientific worldview because it is nonphysical, and thus the fact that its "reality" can't be adequately explained by science has been somewhat of an embarrassment. But since about 1990, due to advances in neuroscience and brain imaging technologies, we have witnessed a "consciousness boom" as scientists have become able to investigate the correlations between brain function and human experience. However, while progress in the science of consciousness is certainly a good thing, in many ways this has only tended to strengthen the conviction of scientific materialists that all human experience will eventually be explained in purely physical terms.

For example, if you go to the University of California at Berkeley and ask John Searle, one of the academic world's leading experts on consciousness, what consciousness is, he will tell you that it is simply a function of the human brain. Professor Searle will admit that much is unknown about the nature of consciousness, but he will also claim that there is a general consensus among academics that mental awareness can be reduced to the physical activity occurring in brain cells, and that it is just a matter of time before science is able to clearly explain how brain states produce the sensations of awareness. Searle and his colleagues reject the idea that "mind" is separate or even much different from matter, and their worldview currently dominates the institutional study of both consciousness and evolution.

However, despite the recent advances in neuroscience, when it comes to the study of consciousness, the scientific materialists have a crucial problem—it's called the "mind/body problem," and it has been recognized as a significant dilemma for over three hundred years. The issue is the undeniable fact that we each have a direct experience of the content of our own consciousness. We know "what it is like" to be us, to have our experiences, to think our thoughts and feel our feelings. Further, this sense of self-awareness carries with it the distinct feeling of an *inside*; each of us has a rich experience of the tremendous depths of our own subjectivity. But from a perspective that sees everything as material and objective, the experiential reality of subjectivity is hard to explain. From the perspective of the integral worldview, however, the mind/body problem is seen as merely a conundrum that arises from the limitations of a materialist metaphysics. That is, the very idea that the universe is purely material, that all phenomena can be explained by or reduced to the laws of physics, is itself highly metaphysical because it is ultimately a proposition that must be taken on faith. As science progresses, it is becoming increasingly clear that materialism is a metaphysical belief system that is just as all-encompassing as a belief system that insists God created the world in six days. And just as the metaphysics of creationism has become evidently wrong, so too is the metaphysics of *scientism*—the materialist belief system that has become an embedded feature of the institutional culture of science.

Many of you may not have a problem with this one-paragraph dismissal of the materialistic paradigm. For many, the absurdity of scientism is self-evident. Yet for others of good sense and good faith, a more realistic explanation of reality has yet to be advanced. Pre-modern cosmologies are clearly mythological, and as we will see, most postmodern ones are hardly coherent. Despite its limitations, the worldview of science has greatly benefited humanity and has brought a tremendous amount of light to our world. So it must be taken seriously—it must be honored and included by integral philosophy if the integral worldview is to produce the kind of significant cultural evolution that it promises. In order for us to move forward into a larger understanding of our world, we now need to find a way to grow beyond the limitations of the scientific worldview while simultaneously bringing along its clear-eyed realism and evident power. Fortunately, this is exactly what integral philosophy does—it *transcends and includes*. It works like evolution itself by carrying forward the best and pruning away the worst of all previous developments. And the task of transcending and including both modernism's materialism and postmodernism's relativism is one that must be done well and done thoroughly by integral philosophy. So throughout this book, and especially in chapter 4 and chapter 8, we will see how the integral worldview overcomes the limitations of these previous worldviews while simultaneously preserving their enduring contributions to human civilization.

But assuming that you don't insist that there is nothing more to consciousness than the electrical activity in your brain, we are ready to broaden our discussion of the nature of consciousness. First, a reasonably safe, one-sentence definition of human consciousness can be stated as follows: Human consciousness is our experiential awareness, consisting of feelings, thoughts, intentions, and our personal sense of identity.

Although consciousness is definitely real, it is not a *substance*—consciousness isn't "stuff." Yet it's more than just a "clear emptiness," merely disclosing that which it contains. Consciousness is the subjective presence of every living person—a presence made precious by the inevitability of its eventual death. Consciousness is contained and upheld not only by its biological host, but also by the culture in which it participates. Our bodies "hold up" our consciousness from the outside and our culture holds up our consciousness from the inside. As we will see, the development of consciousness and the development of culture are mutually dependent, and thus their interactive coevolution is best understood when considered together as a whole.

Now there is, of course, more to consciousness than human consciousness. In fact, as a technical matter, the most advanced understanding of consciousness recognizes that some primitive forms of it go "all the way down," that awareness pervades the entire universe and can be found at the heart of every naturally occurring form of universe organization. Human consciousness thus shares a connection with all forms of consciousness. Yet human consciousness is also unlike any other form of consciousness we know of because human consciousness has demonstrated its ability to evolve in ways that do not depend solely on the corresponding evolution of its underlying biology. And it is this unique ability of human consciousness to determine the course of its own evolution that most interests integral philosophy.

The Evolution of Consciousness

Through the accomplishments of science, a relatively complete account of the genesis of the physical universe can now be told. As we look at science's story of the universe (setting aside any consideration of the ultimate source or destiny of this creative unfolding), we can see in the timeline of evolution from the Big Bang onward, long before the appearance of life, how matter came to be organized in increasingly complex arrangements, eventually resulting in the formation of our solar system and our planet. We can see, for example, how the very structure of the periodic table of elements is a biography of preliving matter as it passed through its sequential stages of increasing complexification. Then, once our planet had consolidated, material evolution continued to progress until it produced the dramatic emergence called *life*. Once life appeared, evolution demonstrated new capacities. Life used new methods of development and evolved at a faster pace than matter. Life became increasingly more organized and complex until it produced what can now be recognized as the dramatic appearance of human consciousness.

The evolutionary novelty of humans was not really a biological breakthrough. In fact, the biological differences between early humans and their immediate animal ancestors were barely noticeable. The evolutionary leap constituted by the appearance of humans was *internal*—it came about through the advent of a dramatic new type of *self-consciousness*. This self-awareness, this consciousness of consciousness itself, appears only in humans. It is the emergence of this new self-reflecting ability in humans that marks the real beginning of the developmental domain of cultural evolution. This evolutionary breakthrough is well described by Teilhard de Chardin:

> The being who is the object of his own reflection, in consequence of that very doubling back upon himself, becomes in a flash able to raise himself into a new sphere. In reality, another world is born. Abstraction, logic, reasoned choice and inventions, mathematics, art, calculation of space and time, anxieties and dreams of love—all these activities of inner life are nothing else than the effervescence of the newly-formed centre as it explodes onto itself. …Thenceforward it is easy to decide where to look in all the biosphere to see signs of what is to be expected. We already know that everywhere the active phyletic lines grow warm with consciousness towards the summit. But in one well-marked region at the heart of the mammals, where the most powerful brains ever made by nature are to be found, they become red hot. And right at the heart of that glow burns a point of incandescence. We must not lose sight of that line crimsoned by the dawn. After thousands of years rising below the horizon, a flame bursts forth at a strictly localized point. Thought is born.

The special evolutionary significance of human consciousness is now disputed by some scientific materialists and postmodern academics who often label such thinking as "species-centric." Integral philosophy, however, can see that human consciousness can indeed be distinguished from other types of observable consciousness. It can see that the appearance of human consciousness constitutes an evolutionary breakthrough as significant as the original emergence of life from inanimate matter—because human consciousness is uniquely self-conscious.

Why does this self-consciousness in humans make such an evolutionary difference? It's because with self-awareness comes the ability to take hold of the evolutionary process itself. Through self-reflection, humans have the unique ability to see themselves in perspective within the scale of evolution, and this creates both the desire and the ability to improve their condition relative to the state of their animal cousins. And for generation after generation humans have generally continued to improve their conditions.

The evolutionary significance of human consciousness is clearly demonstrated by the now-obvious fact of global human culture. Development in the complexity of human cultural structures is undeniable. And like the previous evolutionary breakthrough seen in the appearance of life, the appearance of human culture is accompanied by new methods of development and a new pace of progress. Just as life evolves much faster than inanimate matter, human consciousness and culture evolve much faster than life. However, even though the emergence of human consciousness and culture constitute a new domain of evolutionary progress, the methods, habits, and laws of evolution still apply. Indeed, integral philosophy achieves much of its power through its ability to recognize how the influences of evolution are affecting human consciousness and culture in a manner very similar to the way they influence the development of matter and life.

Now we can perhaps all agree that human civilization has developed, and whether this really constitutes true evolution or not is a matter we will discuss below. But, you may ask: What evidence is there that human consciousness has actually evolved much since the appearance of the *Homo sapiens* species forty thousand years ago? Scientists agree that the biology of the human brain has shown few signs of structural development for at least the last ten thousand years. The brain size and overall DNA of the humans who lived during the last ice age are essentially identical to the humans who inhabit the world today. Although there has been practically no biological evolution, there has nevertheless been significant progress in what can best be described as the evolution of the human mind. In the developed world, the amount and complexity of information—the sheer number of words and images—processed by the average citizen is orders of magnitude greater than the quantity of information processed by our prehistoric ancestors. And not only is a modern human conscious of a greater quantity of information, she is also conscious of fine distinctions of quality that would have been lost to her forebears. A modern human's sense of smell or ability to recognize animal tracks may be less than her ancestors, but her ability to discriminate the myriad types of aesthetic experience available today is unquestionably more complex—her access to food, music, art, media, travel, and technology give her a range and degree of choices that are significantly greater than those available to people who lived in the Stone Age. Moreover, educated moderns have a conceptual ability that is not found in tribal peoples; moderns are able to think about themselves and their society from enlarged perspectives that Stone Age peoples clearly do not have.

How do we know this? How can we say for sure that the consciousness of a modern human is "more evolved" than the consciousness of a person living in 8000 B.C.? Well, as we will discuss further in chapter 3 on the "Stages of Consciousness and Culture," numerous studies involving extensive interviews with contemporary indigenous tribal peoples confirm that their thinking and perceiving is largely "representational," that the words they use can usually only match individual objects, not entire categories or larger, more general types of phenomena. As significant research has shown, the consciousness found in most tribal peoples is not capable of thinking in syllogisms or logical types. Comparisons between objects are made purely on the basis of physical attributes, with functional or conceptual similarities being largely ignored. This research does not suggest that there are any biological or racial differences between peoples who live "in different times in history," but it does confirm that there are significant, measurable differences in the development of their respective stages of consciousness.

How does this happen? How is it that our minds can evolve without our brains evolving? As noted, an infant born today has pretty much the same biological equipment as an infant born ten thousand years ago. Yet an infant born today in the developed world will be able to stand on the shoulders of the giants of history and assimilate the lessons of the last five thousand years of human cultural evolution by the time she graduates from college. Obviously, the reason that the consciousness of moderns is measurably more developed than our prehistoric ancestors is that the achievements of each generation have been accumulated and passed on through the development of things such as language, art, and technology. As human culture develops and evolves, human consciousness evolves along with it.

Integral philosophy recognizes that the evolution of human consciousness actually occurs in a distinct "domain of evolution" apart from biology. It can see this in the way that the inside of an individual (her consciousness) can evolve and develop without the outside of that individual (her biology) evolving much at all. Although there are measurable differences in neurological activation (electrical activity) between the brains of primitives and moderns, the biological structure of the brain is effectively the same. Before the appearance of humans, an organism's inside mind and outside brain evolved together in lockstep. For an animal to become appreciably smarter, it had to evolve biologically. But with the advent of humans, the internal domain of consciousness is partially liberated from its biological constraints and is able to embark on the path of a whole new type of mental, emotional, and spiritual evolution. However, the essence of this development is *within* consciousness and culture; it is occurring in a domain that is best described as the *internal universe*.

The "Within of Things"

When we talk about the evolution of stars and planets, or the evolution of life forms, we're talking about the development of visible material structures. But when we talk about the evolution of culture and consciousness, we are talking about development that is for the most part, invisible. We can certainly see outward manifestations of these developments, such as changes in behavior or bigger buildings. But according to integral philosophy, a big part of that which is actually evolving is internal.

I use the word "internal" to refer to what might be understood as "locations" within subjective consciousness and intersubjective culture (which I'll explain below). As noted earlier, we all have a direct experience of the inwardness of our own minds. We use phrases like "in my head" and "in my heart." The experience of an inner life defines what it means to be human. Yet behind the commonplace notion of an external, objective, outside world and an internal, subjective, inner experience is an important chapter in the history of ideas.

Today, we take the idea of "objective facts" and "subjective opinions" for granted. But there was a time in history when most people didn't think in terms of the distinction between objective and subjective. It was the French genius Rene Descartes who really systematized this way of thinking back in the seventeenth century. Descartes methodically questioned the relationship between mind and world, and in answer to his questions he proposed a radical distinction between the physical body and nonphysical consciousness. According to Descartes, mind and matter were distinct entities composed of entirely different substances—matter was natural, and mind was supernatural. This distinction proved very useful at first. The trend of thinking represented by Descartes provided Europeans with a new "objective" way of seeing the world. With mind and matter separated, the objective world could be examined scientifically, it could be studied from the perspective of an "outside observer." Perhaps more than any other single person, it was Descartes who triggered the scientific revolution that resulted in what is now called *modernism.*

The emergence of modernism in the seventeenth century constituted a new stage or level of consciousness. As we will explore more fully in the pages ahead, "modernist consciousness" brought a new way of seeing things; it offered a new set of values, a worldview that was distinct from the more mythological worldview of medieval Christianity that preceded it.

The modernist worldview epitomized by Descartes allowed people to see the world in a fresh way; it opened up the external universe to new discovery. Through the lens of this new philosophy, early modern intellectuals could, for the first time, see things scientifically. And this new way of seeing things, this new scientific method, eventually resulted in unprecedented material progress. The liberated mind of the modernist produced what historian Richard Tarnas calls "spectacularly tangible results." So it is important to look back at this chapter in history because it tells us a lot about what is happening now. Just as the emergence of modernism produced cultural evolution through its new understanding and mastery of the *external* universe, we will soon begin to see how the emergence of the integral worldview will result in similarly dramatic cultural evolution through its new understanding and mastery of the *internal* universe.

As I explain in detail in chapter 8 on "The Integral Reality Frame," today, Descartes' distinction between mind and matter (now known as "dualism") has been largely rejected by the materialists who maintain that mind is just an aspect of matter. So as integral philosophy includes and transcends the scientific worldview, it takes notice of the problems of dualism, and thus avoids naively proposing a return to this way of seeing things. According to integral philosophy, the reality we are familiar with does not consist of a natural world and a supernatural world—the external and the internal are both essentially natural. But although the internal and external are recognized as different phases of the same thing, that "thing" is not merely particles of matter.

Like the evolution of consciousness, the evolution of human culture also has an inside and an outside. On the outside of cultural evolution we have what are defined as the external artifacts of civilization—these include the development of words and languages, tools and technology, art and architecture, and organizations such as governments. These human-made artifacts serve as the external manifestations of cultural evolution. But these artifacts of civilization are obviously not living evolutionary systems; they depend on underlying human relationships to give them life. Words, for example, have no meaning unless there is an agreement between at least two people as to what they mean. Similarly in a human organization, if there are no agreements about shared purposes, the organization usually collapses.

When we look at human culture and ask: "What is it that is actually evolving?" we can see that it's the quality and quantity of connections between people, taking the form of shared meanings and experiences, agreements, relationships, and groups of relationships—these constitute what we might call the organisms of cultural evolution.

This cultural domain of evolution I'm describing is known as the *intersubjective*—it exists between subjects. And these agreements and relationships that are the structures of cultural evolution have their existence in the internal universe. That is, the substance of a human relationship is the experience that is in our minds and also in the minds of others. Relationships exist in the internal space "in between us," not wholly in our minds and not wholly in the minds of those with whom we are related, but mutually inside both of our minds, and often simultaneously. These relationship structures are partially independent from our individual subjective consciousness, but at the same time internal and invisible.

When we think about the idea of an internal and external universe, there seems to be a mismatch. The external universe is vast; it stretches to unknown frontiers of space and time. The objective world "out there" seems so much larger and significant than the subjective world "in my head." And when viewed from this perspective it is no wonder that the scientists who focus on the objective universe often dismiss the nonphysical, internal phenomenon of consciousness as "merely subjective." In the modernist worldview much greater degrees of reality and significance are attributed to objective entities than to subjective entities. However, when we enlarge our conception of the internal universe to include not only the subjective domain of individual consciousness, but also the intersubjective domain of relationships and human culture as a whole, the internal universe begins to look more substantial. It is important to have some idea of "where" the internal structures of cultural evolution actually exist. These systems of human relationships are not "in the air," nor are they merely in our minds. They exist in the intersubjective domain of the internal universe.

The idea of the intersubjective domain of evolution can sometimes be difficult to grasp, but one way to see its significance is to ask: What is real? Well, objects are real, consciousness is real, and relationships are real. Indeed, when faced with death, humans fear the loss of their relationships—separation from their loved ones—as that which they dread the most. Relationships have a definite ontological status—their being is as real as anything else. The difference between a real intersubjective relationship and an imagined (and thus merely subjective) relationship is that real relationships impact us in ways we can't always anticipate or control. Real relationships move us. And the relationships found in the intersubjective domain encompass more than our personal relations with family, friends, and colleagues, they also include what we might call "indirect" relationships—relationships with our favorite authors, artists, musicians, and public figures, living and dead. Indirect relationships can be remote in space or time—they do not require direct contact or real-time communication—yet such relationships can be very significant to our consciousness. Meaningful relationships need not be directly personal to move us; we can engage in meaningful relationships with our heroes by simply allowing their words, deeds, or art to communicate with us in the present. As long as there is communication (even one-way communication), there is a relationship.

A recent example of the evolution of culture produced through the development of indirect intersubjective relationships is found in the significant impact made by the music of Bob Dylan in the 1960s. When Dylan sang "The Times They Are a-Changin'" he "sat behind a million eyes and told them what they saw." His music caused people to agree with him at a deep level of feeling, and those who together formed Dylan's audience found themselves to be in a kind of indirect relationship with each other to the extent that they were all deeply moved. The beauty and truth communicated by the music of Dylan and his contemporaries in the 1960s produced a solidarity of understanding that helped a new type of culture to be born. We can see the importance of these indirect relationships in the evolution of culture when we realize that all culturally significant works are forms of communication, and that the receipt of this communication always creates an intersubjective relationship between the receiver and the person or group that created it.

When we begin to see the evolving reality of not only the objective external universe and the subjective interior of consciousness, but also the intersubjective realm of relationships, this constitutes a significant new way of seeing things. Just as Descartes' vision of the objectivity of external reality resulted in the opening of a new frontier of human progress, so too does integral philosophy provide a new way of seeing things by revealing how intersubjectivity (in concert with subjectivity) comprises the internal universe. This idea of intersubjective evolution emerges out of murky abstraction when we begin to see the presence of living systems within the intersubjective realm exhibited in the reality of human relationships. That is, relationships are the real, evolving, living systems of human culture. And, as we will examine below, this vision of relationship systems is fortified by the integral worldview's recognition and incorporation of the recent discoveries of systems science. As we will see, it is this new understanding of the systems of cultural evolution that endows integral philosophy with the ability to positively impact the condition of human society everywhere.

The diagram shown in Figure 2-1 below illustrates the nested nature of the internal domains of evolution. The concentric circles show how life emerges from inside matter, how consciousness emerges from inside life, and how culture develops, in a way, inside consciousness through the relationships found in the inter-

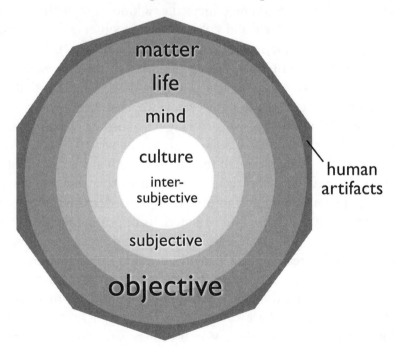

Figure 2-1. The basic types of evolutionary development shown within the essential domains of evolution.

nal domain that exists "in between" the consciousness of individuals. Figure 2-1 also shows human-made artifacts in the objective domain (such as languages, technologies, art, architecture, etc.), because even though artifacts are not natural evolutionary systems, they are significant in the way their development objectifies the intersubjective evolution of culture. This diagram shows all the various types of evolution—the chemical and geological evolution of matter, the biological evolution of life, the personal evolution of consciousness, the collective evolution of culture, and the corresponding development of material artifacts. Figure 2-1 also shows how these different types of evolution fall into three main categories: objective, subjective, and intersubjective. These three great domains of evolution are what Ken Wilber calls "the IT, the I, and the WE"—objective, subjective, and intersubjective, or simply: nature, self, and culture.

Integral philosophy's explanation of the evolving universe, which relies on the recognition of these three evolutionary domains—nature, self, and culture—could be criticized as a kind of metaphysics. And to the extent that "self and culture" are not observable objects, to the extent that these realities are distinguished from "nature," their investigation does literally go "beyond physics." Thus the exploration of these realms can be characterized as "metaphysical," as that term was originally understood. However, as we have seen, a reality frame that insists that nothing is essentially beyond the laws of physics is itself highly metaphysical. So no matter how you try, when you ask questions about the nature of the universe—when you ask questions about the real nature of evolution—you can't avoid metaphysics. Whether your viewpoint is informed by premodern mythology, early modern dualism, late modern materialism, postmodern subjectivism, or integral philosophy's recognition of objective, subjective, and intersubjective realms, it is framed by assumptions that are essentially metaphysical. However, the idea of the objective, subjective, and intersubjective domains of evolution seems far less metaphysical when we see how these categories are simply descriptions of the different types of evolution. Matter evolves, life evolves, consciousness evolves, and human history evolves, and these different types of evolutionary activity are what make these categories real.

So although we cannot completely avoid metaphysics, we can continually refine our metaphysical understanding through observation and agreement. As we'll discuss more fully in chapter 8, integral philosophy strives for a *minimalist metaphysics*, and it is thus careful to avoid becoming just another belief system. Integral philosophy recognizes that while truth is never fully absolute, it is also not completely relative—truth is best understood as an actual direction of evolution in consciousness and culture. So as we strive for a minimalist metaphysics, we hold onto our integral reality frame very loosely, recognizing that it serves merely as the scaffolding for the construction of the next level of civilization.

Nevertheless, we also have to remember why having a conceivable reality frame is important in the first place. History clearly teaches that the emergence of new and more complex worldviews relies on expanded reality frames. As we've seen, during the Enlightenment the new agreement about reality facilitated by Descartes' metaphysics provided the vision that resulted in scientists being able to literally grab hold of the stuff of the external universe, producing the spectacular achievements of modernism. And now, the new metaphysics of integral philosophy promises to produce similarly spectacular advances. As we come to see how culture and consciousness actually evolve, we can likewise grab hold of the "stuff" of the internal universe. With the new understanding provided by the integral worldview we can begin to realistically address the significant global problems that confront our civilization here at the beginning of the twenty-first century. According to integral philosophy, just about every problem in the world can be identified, at least partially, as *a problem of consciousness;* and with integral philosophy we can now begin to see how a key part of the solution to every problem in the world is found in the opportunity to raise or evolve consciousness. As we will explore in the pages ahead, the integral worldview provides a clear vision of how the human condition can be dramatically improved everywhere.

In summary, the period of history known as the Enlightenment opened up the external, objective universe to exploration and discovery. Now in our time, as we look forward into future history, we can see the beginnings of a Second Enlightenment, wherein we can anticipate an "opening up" of the internal universe of consciousness and culture to a similar period of exploration and discovery. While this new frontier of human understanding is largely approached through philosophy rather than science, there is a branch of hard science that extends itself (although tentatively) into the internal universe. And this branch of science, known as systems science, is the subject of the next section.

The Systemic Nature of Evolution

Systems science is indispensable to integral philosophy because it ties together the three great domains of evolutionary activity (objective, subjective, and intersubjective) at a foundational level. It shows how the influences of evolution gain traction in each of the domains of nature, self, and culture, and how evolution has a similar character in each realm, despite the significant differences between them. Through systems science we can now see more clearly how the evolution of consciousness and culture is *real* evolution. The new science of systems has shown us that within the subjective and intersubjective domains, a unified progressive development occurs—a kind of development that employs similar methods and moves in the same directions as the objective forms of evolution observed in matter and life.

Contemporary systems science arose in the 1970s from the attempt to reconcile the apparent contradiction that existed between the fields of physics and biology. In the first half of the twentieth century, physicists maintained that the universe was "winding down" as a result of the incessant decay of entropy. Biologists, however, demonstrated that life somehow defied this tendency of energy dissipation by actually "winding up"—by developing over time into increasingly higher states of organization. This division between the sciences of physics and biology was not fully reconciled until it was discovered that, like life, certain aspects of matter also "wind up." System science's breakthrough came from the discovery that all evolution in the universe occurs through the processes of *self-organizing dynamic systems* that channel or metabolize energy as a method of developing and maintaining their organization.

Systems science's success in unifying physics and biology through a greater understanding of evolution was then carried forward in an attempt to unify the physical sciences with the social sciences. According to prominent systems scientist Ervin Laszlo:

> Scientific evidence of the patterns traced by evolution in the physical universe, in the living world, and even in the world of history is growing rapidly. It is coalescing into the image of basic regularities that repeat and recur. It is now possible to search out these regularities and obtain a glimpse of the fundamental nature of evolution—of the evolution of the cosmos as a whole, including the living world and the world of human social history. To search out and systematically state these regularities is to engage in the creation of a "grand synthesis" that unifies physical, biological, and social evolution into a consistent framework with its own laws and logic.

The "grand synthesis" claimed by Laszlo and other systems scientists is, however, incomplete. In their attempts to produce "good science," systems scientists focused primarily on what could be seen—what could be empirically demonstrated by sensory evidence. But when it comes to the internal, invisible universe, empirical observation is not an adequate method of discovery. Although the systems scientists recognized the evolutionary significance of consciousness and culture—although they could see that the laws of systems extended into these realms—their sensory-empirical constraints kept them from addressing the depths of the interior side of the equation. This is because the internal universe is known primarily by *interpretation* and not by simple observation. A disengaged observer of the objective phenomena associated with consciousness and culture can never truly know the meanings and values within these realms without some kind of interpretive dialogue. That is, if we want to know the meaning of something, we usually have to ask the people involved what they actually mean; but this is not the kind of research that systems scientists usually do.

These scientists, bound by sensory-empirical constraints, can correctly point out that the development of consciousness and culture exhibits the evolutionary patterns of growing complexity and whole-part hierarchy, but these scientists cannot address the felt presence of quality, the nature of values, or the general richness of the internal realms. In other words, because the evolutionary domains of consciousness and culture are subjective and intersubjective—because they are not external or objective—they can only be *viewed from the outside* by a system of thought that defines itself in objective terms.

Nevertheless, the significant insights of systems theory do form an important pillar of integral philosophy. Understanding the systemic character of evolution disclosed by the new science of systems is thus necessary but not sufficient for the fuller understanding of the evolving universe that we are trying to achieve. I'm bringing in this explanation of systems science here in the Main Narrative because soon we will be examining the series of "internal systems" which are best described as "human worldviews." As we will discuss in detail in the next chapter, historically significant human worldviews are large-scale cultural systems that emerge as a result of the words and deeds of great teachers and leaders. In earlier times in history, worldviews were largely synonymous with religion, but since the Enlightenment, the cultural structures we recognize as human worldviews have grown beyond religious boundaries. Today we can see how these worldview structures are transmitted across generations and come to define the values and cultural orientations of large segments of human society.

One of integral philosophy's most important insights is its recognition of how the distinct worldviews that characterize the sequential development of human history each have a clearly discernible systemic structure. As we will come to see, these historically significant human worldviews (such as modernism or postmodernism) are actually natural evolutionary structures that clearly exhibit systemic behavior. And it is the recognition and understanding of these structures of consciousness and culture that make integral theory so useful and amazing. But without this background understanding of the internal universe and the nature of the self-organizing dynamic systems that inhabit it, our discussion of these worldview structures would lack credibility. However, once we begin to understand how systemic structures arise within the realms of consciousness and culture, the description of the details and dynamics of these structures can be understood within their evolutionary context, and this helps make the truth of their reality more self-authenticating.

Worldview structures can be seen in both the subjective consciousness of individuals and in the intersubjective culture of human societies. Yet although the internal systems of consciousness and the internal systems of culture coevolve together, they are significantly different in character. The subjective system that is the consciousness of every human is self-aware; it has free will and is endowed with spiritual presence. Intersubjective systems (relationships and groups), however, are not self-aware; although they do cohere as systems with a distinct kind of self-organization, they do not have a will of their own. Thus while cultural entities deserve our respect, although these groups require protection and ethical consideration, they do not have the same moral value as an individual. Individuals are the bearers of evolution; they are the ones who ultimately make decisions and bear responsibility.

Nevertheless, when we look for similarities between subjective and intersubjective systems, we find that what they both have in common is a similar kind of "metabolism." A key insight of systems science is that all evolutionary systems maintain their order through some type of energy metabolism. All self-organizing dynamic systems take in energy in one form or another—the organizational integrity of every naturally evolving system is maintained by the energy that flows through that system. For example, we're all familiar with the way living things use energy to maintain their bodies, and we can see how an organism's relationship to the "food chain" of energy nourishment in which it participates serves to define almost every aspect of its form. The way an animal gathers and uses food (and usually how it keeps from becoming food) determines the structure of its body. Thus when it comes to any kind of dynamic system, understanding that system's metabolism is central to understanding the system as a whole. And if it's true that the internal systems of consciousness and culture share many similarities with the external systems of chemistry and biology, we would expect to see some kind of internal equivalent of this critical systemic activity of energy metabolism.

So how do the internal systems of consciousness and culture use energy? What nourishes them? What is the *input* and *throughput* that drives the metabolism of these structures and allows them to maintain their systemic integrity? Well, as we will explore throughout this book, integral philosophy recognizes that the equivalent of energy that nourishes and maintains the internal systems of consciousness and culture consists of *meanings* and *values*. It is through the giving and receiving of meanings and values that the systemic structures of consciousness and culture sustain their ongoing organization. And these systemic structures actually use meanings and values in a manner that is very similar to the way biological systems use physical energy.

When we attempt to understand cultural evolution by recognizing how the structures of consciousness and culture are actually internal, self-organizing dynamic systems that consist and subsist through a kind of value metabolism, this helps us better see the central role that values play in the human evolutionary process. Indeed, one of integral philosophy's most important insights is that the large-scale worldview structures that have provided the stepping-stones of human cultural evolution are essentially systems of values. These structures provide a source of values for large groups of people by defining what and who is valuable, and this has the effect of bringing orientation and direction to the lives of the people who ascribe to that worldview.

As we will explore in detail in the next chapter, it is by recognizing the evolutionary development and systemic character of the worldview structures that comprise our culture that integral philosophy is actually able to impact the internal universe in new and powerful ways. And so it is to an examination of these specific worldview structures that we now turn.

CHAPTER 3

Stages of Consciousness and Culture

DURING THE FIRST HALF OF THE NINETEENTH CENTURY THE Western world was captivated by the writing of the famous German philosopher Georg Hegel. While the philosophers of the Enlightenment had sought to show that the world was divinely created by pointing to the mathematical rationality found in nature, Hegel went further by demonstrating that reason and divine order could also be found in the development of human history. Despite the contradictions and chaos apparent in the historical record, Hegel showed how history unfolds through a dialectical process wherein conflict makes possible the transformation to higher states of organization. And while Hegel's influence faded in the second half of the nineteenth century, his prescient understanding of the dialectical structure of history began to be validated during the twentieth century through research in the social sciences, and especially in the field of developmental psychology. Developmental psychology serves as an important foundation of integral philosophy because it discloses the stage-wise development of all historically significant worldview structures. That is, the structures that organize consciousness are directly related to the stages of human history. And as we'll explore in this chapter and the next, the expanded vertical perspective that can see the stages of human history within the minds of individuals is the focal point of integral consciousness.

We have all had a direct experience of the development of our own consciousness because we have all grown up from childhood. Our experience of this development includes a sense in which our values have evolved, our perspectives have changed, and our thoughts, feelings, and sense of self have become more sophisticated and complex. The great contribution of developmental psychology has been its demonstration that this growth in consciousness proceeds through discreet, universal stages of development. And even after adulthood is reached, development continues to be governed by a series of distinct stages or waves.

The beginnings of developmental psychology can be traced to the work of American psychologist James Mark Baldwin around the turn of the previous century. Baldwin was among the first to conduct scientific research on the mental and emotional development of children and adults. In his work, he observed that the human mind develops along certain well-defined lines, which he identified as the *rational or logical*, the *aesthetic or emotional*, and the *moral or ethical*. Baldwin's research also revealed that this growth in human consciousness is characterized by distinct stages of development. And these same stages were encountered by psychological researchers throughout the twentieth century whenever they investigated the development of human consciousness.

Although these descriptions of the developmental stages have not all been identical, there is now increasing agreement among academic psychologists that the growth of consciousness definitely unfolds through a series of cross-cultural levels or waves. Despite the objections of the materialist and postmodern schools of psychology, developmental psychology has continued to increase its sway within the larger field of psychology as a whole. In fact, some of the most famous names in psychology have been committed to the idea of progressive stages of human development. These researchers include: Jean Piaget, Lawrence Kohlberg, Jane Loevinger, and Abraham Maslow.

Perhaps the most prominent living developmental psychologist is Harvard's Robert Kegan, whose work carefully incorporates over one hundred years of research in the field. Kegan's perspectives, however, are not always popular among certain of his postmodern colleagues, who continue to reject the idea that some types of consciousness are more evolved than others. Unlike horizontal psychological typologies, such as the Myers-Briggs personality type system, or the Enneagram—which merely identify stylistic differences and are nonjudgmental—Kegan's ideas about the development of consciousness are distinctly hierarchical. Kegan, however, acknowledges the dangers of such a theory by writing that:

> [Because developmental psychology] tells a story of increase, or greater complexity, [it is] thus more provocative, discomforting, even dangerous, and appropriately evokes greater suspicion. Any time a theory is normative, and suggests that something is more grown, more mature, more developed than something else, we had better check to see if the distinction rests on arbitrary grounds that consciously or unconsciously unfairly advantage some people (such as those who create the theory and people like them) whose own preferences are being depicted as superior. We had better check whether what may even appear to be an "objective" theory is not in reality a tool or captive of a "ruling" group (such as white people, men, Westerners) who use the theory to preserve their advantaged position.

Now obviously, Kegan concludes that the findings of developmental psychology do pass this test and are not inherently biased or unfair. And as will become clear by the end of this chapter, the fact that consciousness develops through distinct stages is now becoming increasingly indisputable.

Developmental psychology is a field that has been pursued by many academics, but among developmental psychologists, integral philosophy owes perhaps its greatest debt to the work of American psychologist Clare W. Graves. Graves's research revealed the existence of the same familiar stages of psychological development that had been discovered by previous researchers. Graves's work, however, went farther than the other developmental psychologists in the way that it demonstrated how these sequentially emerging stages are themselves organized within a larger dynamic system. In other words, not only did Graves's research reveal distinct, cross-cultural stages of consciousness, it also showed how these same stages are related to each other in a *dialectical spiral of development*—a living system of evolution. Through his understanding of this larger system of development, Graves was able to discern how each discrete stage of development is shaped and formed by its relationships to the other stages. And it was through this understanding of the formative nature of these interstage relationships that Graves was able to clearly distinguish between what I'll be calling "postmodern consciousness" and the subsequently arising "integral stage of consciousness."

Moreover, although other developmentalists had recognized the parallel between the stages of development in the consciousness of individuals and the stagelike development of history and culture, the dialectical structure revealed by Graves's research showed this parallel more clearly than ever before. By recognizing not only the systemic nature of each individual stage, but also how all the stages were themselves related in a larger encompassing system, Graves was able to convincingly demonstrate how these levels of development in consciousness are actually a recapitulation of the stages of human history. Just as in biological evolution, where we see a human fetus grow through the stages of the entire tree of life as it develops in the womb, we can now likewise see within the development of each human mind, a rough approximation of the evolution of human cultural history.

Following the work of Maslow, Graves studied values. He asked the subjects of his research to describe their ideal person, and after thousands of interviews during the course of over twenty years, Graves saw a clear pattern emerging—a pattern that subsequent research and experience is continuing to validate and confirm. As we'll discuss more fully in Part II, because the Gravesian model of "bio-psycho-social" evolution reveals how each stage is a unified system that encompasses the development of values, worldviews, self-sense, belief systems, neurological activation, and a person's overall "center of psychic gravity;" because the Gravesian model shows how the individual and the culture at large (the micro and the macro) evolve together using the same stages and structures; because the Gravesian model exhibits a conceptual and geometrical elegance that clearly reflects evolution's dialectical method of "transcendence and inclusion"; and most of all, because the Gravesian model clearly identifies the nature, behavior, and antecedent causes of the emerging integral stage of development, his findings serve as an important foundation of the integral worldview.

After his death in 1986, Graves's work was carried on by his colleague Don Beck, who applied Graves's ideas in his work with the leaders of South Africa (both black and white) during the transition out of the apartheid form of government. Beck and his colleague Christopher Cowan later wrote the influential book *Spiral Dynamics*, which served to popularize Graves's work and introduce it to a larger audience.

Now before we begin our discussion of the details of this spiral of development, I need to state a qualification. The systemic structures that populate the internal universe are subtle and complex. They are better compared to ocean currents than to architecture. The very idea of a "stage of consciousness" is something that must be held on to lightly and understood, not as a material object, but as a pattern of relationships that exhibit systemic properties. Understanding the stages of consciousness starts with the kind of discussion we are about to have, but using this understanding to help further cultural evolution involves a practice of seeing that avoids oversimplifying, pigeonholing, or stereotyping. As you will come to see for yourself, the stages of consciousness are real; however, what follows is a description of their reality rendered at a level of generality that facilitates its usefulness. Nevertheless, after reading through this Main Narrative, I recommend that you reconsider this description of the spiral of development in light of the discussion in chapter 9 on the "Structures of the Human Mind." Chapter 9 supplements the following description of the stages of consciousness by exploring the rich complexity of these structures and the scholarly debates that have arisen in response to their discovery.

The Spiral of Development

According to integral philosophy, each stage of consciousness is a *natural epistemology*, an organic way of making meaning with its own

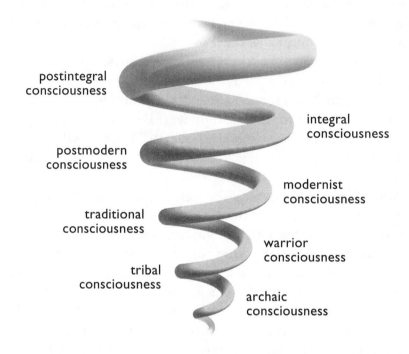

Figure 3-1. The spiral of development in consciousness and culture

distinct view of the world that arises from a specific set of problematic life conditions and their corresponding solutions. These stages function as living dynamic systems that organize both entire human societies as well as the minds of the individuals who participate in those societies. According to Graves:

> Each successive stage, wave, or level of existence is a state through which people pass on their way to other states of being. When the human is centralized in one state of existence, he or she has a psychology which is particular to that state. His or her feelings, motivations, ethics and values, biochemistry, degree of neurological activation, learning systems, belief systems, ...education, economics, and political theory and practice are all appropriate to that state.

These value systems serve to organize a person's consciousness because they engender loyalty and provide identity—they nourish consciousness and contribute to its sense of self.

Each stage of consciousness arises in response to the essential problems of its time in history. Thus, for example, the problematic life conditions of primitive survival result in one stage of consciousness, whereas coping with the problems of the modern world result in others. These stages do not describe "types of people," they describe *types of consciousness within people*. Of course, there are folks who exemplify these stages perfectly and others who defy categorization. In the developed world most people occupy more than one of these stages at different times—for most of us, these levels sound more in chords than in single notes. However, most people do find that they have a general "center of gravity" that can be identified within a specific level. As illustrated in Figure 3-1, the interrelationships between the stages reveal how they are each organized within a larger overall system, and this system demonstrates the unmistakable pattern of a dialectical, logarithmic spiral or helix.

The spiral's structure is dialectical because its growth exhibits the familiar pattern of *thesis, antithesis,* and *synthesis*. This is the same pattern of dialectical development originally recognized over two hundred years ago by Hegel. This dialectical relationship among the stages can be seen in the way that each stage arises in an antithetical reaction to the problems created by the stage that precedes it. And as the stages unfold within the spiral as a whole, we can see how the themes of earlier stages are recapitulated in later stages but with greater degrees of complexity and sophistication. As we are about to explore, the stages illustrated on the right side of the spiral tend to be more individualistic, emphasizing the *expression of the self,* whereas the stages on the left tend to be more communitarian, emphasizing the *sacrifice of the self* for the sake of the group.

This spiral structure is not a deterministic blueprint that cultural evolution is bound to follow, but it does trace a real pattern of development, the recognition of which is backed by decades of research.

Human cultures are not rigidly formed by the pattern, but the pattern does continue to appear in the timeline of just about all

---

Tribal Consciousness

Perceived life conditions:
a mysterious, threatening, and spirit-controlled world where spirits must be placated and fear drives many decisions

Worldview and values:
• sacrifice self for kin and tribe
• respect and obey chiefs, clan, customs, and taboos
• follow sacred rituals, preserve sacred places and objects
• honor the spirits and the ancestors

Contribution to the spiral:
family and kinship loyalty; strong sense of the enchantment of the world; innocence; imagination; closeness to nature

Pathology:
superstitious; violent; slavery to the group; docile; naive

Contemporary examples:
some indigenous peoples, and children

Organizational structures:
tribe or clan

Exemplary leaders:
Chief Seattle; Chief Joseph

Estimated percent of world population: 5%

Estimated percent of wealth & political power: <1%

Techno-economic mode of production:
foraging; herding; early horticultural

Key technologies:
spoken language; fire; stone and bone tools; bow and arrow

Type of medicine:
shamanic; herbal

The true:
tribal myths and stories; pronouncements of chiefs and shamans

The beautiful:
children and family; tribal symbols; fetishes; drumming; dance

The good:
the good of the gods; the good of the tribe

Average neurological activation:
centered in the limbic system

Transition triggers:
suppression of individualism; emerging ego identity; fear of death; attack by outsiders; allures of freedom and power of warrior culture

Other names for this stage:
naive consciousness; magical thinking; purple meme

Chart 3-1. Characteristics of tribal consciousness.

observable forms of cultural development. There are other possible ways to divide up the developmental spectrum of consciousness, but the data does confirm that these specific levels are not merely arbitrary divisions.

A good way to understand these stages is through an analogy using the spectrum of visible color: Think about the wavelengths of color we see in a rainbow—although we can't draw hard lines between them, and although we can identify millions of subtle shades, when we look at a rainbow we do see distinct gradations and specific hues. Each color is a whole in itself, yet it is formed in the relation between its neighbors above and below on the spectrum. And we can see something very similar in the distinct stages found within the developmental spectrum of consciousness and culture.

After we examine each stage in detail below, we'll return to the discussion of the dynamics of the spiral structure as a whole, as well as the variety of research that supports it. However, this broader analysis of the entire spiral of development is best saved until after we have reviewed each stage.

As illustrated in Figure 3-1, the spiral can be traced to the earliest form of human consciousness, called "archaic consciousness," which today can be found only in infants and those who have regressed through illness or injury. Our description of the stages of the spiral, however, starts with the tribal stage of consciousness, because this is where human culture, and therefore human consciousness nourished and molded by culture, arguably begins.

Tribal Consciousness

Every one of us has a tribe or clan in our ancestral past, and the cultural features of tribal peoples from diverse parts of the world are remarkably similar. Moreover, "tribal consciousness" has been identified as a distinct level of development by almost every researcher who has studied the growth of consciousness, so there is more agreement about the contours of this wave of consciousness and culture than probably any of the others. Chart 3-1 provides a general overview of the tribal stage of consciousness.

Every one of the historically significant stages of consciousness and culture provides its adherents with a comprehensive worldview. And what defines a given worldview is what in the world is actually "viewed." That is, worldviews exist as frames of focus that highlight and facilitate the perception of what is most important. For every worldview, that which is most important is that which is valued. And this includes not only the values defined by what is desired, but also the values that are defined in contrast with that which we seek to avoid. In other words, threats, dangers, and those conditions in our environment that cause discontent are always connected to that which we implicitly value as the opposite. For example, if we seek to avoid physical dangers, it is because we value the survival of our bodies; or if we seek to avoid the loss of our homes, it is because we value the comfort and security that our homes provide. In fact, one of Graves's key insights was how unsatisfactory external life conditions work in concert with internal values and desires to define the opportunities for evolution at any given stage of development. Each stage of consciousness thus becomes defined by the natural tension between what that stage defines as negative (the animating life conditions that stimulate needs and identify remedies) and what it defines as positive (the goals of the culture, the good life). And as consciousness evolves through these natural stages of development, the emphasis gradually shifts from a preoccupation with avoiding and overcoming fears and negative life conditions to an increasing focus on achieving what is perceived as positive.

At the tribal stage of consciousness and culture, however, fear is a significant focus of awareness. This stage, also known as "naive consciousness," sees the world as mysterious, threatening, and controlled by spirits. Superstition and magical thinking dominate the mind. For children living in the developed world, this is the fantasy stage that usually begins to appear after the first year and continues until age seven or eight. At this stage the subjective and objective domains of reality are not fully distinguished; in tribal consciousness, objects are often confused with subjects (as rocks and trees are endowed with animistic awareness), and subjects are often confused with objects (as thoughts are imagined to have magical powers).

In tribal culture, social organization remains "close to the body" through kinship relations. In other words, tribes consist mostly of biological relatives, and this form of organization is not fully transcended until the appearance of the ethnocentric values that appear in the traditional stage of consciousness.

The fact that tribes and clans are the organizational structure of all primitive peoples throughout the world is evidence of the universal nature of this stage of consciousness. Tribal consciousness is a stage we must all pass through—a vital foundational level that must not only be transcended but also included in the healthy functioning of higher states of awareness. However, the tribal stage of consciousness and culture can be extremely stable; in fact, it can continue with little development for thousands of years. But as with every stage, as the problematic life conditions that originally gave rise to this stage begin to be resolved, the accumulating excess energy creates a longing for change. As cultural evolution advances and a stage of consciousness and culture becomes more successful at alleviating and improving its value-defining life conditions, this allows higher needs and new values to be awakened. As tribal culture succeeds in reducing fear and providing security, this clears the way for the awakening of the value of individual expression and self-assertion—the tribal organization that was once so important for providing security increasingly comes to seem oppressive and constraining. Thus as one set of problems is solved, the problematic conditions created by these very solutions cause a new set of values to emerge—the solutions of one stage become the problems of the next. And in this case, the next stage to arise is what is best termed "warrior consciousness."

Warrior Consciousness

The warrior stage of consciousness and culture arises as a result of the inevitable transition from the long and stable stage of tribal culture to a more complex form of human social organization. In human history, as tribes become successful, as they develop wealth and new technologies, their expanding populations bring them into conflict with their neighbors. And as life conditions become increasingly warlike, a new worldview emerges. This worldview can be aggressive and egocentric, but it can also be splendid and noble. The characteristics of the warrior stage of consciousness and culture are summarized in Chart 3-2.

One of the most important insights we can glean from an understanding of the spiral of development is how each stage of culture has a healthy aspect and a pathological aspect—a "dignity" and a "disaster." Even after a particular stage has been largely transcended

Warrior Consciousness	
Perceived life conditions: oppressive tribal control and pathology; craves honor; fears shame; the world is a jungle full of threats and predators—dog eat dog, bite or be bitten	**Techno-economic mode of production:** early agrarian; trading; raiding
	Key technologies: weaving; pottery; metallurgy; calendric reckoning; stone architecture
Worldview and values: • express self, the hell with others • gratify impulses now, without guilt • fight to gain control at any cost • trust yourself and no one else	**Type of medicine:** shamanic; herbal
	The true: the existing distribution of power
Contribution to the spiral: individual empowerment; initiative; action orientation	**The beautiful:** the spoils of conquest; symbols of power; rap music; punk rock music
Pathology: violent; ruthless; moral bankruptcy of egocentric ethics; always at war	**The good:** personal power; pleasure; prestige; respect
Contemporary examples: urban street gangs; prisons; Somalia; Afghanistan	**Average neurological activation:** centered in the limbic system
Organizational structures: early empires; warring hordes; gangs	**Transition triggers:** parenthood; spiritual experience; illness or injury; fear of death; allures of traditional culture's security and belonging
Exemplary leaders: Attilla the Hun; Genghis Khan; Shaka Zulu; Kamehameha the Great; Tupac Shakur; Johnny Rotten	**Other names for this stage:** egocentric consciousness; impulsive thinking; preconventional; preoperational; red meme
Estimated percent of world population: 20%	
Estimated percent of wealth & political power: 5%	

Chart 3-2. Characteristics of warrior consciousness.

in a society's overall development, there remains an aspect of that stage which provides an enduring contribution to the spiral as a whole. This is why each stage has an intrinsic value that must be recognized. As a way of understanding each stage's intrinsic value, consider the analogy of our society's children. In our estimates of children, we don't value second-graders less than sixth-graders. We recognize that sixth-graders are more educated and more independent, but certainly not more valuable in an absolute sense. And when it comes to the stages of consciousness, we likewise recognize that every human has a core value as an individual that must be respected, regardless of their level of development.

Although the warrior stage of consciousness can be socially undesirable as viewed by modern sensibilities, some of its cultural expressions have been extremely beautiful. If we consider the historical examples of the ancient Hawaiians or the Lakota Indians, we can see that although these peoples lacked a written language, and although they were brutal warriors and chauvinistic toward women, they also exhibited many "fundamental heroic virtues" and a certain "primordial vigor" that we can still admire today, even if our contemporary idea of these cultures has been somewhat romanticized. An important part of the dignity of warrior consciousness can be found in its motive force, its energetic focus and determination. Because the outlook of this wave of awareness is narrow and immediate, goals are near and visible, and one's energies can be concentrated enthusiastically. Warrior consciousness thus serves to break the inertia of biologically based tribal consciousness and launch consciousness and culture into its developmental progression. But the violence and turmoil that is often seen at this stage of consciousness creates a kind of birth trauma, a fiery ordeal through which developing civilization must pass.

In this chapter's explanation of the historically significant stages of consciousness that form the spiral of development, I've tried to use names for the stages that are both descriptive and nonjudgmental, with the hope that these neutral names will gain generic acceptance as a way of talking about the stages. And with the exception of the warrior stage, the names I'm using for these stages have already been used by others. But despite its novelty in this context, I believe the term "warrior" is the best title for this particular stage because it well-describes the fierce nature of this kind of consciousness while at the same time attempting to uphold its essential dignity. However, it is worth mentioning in this context that the names I'm using for all of these stages must be understood strictly as defined terms. Warrior consciousness is defined as a specific stage of consciousness and culture, it is not meant to describe or include the consciousness of all "warriors." In fact, military culture in the developed world is now centered in traditional and modernist consciousness—the discipline and technological sophistication required of today's soldiers generally precludes those who are not able to make meaning at levels above the warrior stage.

In places like Somalia and Afghanistan, and in the urban slums of America's major cities, warlords and street gangs are clear evidence that this stage of consciousness is still very much active in the world today. And in addition to those populations that have yet to evolve beyond the warrior stage, we can also see how a negative change in life conditions can sometimes cause regression from higher stages of awareness down to warrior consciousness, which is perceived in such cases as a necessary means of survival. Even among youth whose consciousness exhibits a center of gravity at a higher level than the warrior stage, the allure of this value system—the way it nurtures the sense of independent self—can be readily seen in the popularity of such contemporary musical forms as rap and punk rock.

Understanding warrior consciousness and the problematic life conditions its "solutions" create is important for our understanding of the next sequential stage to emerge in history, which is where the largest group of the earth's population now finds itself. The evolutionary appearance of "traditional consciousness" constitutes a significant breakthrough for civilization, because with traditional consciousness, we move from the *egocentric* morality of warrior consciousness to an *ethnocentric* morality that strives for a true sense of brotherhood among the members of the in-group. Today of course, ethnocentrism is something we condemn through our allegiance to a more *worldcentric* morality. But in the course of human history, ethnocentrism is a significant step forward from what came before.

Traditional Consciousness

Traditional consciousness, also known as "conformist consciousness," arises in response to the brutal and chaotic life conditions created by the warrior level that came before it. This is why traditional consciousness tends to perceive the world as "evil," requiring salvation and law and order. While this stage of consciousness can now be identified with the many forms of religious fundamentalism found throughout the world, not all those whose consciousness is centered in this stage are fundamentalists. Military organizations, government bureaucracies, and conservative political groups provide contexts in which this stage of consciousness flourishes. Chart 3-3 provides a comprehensive description of the values and perceived life conditions of the traditional stage of consciousness.

Like the tribal stage of consciousness two levels before it, traditional consciousness is oriented toward the community rather than the individual. This value system emphasizes sacrifice of the self for the greater good of the group. And in today's world, although many traditional consciousness groups are actually multiracial in composition, there remains a solid sense of the referent group (the nation, the religion, or the ideology) being superior to all others. This sense of ethnocentricity or group superiority is closely connected with an essential component of every form of traditional worldview: a transcendent purpose or higher calling. Identification with a transcendent purpose is essential to the formation of traditional consciousness because such a purpose helps lift one's consciousness out of the constraints of the egocentric morality of the previous warrior stage.

Developmental psychologist Jane Loevinger, who conducted extensive research on ego development in adult women, provides a description of what the psychology of traditional consciousness can be like:

> Belonging to a group and being identified with it are the benchmarks for achieving a conformist orientation.... [Women in this stage] strive for approval and acceptance, and especially seek to conform to the dictates of authority within their reference groups. Standards for appearance, behavior, and preferences preoccupy their thinking. Self-esteem is engendered through acceptance and approval by her group rather than through simple hedonistic rewards.
>
> Meeting the needs of others is a major avenue to acceptance. Needs are conceptualized in stereotypical ways, which confuse individual and group differences. Dualistic judgments of "right-wrong" and "good-bad" result in rather sim-

plistic categorization of people.... Niceness and helpfulness are directed toward the groups that define her self-concept. Prejudice and fear are directed toward outsiders.

Traditional Consciousness

Perceived life conditions:
an "evil" world in need of law and order; a suffering world where God's law should reign supreme

Worldview and values:
• sacrifice self for the group's transcendent purpose
• a "black and white" sense of right and wrong
• loyalty to the rules of the mythic order
• salvation through obedience and faith

Contribution to the spiral:
sense of civic duty; law and order; respect for authority; strong moral regard for group members; preserves traditions; loyalty; hope, and a strong sense of faith

Pathology:
rigid intolerance; dogmatic fanaticism; prejudice; fundamentalism; chauvinism

Contemporary examples:
followers of traditional religions; patriotic nationalism; conservative ideologies; military organizations

Organizational structures:
feudalism; dictatorship; bureaucracy; command & control organizations

Exemplary leaders:
Winston Churchill; Pope John Paul; Billy Graham

Estimated percent of world population: 55%

Estimated percent of wealth & political power: 25%

Techno-economic mode of production:
agrarian; trading; maritime

Key technologies:
writing; law; centralized political authority; the wheel; spiritual practices and rituals

Type of medicine:
traditional medicine; folk medicine; faith healing

The true:
scripture of the mythic order

The beautiful:
children and family; art approved by a rightful authority representing the wholesome themes of "the One True Way;" country music; gospel music

The good:
God's will; the eightfold path; the flow of the Tao; the rules of the mythic order

Average neurological activation:
increased neocortical activity with continuing influence of the limbic system

Transition triggers:
higher education; cognitive dissonance caused by scriptural contradictions; the power of science; poverty; allures of modernism

Other names for this stage:
conformist consciousness; absolutistic thinking; concrete operational; blue meme

---

Chart 3-3. Characteristics of traditional consciousness.

Traditional consciousness, however, is more than just a psychological stage of development. Like all the stages of the spiral, this level of development is also a structure of history.

As the stages of consciousness and culture arise from the interplay between changing external conditions and evolving internal values, each stage inevitably develops new technologies. And these new technologies serve to further the development of the stage that creates them. For traditional consciousness, a key technology is the written word. The emergence of the powerful artifact of writing is both a cause and an effect of traditional consciousness. That is, as traditional consciousness emerges from the glorification of its transcendent purpose, there arises a strong need to record and transfix this purpose in a code, law, or scripture. Moreover, traditional consciousness' value of order and central authority endows its rulers with the power to decree the symbols that will be used to stand for the spoken word. And this brings about the advent of writing. Writing thus enacts a new level of civilization in the way that it allows learning and traditions to be more accurately communicated across space and time. It is through this method that traditional consciousness expands the civilizing influence of its value agreements into larger territories and across generations. Thus in a sense, the emergence of traditional consciousness marks the "beginning of history," because the new values of traditional consciousness provide for the better recording of history through the technology of written language.

As we will discuss in detail in chapter 9 on the "Structures of the Human Mind," the process of *evaluation* is an important *technique of perception*. That is, every person uses the values provided by their worldview to see and understand the world around them. And with the emerging values of traditional consciousness comes the new ability to clearly see the difference between right and wrong. The life conditions that originally give rise to traditional consciousness are almost always violent and chaotic. So in response to these life conditions, traditional consciousness recognizes that which is true and that which is good in a kind of black-and-white, cartoon version of reality. And this occurs because in the chaos and brutality of the life conditions that give rise to this stage, shades of gray and moral ambiguity are not very helpful. But what is helpful in dealing with these distressing life conditions is a clear distinction between right and wrong and true and false, and so this is how traditional consciousness perceives the world.

To understand the dignity and the evolutionary necessity of this stage of consciousness it is important to see how traditional consciousness serves as an indispensable foundation for the stages of consciousness that come after it. A good illustration of the foundational role played by traditional consciousness in the later-arising stages of cultural evolution is found in the events surrounding the fall of communism in Russia in 1990. Although Marxism may have originated at a higher stage of consciousness than the traditional stage, by the second half of the twentieth century the Soviet system had come to be dominated by the traditionalist type of conformist worldview. Then when communism was brought down, the transcendent purpose and group identity upon which this level depended largely ceased to exist. It was then assumed by the West that with the fall of communism Russia would be poised for significant economic growth. So substantial foreign investment in the Russian economy ensued. However, Western investors didn't realize that the modernist consciousness required for Western-style economic growth did yet not exist in sufficient numbers among the Russian people in 1990. The loyalties of Russia's traditional stage of consciousness had been swept away by the fall of communism, and much of what remained consisted of the underlying structures of warrior consciousness. So instead of stimulating sustainable economic growth, the foreign investment in Russia in the early 1990s only contributed to the rise of horrendous levels of organized crime. This is because what distinguishes the individualistic orientation of the modernist level from the similarly individualistic worldview of the warrior level is the inclusion of the intervening and moderating values of traditional consciousness, as shown in Figure 3-2. This intervening stage serves to socialize and restrain the individual by providing a clear sense of right and wrong and by emphasizing the importance of law and order.

Without a stable base of traditional consciousness, attempts to evolve to higher stages often collapse back into the chaos of warrior culture as a result of corruption and conflicts between rival groups. In order for higher levels of civilization to be maintained, the enduring contributions of the earlier stages must be in place and functioning. In other words, we have to cultivate and maintain the enduring contributions of the earlier stages in order to make the transcendence to higher stages sustainable.

As we consider the traditional stage of consciousness, it is important to keep in mind that one can achieve a relatively high degree of personal "self-actualization" while still retaining this stage as one's psychic center of gravity. The concept of self-actualization comes from the work of Abraham Maslow, who is perhaps the world's most famous developmental psychologist. Maslow's research led him to propose a "hierarchy of needs," which begins with the satisfaction of basic biological needs, then as those needs are fulfilled, higher needs are awakened until the self is able to focus on the ultimate need for self-actualization. Although it is possible to roughly align Maslow's hierarchy with Graves's stages of development, it seems to me that Maslow's hierarchy can also be seen functioning as an organizing principle within each stage. That is, just about all the needs of the self identified by Maslow can be satisfied within the traditional stage (or within any of the higher stages for that matter). Let's use the Reverend Billy Graham as an example. Billy Graham has had a long and distinguished career; he has been the spiritual adviser of

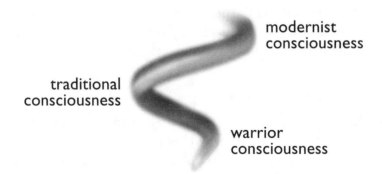

Figure 3-2. The sequential developmental relationship among the warrior, traditional, and modernist stages of consciousness.

numerous U.S. presidents, he has inspired millions of people world-wide, and he has built a substantial ministry that is now run by his adult children. Few would argue that Graham has not fulfilled at least some of his self-actualization needs. And although Graham is certainly able to make meaning at levels of consciousness above the traditional stage, the center of gravity of his consciousness appears firmly embedded within this level. This serves to underscore the fact that spiritual development and self-actualization are available to all levels of consciousness, regardless of one's position on the spiral.

However, like all evolutionary stages of consciousness, the traditional level certainly has its downside. Pathology typically appears when the existential problems that give rise to a particular stage begin to be resolved. Because a level's animating life conditions are necessary for its existence, when those life conditions begin to disappear, it is common for that stage to begin to invent or project those life conditions onto situations where they don't actually exist. For example, we saw how the life conditions that give rise to the traditional level of consciousness are perceived as an evil world in need of redemption. Yet as the worst excesses of the warrior stage are brought under control, the traditional level begins to focus on new "evils." Attention shifts away from the past evils of egocentric violence and begins concentrating on falsely perceived "evils" such as homosexuality or other relatively benign aspects of society that the fundamentalists condemn. And so the process continues: As consciousness becomes successful at addressing the problems of one level of evolution, those very solutions result in a new set of problems that can be addressed only by the next emerging stage of development.

Modernist Consciousness

Traditional consciousness has been present in various forms for at least the last five thousand years. However, only the most successful versions of it have led to the transition to the next stage known as "modernism." The first significant emergence of modernist culture appeared in the fifth century B.C. during the Golden Age of ancient Greece. The triumph of reason over myth was evident in Greek philosophy, mathematics, engineering, politics, and art. Indeed, the appearance of realism and perspective in art is always a good marker of emerging modernist consciousness. However, although the Golden Age of ancient Greece has served as a kind of "Platonic essence of civilization," a romantic ideal that has captured the imagination of latter-day modernists for the past five hundred years, this level of civilization was premature; it could not be sustained. And even though traces of modernist culture can be seen in the Roman Empire up to its final collapse (and to a degree in ancient Islamic, Indian, and Chinese civilization), modernist consciousness did not emerge in a sustainable form until the European Renaissance, with it then coming to complete fruition during the Enlightenment of the seventeenth and eighteenth centuries. The basic features of the modernist stage of consciousness are outlined in Chart 3-4.

The values of this individualistically oriented stage of consciousness include progress and improvement, material wealth and status, and, of course, individual autonomy and independence. As it breaks out of the conformist mentality of the traditional stage of consciousness, modernist consciousness achieves power through the initiative, confidence, and sense of liberation that arises from the rejection of traditional culture's received authority and historical abuses.

In our discussion of traditional consciousness we saw how the emerging values of the traditional worldview provide new powers of perception and an enhanced ability to distinguish right from wrong. Similarly, the emerging values of modernist consciousness provide new powers of perception that arise from an enhanced ability to reason beyond the received explanations of the traditional worldview's "mythic order." That is, the clear-eyed realism derived from the rational values of the modernist worldview leads its adherents to question the nature of things and to measure and experiment with the material universe through the scientific method. And in the realm of politics, modernist values provide a new vision of "natural law" and the "rights of man." Modernism's new sense of the dignity and authority of the individual provides the courage to boldly challenge the corrupt structures of feudalism and Church-sponsored social hierarchy. It is thus through this new political confidence that modernism gives rise to

Modernist Consciousness

Perceived life conditions:
opportunities for a better standard of living and improved social position for the individual; need to escape oppressive dogmatic systems; need to demystify material world

Worldview and values:
• achieve wealth, status, & "the good life"
• progress through science, technology, and the "best" solution
• winning, competition, and striving for excellence
• individual autonomy and independence—liberty

Contribution to the spiral:
meritocracy; upward mobility; the middle class; excellence through competition; science; technology; confidence in progress

Pathology:
materialism; nihilism; exploitive; unscupulous; selfish; greedy

Contemporary examples:
corporate culture; modern science; mainstream media; professional sports

Organizational structures:
democratic capitalism; corporations; strategic alliances

Exemplary leaders:
John F. Kennedy; Bill Gates; Margaret Sanger; Carl Sagan; Isaac Newton

Estimated percent of world population:
15%

Extimated percent of wealth & political power: 60%

Techno-economic mode of production:
industrial economy

Key Technologies:
scientific method; advanced mathematics; reason; logic; industrial technologies; transportation technologies; communication technologies

Type of medicine:
scientific and allopathic medicine

The true:
objective truth; reason; that which can be materially proved

The beautiful:
fashionable symbols of power and prestige; glamour; classical music; jazz music

The good:
progress; liberty; material wealth; status; opportunity; higher education; "the good life"

Average neurological activation:
left brain dominated

Transition triggers:
spiritual experience; dissatisfaction with possessions; feelings of emptiness; guilt; allures of counter culture

Other names for this stage:
achievement consciousness; strategic thinking; formal operational; orange meme

Chart 3-4. Characteristics of modernist consciousness.

democracy. Thomas Jefferson understood the power of the values of modernist consciousness through the concept of "public virtue." Jefferson recognized that in order for a democracy to succeed, a good portion of its population must have a strong sense of its duties of citizenship, an intolerance of corruption, and a willingness to take personal responsibility for the improvement of their government.

The emergence of the modernist level of consciousness can be associated with increasing use of the neocortex and especially with the left hemisphere of the brain. This explains how logic and reason become more available at this stage of development. Integral theorist Jenny Wade calls this wave "achievement consciousness," and in summarizing the findings of a wide range of researchers, she concludes:

> Achievement orientation allows a person to conceptualize plans from a vantage point partially removed from the system, that is, to figure out the "rules of the game" in order to "cut corners," "play the angles," increase his 'odds' and gain an advantage over [those] less able (or less constrained).... Sensitivity to status keeps the Achiever focused on everyone's relative positions concerning differential social power (money, position, prestige) in what is presumed to be a fixed "pie." People at this level of consciousness work to keep ahead out of a sense of personal achievement and competition. While the need for power and dominance resembles some aspects of Egocentrism [warrior consciousness], the socially constructed world view at this level of awareness creates much more complex dynamics. The achievement-oriented person not only judges himself and his performance relative to others, he is very concerned about his public image. He is no longer embedded in the social roles and rules of Conformist [traditional] consciousness; nevertheless, he remains in a dialectic with the social system, needing to "win" in acceptable ways.

This quote by Wade brings out an important feature of developmental theory that is most closely associated with the work of Robert Kegan, quoted earlier. Kegan's "subject-object theory" charts the progress of consciousness through the stages by observing that a person transcends a given stage when what was previously embedded in that person's subjective consciousness becomes objectified, or recognized from an external perspective. According to Kegan, "[T]ransforming our epistemologies, liberating ourselves from that in which we were embedded, making what was subject into object so that we can 'have it' rather than 'be had' by it—this is the most powerful way I know to conceptualize the growth of the mind." For example, in the traditional stage of consciousness, one's religious belief system is a part of their subject—the person's subjective consciousness is embedded in their belief system and the objective world is thus perceived and constructed to satisfy the demands of this belief system. However, when a person transcends the traditional stage and achieves the increased "epistemological capacity" of the modernist order of consciousness, he may still hold the same essential religious beliefs, but these beliefs are now objectified, he can see beyond the beliefs, he has a greater capacity to adopt the perspective of others and see the world through their beliefs as well as his own. As a person's consciousness evolves, he can still "have his beliefs," but in more evolved stages those beliefs no longer "have him."

With the emergence of modernist consciousness comes the liberal ideals of religious freedom, gender equality, democracy, freedom of speech and press, and the equality of all persons before the law. And even though the modern world has yet to deliver these "dignities" in a fair and universal distribution to all citizens, it was through the rise of modernist culture that these rights and freedoms were originally conceived as achievable ideals. But perhaps the greatest gift of modernist consciousness was the emergence of science and the scientific worldview. It was science that first gave us a form of seemingly universal truth, an "objective" truth that transcended cultures, languages, and nations. Science produced the technology to explore and connect the world; it gave Europe the knowledge and the power to colonize the globe and forge the foundations of the Industrial Revolution, world trade, and international relations. And the science of Western medicine, along with agricultural technology, was so successful in reducing mortality rates that it eventually produced a population explosion of unprecedented proportions.

Now if you don't agree that these "gifts" of science have been all that good for the world, you are not alone. Obviously, strong arguments can be made that the disasters of modernism far outweigh the dignities. But from an evolutionary perspective, this is just another example of one level's solutions creating the next level's problems.

Because the culture of modernism was more complex, because it contained greater *depth* than previous stages, its potential for good and bad were both magnified. As science and reason separated itself from mythic thinking and the constrictions of the authority of the Church, as it became increasingly differentiated from the moderating influences of other spheres of knowing such as the arts and the humanities, this initially healthy differentiation eventually became a pathological dissociation (too much transcendence, and not enough inclusion). Science eventually came to "colonize" and dominate other spheres of knowing, often going so far as to deny their validity. In many significant areas science developed into scientism, the pathological form of modernist consciousness we noted earlier which maintains that the only "real" reality is objective, material reality. According to Ken Wilber:

> Put bluntly, the I and the WE were colonized by the IT. The Good and the Beautiful were overtaken by a growth in monological Truth that, otherwise admirable, became grandiose in its own conceit, and cancerous in its relations to others. Full of itself and flush with stunning victories, empirical science became *scientism*, the belief that there is no reality save that revealed by science, and no truth save that which science delivers. The subjective and interior domains—the I and the WE—were flattened into objective, exterior, empirical processes, either atomistic or systems. Consciousness itself, and the mind and heart and soul of humankind, could not be seen with a microscope, a telescope, a cloud chamber, a photographic plate, and so all were pronounced epiphenomenal at best, illusory at worst.

Eventually, the inherent limitations and growing ideological oppression of the "Newtonian-Cartesian paradigm" caused many thinkers to look for new ways of understanding the world. Today, the scientific worldview has, in a sense, partially deconstructed itself through its own advances in theoretical physics. The dethroning of positivism as the ultimate authority has also been aided by critical academia's exposure of the "Myth of the Given"—the naive assumption that actual reality can be objectively perceived without the distortions of interpretation. Nevertheless, despite the inroads of postmodernism, the materialistic prejudices of the scientific worldview continue to dominate many of the institutions of the developed world.

Scientism, however, is not the worst of modernist consciousness' problems. Modernism's principle pathology is found in the continuing threat that the horrors wrought by its industrialized military technology during the twentieth century will be unleashed again in another world war. And now, this same modernist military technology threatens us in new ways as it becomes adopted by premodern militants bent on destroying the developed world through terrorism. Moreover, the growth of modernism has also been largely responsible for producing the world's growing environmental crisis, which may eventually prove to be more destructive than any conceivable weapon.

Modernism's abundant pathologies, and the moral bankruptcy of some of its most prominent leaders, have caused many to question whether the advance of Western civilization has actually resulted in any real "progress." Throughout the twentieth century, and especially after World War II, some of the Western world's most gifted thinkers began to lose faith in the whole Enlightenment project. Modernism's moral failures spawned a wide variety of antimodern movements, and over the last fifty years these various forms of alternative culture have become loosely consolidated within a now distinctly identifiable wave of postmodern consciousness, which we examine next.

We'll return to our discussion of modernist consciousness throughout the chapters ahead, but in order to fully understand the modernist worldview it is necessary to see it in the context of what has come after it.

Postmodern Consciousness

Modernism has achieved a great deal of success, and its greatest success is demonstrated by the fact that it provided the platform for its own transcendence by an alternative form of culture, which is best termed "postmodernism." It is worth repeating here that although the term postmodern has many meanings, and although it has been used to describe certain discrete aspects of contemporary culture that are merely subsets of the larger cultural worldview that has emerged beyond modernism, I will use this term as the label for this world-view because it is already being used by others in this context, and because it well-describes the antithetical relationship that much of this worldview has with modernist culture.

Most developmental psychologists either end their description of the stages of consciousness at the modernist level, or confuse the postmodern level with the integral stage that comes after it. Thus as we've discussed, a distinguishing advantage of Graves's model is its clear identification of the communally oriented stage of consciousnes that intervenes between modernism and later-appearing integralism.

Postmodern consciousness (summarized in Chart 3-5) is charac-terized by a high degree of sensitivity—sensitivity to those who have been previously marginalized or exploited, sensitivity to the needs and fragility of the environment, and sensitivity to the charms of the feminine way of knowing. The postmodern stage arises in response to the "push" of the pathologies of modernism, and many of its val-ues are defined in reaction to these pathologies. For example, mul-ticulturalism is a reaction against Eurocentrism; environmentalism is a reaction against industrial degradation and exploitation; and the preference for consensus, bonding, and "linking" is a reaction against modernism's ubiquitous hierarchical ranking. Even postmodern consciousness' feeling, caring, sensitive orientation is itself largely a reaction against the cold rationality and dispassionate perspective of scientific materialism.

Also known as "affiliative consciousness" and pluralistic relativ-ism, this worldview can first be seen emerging in the Enlightenment itself in the writings of Jean Jacques Rousseau and the Romantic movement, and then in the nineteenth century in the writings of Walt Whitman, Henry David Thoreau, and Ralph Waldo Emerson. However, it was not until the 1960s that the first authentic large-scale postmodern cultural structures began to emerge. The lure or "pull" that caused the baby boom generation to embrace postmodern consciousness in large numbers was found in the power of sixties music and the moral agendas of civil rights and peace in Vietnam.

In academia the rise of postmodern values produced a new "critical paradigm" that sought to deconstruct the canon of Western knowledge by showing the subjectivity of what had been previously understood as "objective."

Postmodern Consciousness

Perceived life conditions:
presence of exploitation; corrupt hierarchy; environmental degradation; shallow materialism; suffering of others

Worldview and values:
• inclusion of those previously marginalized or exploited
• consensus decision making and egalitarianism
• environmentalism and preference for "natural"
• multiculturalism and spiritual diversity
• personal growth of the "whole person"
• sensitivity

Contribution to the spiral:
worldcentric morality; recognition of human potential; increased responsibility for people and the planet; compassion and inclusion; celebration of the feminine; renewed spiritual freedom and creativity

Pathology:
value relativism; narcissism; denial of hierarchy; contempt for modernism and traditionalism

Contemporary examples:
progressive culture; critical academia; environmental movement; political correctness; the Netherlands

Organizational structures:
democratic socialism; consensus committees; self-directed teams

Exemplary leaders:
John Lennon; John Muir; Martin Luther King Jr.; Margaret Mead; Joan Baez; Allen Ginsberg

Estimated percent of world population: <5%

Estimated percent of wealth & political power: 10%

Techno-economic mode of production: informational economy

Key technologies:
non-violent resistance; postmodern music; art and poetry; constructivist critique; entheogens; spiritual practices

Type of medicine:
holistic—scientific, traditional, naturopathic, homeopathic, herbal, shamanic, psychological

The true:
subjective truth; whatever is true for you

The beautiful:
nature; modern art; tribal art; new age music; 60's music; psychedilia

The good:
sustainability; that which is best for all the people and the planet

Average neurological activation:
right brain dominated

Transition triggers:
dissatisfaction with seeking; failure of alternative culture to provide cures or answers; growing "expense" of rights and entitlements; desire for greater results; allures of integral solutions

Other names for this stage:
affiliative consciousness; holistic thinking; postformal; consensus; green meme

Chart 3-5. Characteristics of postmodern consciousness.

The dignity of the postmodern stage of consciousness and culture can be seen in the way it has sensitized and feminized much of Western society. The cultural hegemony of the monolithic values of the two previous stages (modernist and traditional, which together comprised the overall worldview of the West) were significantly diminished in their influence as the new worldcentric morality of the postmodern stage began to recognize the value of the previously marginalized stages of evolution—especially the warrior and tribal stages still exhibited by many indigenous and non-Western peoples. Thus, one of the most important legacies of the postmodern worldview is how it has sought to reinclude at a higher level what the modernist stage had previously left behind in its transcendence.

The rise of postmodern consciousness has now had a significant impact on the politics of the Western democracies. In fact, each new stage of consciousness that has emerged in the sequence of historical development has been endowed with an advantage over the stage that preceded it by virtue of the increased depth and complexity of its values. Warrior consciousness defeats tribal consciousness because of its ruthless ferocity and energetic determination. Traditional consciousness is usually able to defeat warrior consciousness because of its superior organization and group discipline. Modernist consciousness overcomes traditional consciousness as a result of its technological and industrial superiority. And postmodern consciousness finds its advantage over modernism in its unique ability to bring about change through nonviolent political action and moral strength. Examples of this can be seen in the success of the political strategies of nonviolent resistance conceived by Thoreau and applied by Gandhi and Martin Luther King Jr. In fact, the potency of nonviolent resistance to bring about meaningful social change can now be recognized as a significant moral legacy of postmodern consciousness. Although many exceptions to this trend can be thought of, the increasing relative power of each stage of consciousness is evidence of that stage's evolutionary transcendence over the levels that came before it.

In our discussion above we saw how the values of traditionalism provide a new vision of right and wrong, and how the values of modernism provide a new vision of the material universe and human rights, and now with postmodern consciousness we can also see how its emerging values provide a new kind of perception. Postmodern consciousness sees with fresh eyes the value of what had been previously ignored or discarded in modernism's advance. For example, the new vision of postmodernism perceives the value of alternative and traditional medicine, it discovers the deep truths of Eastern spirituality, and it becomes angry and ashamed of the legacy of modernism's racist and sexist exploitation. Again, these fresh insights are achieved through the "perception power" of new values. Just as modernism makes progress through its adoption of the scientific-objectivist standard of truth, postmodernism swings the other way in its concern for the role of subjectivity in any estimate of truth. And postmodernism's discernment of the socially constructed nature of truth can be recognized in many areas of progressive culture. While modernist standards of truth tend to become increasingly constrained by scientific facts, postmodern standards of truth tend to become increasingly pluralistic—truth for postmodern consciousness might be described as "whatever is true for you."

Because of the vulnerability inherent in its complexity and depth, like the stages before it, the postmodern level brings pathology as well as progress. One of the downsides of the postmodern stage is found in its "value relativism." Examples of the "anything goes" inclusiveness of value relativism can be seen in many areas of contemporary society such as New Age spirituality, alternative medicine, multiculturalism, and victim politics. And value relativism is especially prevalent at elite universities. Within academia and much of our education system there are many postmodernists who firmly believe that all social hierarchies are essentially subjective, and that modernism is in no way superior to what came before it. This is not to say that every one of these expressions of the postmodern worldview are necessarily pathological, but in these areas of our culture the values of comparative excellence and the hierarchy of achievement are generally subordinated to the preferred values of equality and inclusiveness. However, in an evolutionary universe organized by hierarchical development at every level, to attempt to eliminate hierarchy is to deny what is real.

Just as the modernist stage before it had gone too far in its differentiation by becoming disconnected from the healthy aspects of the previous stages, the postmodern stage likewise often goes too far in the other direction in its attempted integration of previously transcended levels. When differentiation (transcendence) goes out of balance, it becomes dissociation. And when integration (inclusion) goes out of balance, it results in fusion. Postmodernism's pathological fusion is found in the way that it fails to differentiate between the healthy aspects of the previous stages—aspects that we want to carry forward into the future and include—and the immature and pathological aspects of the previous stages that we would do well to leave behind.

Postmodernism's value relativism leads to what might be called the "green dilemma." This arises from the fact that postmodernism's worldcentric morality is an evolutionary improvement over the less-developed forms of morality that accompany the previous stages of consciousness. Postmodernism's sensitivity and compassion for the less fortunate heightens this stage's ethics and generally attunes it to suffering and injustice that had previously gone unnoticed. Yet because of its aversion to being "judgmental," postmodern consciousness often finds it difficult to justify the imposition of its values on even some of the worst abuses of the lower levels. Postmodernism is thus often stymied in its efforts to bring about positive and sustainable changes in a society. But as we will shortly examine, integral consciousness, which has the ability to evaluate more effectively, is better able to use the worldcentric morality developed by postmodernism to bring about lasting social evolution.

Another problematic aspect of the postmodern stage of consciousness is that it is so "expensive." This worldview is quick to recognize rights but rarely does it see the corresponding responsibilities. This stage relies and depends on the material prosperity created by the modernist level, while often simultaneously denying its validity. In its attempt to redistribute the wealth, it often does damage to the systems that produced the wealth in the first place. But when it attacks the values of both the modernist and traditional stages of culture, the postmodern stage unwittingly destroys the means to its own evolution. As Don Beck has said, "It's like a person who climbs to the top of a house and then throws down the ladder that got him up there." According to Beck, when we consider the health or pathology of any developmental level, it is important to look at three things: the life conditions, the general values of the stage being considered, and the particular expression of that worldview in the specific context being examined. He explains why we must consider these three factors in the following example:

> If we don't like capitalism or consumerism, which are expressions of the [modernist stage], it's not the same thing as the [abilities of the modernist level], which is the capacity to engineer things, to make things better. The creativity and ability to engineer that are inherent in the same [modernist stage] can now be used to clean up the environment. That's why we can't afford to bash any of these [stages of consciousness]. We can challenge a manifestation of it, but without the [modernist] thinking system, we couldn't solve medical problems, we couldn't figure out how to clean up the water or air, and we would sink back to the myth and mysticism of [traditionalism]. I don't think anybody wants that to happen.

Because it is the most recent stage that has emerged in history, postmodernism is thus the most evolved stage of consciousness that has yet to appear in the culture of the world. And because it is the most evolved, it is therefore the most morally advanced of the established stages of culture, and deserves to be honored and praised. However, as its inherent limitations (which we will examine more fully in the next chapter) start to become apparent, we can begin to see why the postmodern worldview needs to be transcended and included by a new evolutionary development in consciousness. Further cultural evolution will be required in order for our society to find realistic solutions to the growing problems of the world. And this further cultural evolution can now be recognized in the form of the newly emerging integral stage of consciousness.

We will return to our discussion of postmodern consciousness and its role in catalyzing the emergence of the integral worldview in the next chapter. But before we begin our exploration of the integral stage of consciousness, it is necessary to say a few more things about the spiral of consciousness and culture as a whole.

The Spiral as a Whole

As the manifestations of these stages of consciousness and culture become increasingly easy to see, it is important to keep in mind that these worldview systems are broad and fluid. As Beck often repeats, "The spiral is messy, not symmetrical, with multiple admixtures rather than pure types. These are mosaics, meshes and blends." Again, these stages need to be understood not so much as types of people, but rather as types of consciousness within people. And people often employ different value systems when dealing with different aspects of their lives. Moreover, the stages can often be found working together in pairs. For example, most manifestations of warrior consciousness retain a connection to the kinship loyalty of the previous tribal stage. Despite the ruthlessness of warrior culture, there is usually a felt-sense of the need to protect (and avenge) "la familia." Similarly, although modernism emerges in antithesis to traditional consciousness, the legacy of its native traditionalism continues to inform the modernist worldview until the appearance of the challenge of postmodernism. As we can see today in America, postmodernism is engaged in an intense struggle with traditionalism to define the morality and attract the allegiance of the modernist majority.

As we look at the spiral as a whole we can see that as each stage matures, it increasingly develops its own unique form of orthodoxy or what might be called "stage absolutism." Throughout the twentieth century we have seen the rise of orthodox religious fundamentalism in almost every great world religion as these traditional worldviews are increasingly threatened by the success of modernism and the rise of postmodernism. Similarly, modernism's orthodoxy can be seen in its atheism and scientific materialism, which insists that talk of anything nonmaterial is nonsense. And now as postmodernism is maturing, we can see manifestations of its orthodoxy in the strict political correctness that characterizes much of the education and entertainment establishments. Thus, not only can we see the dialectical pattern of thesis-antithesis-synthesis in the development of the spiral as a whole, we can also see a dialectic of development within the life span of each stage. Every new level begins as an antithesis to what came before. In the course of healthy development, this is then followed by a season of synthesis wherein a stage's primary work is accomplished. Then after its "prime time," a stage of culture usually matures into a more orthodox thesis of itself that eventually calls forth its own transcendence by a new level's fresh antithesis.

We can see the stages of development from a completely different angle by observing how, as new worldviews emerge sequentially, they provide additional perspectives for those who use them. For example, the research shows that tribal consciousness is usually limited to a "first-person perspective" and cannot always make clear distinctions between subjects and objects—as we've discussed, in tribal consciousness objects are confused with subjects and subjects are confused with objects. But with the rise of traditional consciousness a "second-person perspective" appears that can more clearly distinguish between self and other. And this new second-person perspective contributes to the higher level of morality that results in the appearance of "the golden rule," an ethical directive found in almost every form of traditional culture. Then with modernist consciousness we see the emergence of a "third-person perspective," which enacts the scientific viewpoint of the "objective observer" and eventually results in the field of science being separated from philosophy and religion.

As a map of the historical evolution of the culture of humanity, the spiral of development clearly shows how the stages of the history of consciousness are still very much alive today. When we consider how the development of consciousness is spread out all over the globe, we can see that not everyone is living in the same "time in history." Moreover, because every infant begins life at the archaic level of consciousness, "the battle has to be fought anew with every birth." However, when we begin to recognize how the unfolding of history occurs within this dialectical evolutionary system, we can better see what can be done to help people move forward and improve their conditions from wherever they find themselves. Problems that once seemed hopeless begin to appear more as exciting opportunities for the raising of consciousness. As we've discussed, every problem in the world is ultimately a problem of consciousness, and every solution can thus be recognized as an opening for further evolution.

For example, if we look at the problems of the Middle East, we can see that a central challenge faced by the Muslim nations (most of whom, with the partial exception of Turkey, are centered in traditional consciousness, although a few remain centered in earlier stages) is to develop an authentic form of Islamic modernism—not a transplanted European modernism, but a native modernism with its roots in the soil of the once-great Islamic civilization.

A successful model of homegrown non-Western modernism is found in the recent history of the Japanese people. Because the Japanese had a strong and healthy version of traditional consciousness (nurtured by two hundred years of self-imposed isolation and unfettered refinement), when they made the leap to modernism in the late nineteenth century they were extremely successful (even after the devastation of World War II) because their strong base of traditional consciousness served as a supporting foundation for their uniquely Japanese form of modernist culture. By contrast, here at the beginning of the twenty-first century, the traditional structures of Islamic culture are apparently not yet healthy enough (and not sufficiently free from outside interference) to support the sustainable development of a modernist society. This is because much of Islam's traditional consciousness is compromised by admixture with excessive amounts of warrior and tribal consciousness. And this results in the status of women in traditional Islamic societies remaining generally so low. Although in all traditional cultures women are subordinate to men and chauvinism is a clear pathology, Islam is undoubtedly the worst on this account because of the degree to which these earlier stages of consciousness remain so prevalent in its culture. And this emphasis on male superiority has rendered the moral power of traditional Islam vulnerable.

Unlike the form of traditional consciousness found in European Christianity, the traditional consciousness of the Islamic world has not yet been able to evolve sufficiently away from warrior consciousness and toward modernism. Part of this stagnation has resulted from the Islamic world's military defeat and resulting colonization by the European powers, which left it humiliated and sapped of its moral authority, crippling it as a force for good. And because it had lost much of its moral authority, it has not been able to effectively work as traditional consciousness must to bring about enough of the civil obedience, honesty, respect for authority, and good citizenship that are all prerequisites for functional modernism.

But once we can see exactly how Islam needs to be strengthened, once we can see what can be done to restore the moral authority of this traditional culture, we can begin to help create sustainable evolution in this part of the world. Viewed through the lens of the spiral of development, we can see that the phenomenon of Islamic terrorism is not so much a challenge to the West as it is a challenge to Islam itself—a challenge for the Islamic world to unite and righteously condemn the warrior consciousness–infected suicide cults and radical fundamentalist mentality that is in a death-struggle for the soul of this great world religion. It is by supporting and encouraging Islam to subdue the warrior consciousness within its midst—it is by helping Islam become more moral—that the developed world can assist Islam in achieving a form of traditional consciousness that will be successful enough to provide a platform for its own transcendence through the emergence of a native version of Middle Eastern modernism.

We can have confidence in this prescription for development (which could obviously be the subject of an entire book) because we can see in history that this is exactly what happened prior to the emergence of modernism in Europe during the Enlightenment. The reformation of Christianity during the sixteenth and seventeenth centuries purged this religion of much of its warrior consciousness (seen clearly in the excesses of the Renaissance popes). Protestantism constituted a more successful form of traditional culture because it had achieved a higher level of morality than the Catholicism of the time. It thus paved the way for its own transcendence during the subsequent Enlightenment. And we can still see the ongoing successful functioning of these stages of history in the way that postmodernism has only really flourished in the countries where modernism first developed. The original success of modernist consciousness in the Protestant countries of England, America, Germany, Scandinavia, and the Netherlands itself formed the foundation for its subsequent transcendence by postmodernism, which today represents a significant percentage of the population in these countries.

We can clearly see the structure of the spiral of development in both the historical progression of culture and in the growth of consciousness in individuals. And we can use this understanding to predict the future and heal the past, not just on a global level, but in our own families and communities—indeed, even within our own psyches. This process of discerning the stages of history within the spectrum of consciousness, guided by the values of the integral worldview, will eventually lead to a new kind of political reality which we'll discuss in chapter 5 on *"Integral Politics."*

In our consideration of the spiral as a whole, it is important to remember that just as the external universe extends to the far reaches of space and time, the internal universe is also vast; within its confines we find a continuous outpouring of creative originality. So as we think about the structures and identifiable "locations" of consciousness and culture within the internal universe, we do well to keep in mind how much diversity and complexity there is. For instance, within the consciousness of individuals there are multiple lines of development and different types of intelligence. As we have seen, although values and worldviews serve to define and unify people's overall motivations and loyalties, within these worldviews there can be found a wide variety of cognitive and emotional development. For example, people who are centered within traditional consciousness can nevertheless exhibit genius-level intelligence. And conversely, people who may have highly evolved values might at the same time be somewhat emotionally immature.

Although we can trace multiple currents of development within any individual, these different types of consciousness can generally be grouped within three overall lines of development, which we can identify as *emotional intelligence, cognitive intelligence,* and moral development or *values intelligence*—these three main types of intelligence can be abbreviated as *EQ, IQ,* and *VQ.* The idea of an intelligence quotient, or "IQ," has been around since the beginning of the twentieth century. The emphasis on IQ, however, led to a rather narrow assessment of mental excellence. But recently, the importance of emotional intelligence, or "EQ," has also begun to be recognized, and this has served to broaden our appreciation of the many ways that a person can be "smart." And now, in addition to the assessment of consciousness through EQ and IQ, the enlarged understanding provided by integral philosophy allows us to recognize "VQ"—values intelligence—as an important indicator of one's "location" within the internal universe. However, this is just a preview of the deeper discussion of these issues, which we will undertake in chapter 9, on the "Structures of the Human Mind."

What Is the Real Evidence for the Spiral?

In my experience, the most powerful and practical aspect of integral philosophy is its understanding of the spiral of development in consciousness and culture. So before we turn to our discussion of the integral stage, it will be useful to briefly review the evidence for this internal universe structure. As you consider these stages of development, you may be led to ask: Even if these stages do have some validity, why can't they be seen merely as a series of steps instead of some kind of "dialectical spiral or helix structure"? Well, there is a variety of evidence; some of it is based on psychological research on individuals, some of it is based on sociological research on groups, and some of it is based on observation of the clearly identifiable dialectical relationships that exist between different aspects of human culture.

First, as we discussed at the beginning of this chapter, the psychological evidence that these stages exist within the minds of individuals is overwhelming. Following the work of James Mark Baldwin, Swiss psychologist Jean Piaget amassed a tremendous body of research that showed how cognition develops through a series of distinct stages, which he labeled: sensorimotor, preoperational, concrete operational, and formal operational. Piaget demonstrated how each of these stages of development brings with it a unique set of values and an overall worldview. Piaget's research has garnered significant respect from academics in a wide variety of disciplines. After careful review and intense scrutiny, his work has been found to be scientifically valid and cross-culturally universal. Piaget's work has thus served as a foundation for the many developmental psychologists who have followed him. And although there has not always been complete agreement among these developmentalists about the *exact* details of the stages, there is a remarkable degree of *general* consensus among them. Clare Graves did discover some new and important aspects of these stages, but his overall findings on the levels of consciousness were in general accord with the well-researched conclusions of the other developmentalists.

In addition to the significant psychological evidence that has been collected through research on individuals, we also have further credible evidence of the stages of consciousness from the field of sociology. In 1995, sociologist Paul Ray published the findings of his national survey on the role of values in American life sponsored by the Fetzer Institute and the Institute of Noetic Sciences. Ray's research, which drew upon more than 100,000 questionnaire responses and hundreds of focus groups, revealed the existence of three large and distinct subcultures in America. Ray identified these groups as "Traditionals, Moderns, and Cultural Creatives." Ray's research revealed further that the "Cultural Creatives" first emerged as a significant subculture of American society in the 1970s. And not surprisingly, Ray found that the values and worldviews of each of these distinct subcultures correspond almost perfectly to the stages of consciousness revealed by the research of Clare Graves (which was unknown to Ray until after he published his findings). According to Ray, in the 1990s, 51 percent of the American population were "Moderns" (corresponding to the stage I'm calling modernist), 25 percent were "Traditionals" (corresponding to traditional consciousness), and 24 percent were "Cultural Creatives" (whom I label postmodern). Ray's findings made a big impact and were immediately adopted by the publishing and natural foods industries as a useful way of identifying and describing their demographic target markets. And recently, Ray's research has been confirmed and supplemented by the findings of the University of Michigan's *World Values Survey*.

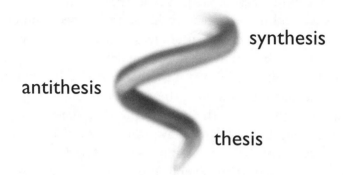

Figure 3-3. The dialectic of development.

So without belaboring the point, I think it's fairly safe to conclude that within the developed world there are at least three major
and distinct stages of consciousness and culture: traditional, modernist, and postmodern. And it is clear that these stages have arisen
in an historical sequence with the traditional being the oldest and
the postmodern the most recent. But again, how do we get from this
simple conclusion about subcultures to the elaborate idea of a dialectical spiral? As we have already discussed, and as we will explore
further in chapter 10 on "The Directions of Evolution," the answer is
that the spiral structure results from the natural geometry found in
the relationship of thesis-antithesis-synthesis (illustrated in Figure
3-3), which can be seen in the pattern of development exhibited by
the stages of consciousness. This pattern of development defines the
character of the stages and is critical to their understanding. One of
Piaget's most memorable quotes is that "there is no structure which
lacks a development, and that the process of development can only
be understood in view of the structure which exists at the beginning
and the structures into which it will evolve." In other words, as we
have seen, the stages arise in relation to each other and actually form
each other through these relationships. Thus, if we are to acknowledge that the stages themselves are observable, if we are able to see
the stages for ourselves, then we may also be able to discern how the
character of each stage is shaped by the problems and deficiencies of
its previous stage, and how each stage's own problems in turn shape

the character of the stage that comes after it in time. And when we once recognize these structural connections, we can see that these relationships are unmistakably dialectical.

A good illustration of a dialectical relationship among the stages is found in the development of the idea of "what is true." At the warrior stage of consciousness, the value of truth relates to the real distribution of power—what's true is what is powerful. Truth for traditional consciousness is usually defined by a particular tradition's holy scripture, such as the Bible. Truth for modernist consciousness is generally defined as objective scientific fact, and that which can be materially proved, whereas truth for postmodern consciousness is far more contextually dependent. As we have seen, postmodernism's subjective approach to truth is found in both the subjectivism of critical academia as well as in the "anything goes" culture of New Age spirituality. An important part of postmodernism's definition of truth can thus be seen as an antithetical reaction to modernism's version of the truth. And as we will explore in the chapters ahead, with integral consciousness, truth is increasingly recognized in the synthetic integration and harmonization of science and spirituality.

Figure 3-4 shows how the value of truth evolves along a dialectic path with the individualistic stages on the right defining truth with reference to an exterior or "actual" reality (such as military power or sensory-empirical proof) and the communal stages on the left defining truth more through reference to a socially constructed or interior reality (such as holy scripture or cultural relativism). But in this illustration, even though the understanding of the truth swings back and forth from thesis to antithesis, we can observe overall synthetic progress as the spiral is ascended, and this is especially true of the synthesis achieved at the integral level.

The dialectical spiral structure thus serves as a powerful hypothesis that explains the developmental relationships between the stages, and so like any theory, its relative accuracy is recognized in the way its explanation fits the observable data. That is, because so many of the facts of history exhibit dialectical development, their very existence suggests the underlying pattern of the spiral. As we come to understand how human history develops according to this systemic evolutionary pattern, we can begin to recognize more clearly why

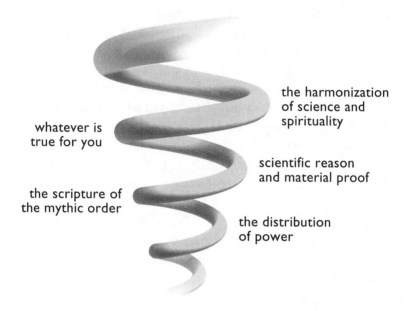

Figure 3-4. The dialectical progression of the recognized source of "Truth".

some societies have progressed and others have remained stagnant. We can see where a stale thesis requires the challenge of its antithesis, and we can also see where conditions may be ripe for an emergent synthesis. And while these relationships do become more obvious when viewed from an integral perspective, it is possible to recognize the dialectical progression of history even from the vantage point of modernist or postmodern consciousness. Thus by more fully appreciating the way the stages of history continue to exist and shape our world in the present, we can use the spiral to better understand why things have gotten stuck, and we can help people move forward in ways that are most appropriate for them. As we will see throughout this book, the truth of the spiral is evinced in the way that it yields accurate predictions about what will work and what we can expect in the future.

My diagram of this structure of development is drawn as a logarithmic spiral, growing wider as it ascends, because this also fits the data: Developing consciousness is becoming more complex, yet with each new level to emerge we see a recurrent pattern wherein there is a return to either the individualistic or communitarian orientations of the previous stages, but at a level that better integrates what came before. The conceptual image of the spiral structure thus helps us see how the stages are related; it reveals their dynamic tensions and cross-level affinities. This geometrical model also illustrates how the stages of consciousness function together as a relational system of evolution, similar to an ecosystem. And as we have seen, the health of this internal ecosystem must be maintained to preserve both the path of development of each individual as they grow up from infancy, as well as the functional stability of complex civilizations.

We will return to our discussion of the dialectic character of evolutionary development in chapter 10 on "The Directions of Evolution." But now, as we keep in mind this understanding of how development unfolds through the pattern of thesis, antithesis, and synthesis, we turn to our discussion of the extraordinary synthesis found within the integral stage of consciousness.

CHAPTER 4

The Integral Stage of Consciousness

WITHIN PROGRESSIVE CULTURE AS A WHOLE THERE IS A DEEP yearning for some kind of large-scale social awakening. Many are stirred by the poverty of values they see all around them and long for some kind of breakthrough that will pull us out of what often seems like a hopeless mess. Yet many of those who call for such a great awakening vaguely envision it as a kind of miraculous revolution, a crises-induced change of heart that will bring us all together through a new vision of our essential unity within the greater earth community. Such sentimental hopes for global transformation are indeed charming, but hardly realistic. While it is realistic to recognize that some kind of significant transcendence is now required, it is not realistic to assume that a revolutionary change would produce the kind of sustainable advance that our civilization requires. To be sustainable, the transformation we seek must come about as a result of evolution, not revolution. However, when we look closely and carefully at the historical phenomenon of cultural evolution through the lens of integral philosophy, we can begin to see what can be expected next. The cultural evolution that we need will come to us as it has always come before: in the form of a new values-based worldview forged through the interpenetration of increasing problems and newly perceived opportunities.

Although postmodernism's contribution to humanity's evolution is not yet complete, there are many signs that it is reaching maturity as a level of culture. So as we look beyond postmodernism in anticipation of the bound-to-be-thrilling history of the twenty-first century, we can begin to see the contours of the next emerging wave of consciousness and culture. The integral worldview, which we now explore in detail, represents a transcendence of postmodernism because it does what postmodernism cannot: It fully recognizes the legitimacy and evolutionary necessity of all previous stages of development. Integral consciousness thus grows up by reaching down. It produces evolution more effectively because it understands evolution more thoroughly. And as we come to better appreciate the subtle habits and methods of evolution—its gentle persuasion, and the way that it grows from within itself, always building on what came before—we can begin to see how *the degree of our transcendence is determined by the scope of our inclusion.*

Like each of the previously arising, historically significant worldviews, integral consciousness is emerging in response to what might be characterized as a "push" and a "pull." As we've seen, the push toward a new stage of consciousness comes from the pressure of unsatisfactory life conditions and the accumulating pathologies of previously existing stages. The pull arises from the attraction power of a new stage's fresh values—new truth, new beauty, and new ideals of morality that always accompany the birth of a new historical level. So first we'll look at the push toward integral consciousness, and then we'll examine the pull of the values of the integral worldview.

Life Conditions for Integral Consciousness

Due to the dialectical current of conflict and resolution that apparently underlies all forms of evolutionary development, we must begin our search for the course of our future development within the confines of conflict that currently afflict our culture. There is in the developed world an increasingly bitter clash of worldviews wherein these stages are battling for control of the laws and mores of their societies. This cultural struggle is found not simply between liberals and conservatives; in the developed world, we actually face a three-way conflict between the values of traditionalism, modernism, and postmodernism. Or perhaps more accurately, we are faced with a tug-of-war between traditionalism and postmodernism for the soul of the modernist majority. But however we characterize the culture war, we can see that the stakes are high. Because progressive development is sorely needed, and because the cost of the culture war is developmental stagnation, we need to find the peace of greater agreement in order to make meaningful progress. With integral consciousness we can see how the values of each worldview stage are both part of the solution and part of the problem—each stage embodies both dignities and disasters: Traditional consciousness identifies the need to reduce lawless violence and evil in the world, yet it creates oppression. Modernist consciousness identifies opportunities for development and discovery, yet it creates gross inequalities. And postmodern consciousness identifies the need to honor and include everyone, yet it also creates blindness to comparative excellence. Because each of these worldviews are very much alive and well within the developed world today, not only are they each continuing to produce their particular kind of progress, each of them are also continuing to act out their particular kind of pathology. And this is where the cultural battle is joined.

Moreover, this social acrimony is exacerbated by the tendency of each of these stages to see the other existing worldviews primarily for their pathologies, discounting the progress and stability these other worldviews are continuing to bring to the world. There is a general lack of understanding about how the other worldviews are actually most appropriate for a given set of life conditions. For instance, modernists tend to view the postmodern worldview as some kind of politically correct fashion. Postmodern sensibilities are often dismissed as "airy fairy." Likewise, traditionalists often see those who fail to ascribe to their worldview as misguided sinners or worse. And postmodernists also tend to vilify modernists and traditionalists as the real cause of the world's problems. In fact, postmodernism can be intensely antimodern, despite the fact that modernism represents the next crucial step for the majority of the world's population.

When we look at the culture war from inside any one of these worldviews, we can sympathize with their respective frustration; it's not hard to imagine just how wrongheaded the others look when we ourselves adopt any one worldview to the exclusion of all others. But from an integral perspective we can also see that when we fight the culture war, we only strengthen the more regressive segments of these worldviews. The more we condemn the value poverty of these respective worldviews, the more we push people into their corners, feeding into the fears that give rise to each stage's particular kind of orthodoxy. And as the orthodox segments of each worldview become more powerful, this makes positive progress more and more difficult.

However, integral consciousness recognizes that this seemingly unresolvable culture war in fact presents a powerfully problematic life condition that helps define integralism's own transcendent vision. Unlike the previous stages, each of which take as their animating life conditions the problems of the immediately preceding level, the life conditions for integral consciousness can be found in the set of problems created by all of the previous levels at once. Integral consciousness finds its value-solutions by understanding how to harmonize and integrate the distinctive values of each historically significant worldview. Because integral consciousness can better listen to and understand the legitimate concerns of every worldview, it can help heal the rifts created by the culture war by appropriately validating each set of values and by championing the essential core of those values at a more inclusive level. It's by showing that we actually care deeply about the enduring ideals and rightful concerns of each previous worldview that we can disempower each level's extremists and achieve the kind of higher-level agreement that will help quell the current conflict. Integral consciousness is thus required—and it is actually brought into being—as the only realistic solution to the inherent incompatibility of these previously arising evolutionary stages of consciousness.

In addition to the problematic life conditions caused by the increasing conflict between the stages, integral consciousness also finds its animating life conditions in the growing global problems that are increasingly affecting everyone: environmental degradation, injustice and oppression, terrorism, unfettered corporate globalization, hunger, poverty, disease, and war. Now, these global problems have already been well identified by postmodern consciousness; postmodernism's worldcentric morality naturally sees the urgent need to protect the environment and care for the needy. Indeed, most of us can clearly see how the problems identified by postmodernism are very real and very threatening. Yet it is postmodernism's failure to offer effective and realistic solutions to the problems it identifies that creates a need for the integral vision. As we've discussed, postmodernism's solutions usually call for a "transformation of global consciousness," and this is often accompanied by the admonition "that we all need to come together, and wake up to the fact that we're really all one people." And if it were possible for the world to come together like this, it would indeed provide many solutions. However, these calls for a great awakening ring hollow because they are usually addressed to humanity as a whole without regard for the fact that the majority of humanity is not yet able to make meaning in the way that the postmodernists implore. Thus, because most postmodernists generally fail to understand how consciousness and culture actually evolve through a series of specific stages, they do not really know how to bring about the change of mind they seek. This is well-articulated by Ken Wilber, who writes:

> Simply asserting that we should all learn a worldcentric ecology, or embrace a global compassion, is a noble but pragmatically less-than-useful project, because worldcentric waves are the product of development, not exhortation. As noted, the "new paradigm" approaches exhort a goal without elucidating the path to that goal—they are cheerleaders for a cause that has no means of actualization, which perhaps explains the deep frustration among new-paradigm advocates who know they have a better ideal but are disappointed at how little the world responds to their calls.

However, once we recognize how consciousness is distributed across the spiral of development, we can see that the next step for the majority of the world's population is the transition into traditional consciousness or modernist consciousness. This increased understanding of the evolution of consciousness and culture shows that a majority of the world's population has not even reached the modernist stage, and therefore is not going to adopt the values of postmodern consciousness anytime soon. Thus we need to find solutions that don't require the entire world to become postmodern in some kind of miraculous transformation.

Most of us can see that many of the significant problems of the world are getting worse. The question now before us is whether these problems must reach a point of acute crisis before they exert sufficient pressure to produce the kind of cultural evolution that will result in their alleviation. It may indeed take a global crisis to trigger the emergence of the integral worldview as a significant cultural structure. But regardless of what happens in the future, hopefully, these global problems are troubling enough in the present to stimulate the emergence of the integral worldview in a critical mass of people. Hopefully, our culture will evolve fast enough to prevent the kind of crisis that could actually cause culture to regress. However, we can do more than just hope. Through the adoption of integral values we can begin to see, agree, and participate in the realistic solutions offered by the integral worldview (which we'll discuss below).

As we can see throughout history, problems often remain invisible until solutions appear—until a better way is shown, people often become resigned to seeing current conditions as just "the way things are." Some think that human nature never changes, that we will always have war, haves and have-nots, and the kind of exploitive selfishness that makes a better world seem impossible. But when we see how values and the worldviews they construct actually do evolve—that as the spiral is ascended "human nature" does evolve— we can begin to perceive the new set of life conditions which contain the new opportunities for evolution that are now before us.

In summary, it is the contemporary life conditions of the stagnation of social progress brought about by an increasingly bitter culture war, looming global disasters, and the failure of postmodernism to offer realistic solutions to the problems it identifies that serve as the push, the pressure that is resulting in evolutionary development toward the integral stage of consciousness.

The Values of Integral Consciousness

Integral values arise out of an enlarged understanding of value itself. With integral consciousness comes a new appreciation of how values are the substance of every worldview, serving as the energy-like source of systemic metabolism for these internal universe structures. Integral consciousness thus recognizes the importance of values because it can see that it is values themselves that are actually evolving within the realm of consciousness and culture.

Of all the values of the integral worldview, that which it most esteems is the value of evolution itself. And with this exaltation of the value of evolution comes the ideal of "the prime directive." The prime directive is to work to maintain the health and sustainability of the entire channel of cultural evolution, the spiral of development as a whole. Because every infant begins life at the level of archaic consciousness, the flow of evolution through the levels is unceasing. So the prime directive instructs us that for cultural evolution to be sustainable, the enduring contributions of each stage of the system must be healthy and functioning within the greater society. Caring for the spiral as a whole means preserving the evolutionary opportunities for every person, regardless of that person's place in the sequence of evolution.

However, the values of the prime directive include not only the values of progress and development through the stages, but also the inherent value of each stage as it is in itself. One of my favorite quotes by Clare Graves is his famous exclamation: "Damn it all, a person has the right to be who he is." And this of course applies not only to the people living in fragile tribal cultures, whom we all want to protect, but also to people living in fundamentalist cultures who may not be as appealing to postmodern sensibilities. So in addition to valuing the channel of evolution of consciousness and culture as a whole, integral consciousness is also able to appreciate the healthy values of each stage in a new way.

Integral consciousness achieves its evolutionary advance partially by being able to metabolize all the values of the spiral. This does not mean that integral thinking values everything equally (a pathology of postmodern consciousness), but rather, that it recognizes how the real values of every historically significant worldview must be included within our larger estimates of what is good and worthwhile. And this applies even to the oldest human worldviews. For example, an enduring contribution of tribal culture can be seen in the necessity of family loyalty—and this same sense of primal loyalty can be magnified by the values of the higher levels to include not just loyalty to our blood kin, but loyalty to the entire family of humanity. Similarly, the fierce sense of individual autonomy that arises with warrior consciousness can be carried forward to preserve personal freedom and individual liberties even within complex, interdependent societies.

People whose center of gravity is within integral consciousness are able to effectively use the appropriate reactions for all life conditions that have evolved over the millennia. For example, when it comes to setting up an organization, postmodern consciousness naturally wants to create a nonhierarchical, consensus type of organization. And for some conditions this is entirely appropriate. But for other life conditions, such an organization can be highly dysfunctional. Integral consciousness, however, can better read life conditions and thus create the kind of organization most appropriate for the members and for the task. If the situation calls for a command-and-control military-style organization, integral consciousness can create this, or if a group's purposes can best be served through an incentive-based corporate organization, integral consciousness can create this as well.

A similar example of how integral philosophy can be applied within an organization comes from the management of my own company. Every time I hire a new employee, after discussing the company's mission statement, I go through our organization's "basic agreements." The first agreement is the honor code: no lying, cheating, or stealing—this simple black-and-white expression of our value of honesty honors the foundational values of traditional consciousness. Next comes the agreement to strive for excellence—here we define performance goals and express our value of continuous improvement that arises from the modernist worldview. Then we discuss the agreement of mutual respect and interpersonal fairness, which specifies that despite the hierarchy of management authority, everyone in the organization has a right to be respected, informed, and treated as a valuable human whose intrinsic worth is not limited to their role in the company. With this agreement of mutual respect comes the responsibility to treat the other members of the organization, as well as the suppliers and customers of the business, with this same type of basic regard. This agreement of mutual respect thus attempts to honor the sensibilities of postmodern consciousness. These "value agreements" serve to supplement the company's mission statement by affirming the type of organizational culture to which we aspire.

However, the best examples of how integral consciousness can use the values of the spiral as a whole are found in the context of politics. As we will examine in more detail in the upcoming chapter on "Integral Politics," integral consciousness transcends the politics of left and right by recognizing how the values and programs of traditional consciousness, modernist consciousness, and postmodern consciousness each have appropriate applications to different sets of life conditions. Sometimes the solutions of traditionalists apply, sometimes a modernist's approach is best, and sometimes the sensibilities of the postmodern worldview should prevail. Again, it's not that integral consciousness values these approaches equally—it can see that postmodernism is more evolved than the others—but integral consciousness can also see where postmodernism is not evolved enough to always work for the benefit of the spiral as a whole. Thus, by including the best of all worldviews in life condition appropriate proportion, the integral worldview is able to transcend all previous worldviews in its power to produce cultural evolution.

In our discussion of the stages of consciousness in chapter 3, we examined how the emerging values of every historically significant new worldview provide their adherents with an increased perception power that allows them to see new aspects of reality. Traditional consciousness provides an increased ability to see the difference between right and wrong. Modernist consciousness provides new insight into the material nature of the external universe and the natural "rights of man." Postmodern consciousness provides the ability to recognize the excesses of modernism, as well as the many alternatives to the modernist way of seeing things. And now, through the emerging values of integral consciousness we are given fresh insight into how consciousness and culture develop and evolve, and this shows us how we can become agents of evolution by participating more directly in its unfolding.

Integral consciousness, however, provides not only a new way of seeing things, but also a new way of arriving at creative solutions—a *new epistemological capacity*. This emergent capacity can be compared to the earlier emergence of reason and rationality within modernist consciousness—an ability rarely seen in earlier stages. While it is certainly possible for earlier stages of consciousness to use forms of reason and logic, premodern consciousness generally fails to see how the myths that dominate its ways of thinking are inherently unreasonable, if not completely irrational. Premodern consciousness thus cannot use reason like modernist consciousness does to demythologize the world and see nature with the new clarity that only a thoroughly rational worldview can provide. So just as the rise of modernist consciousness brings the new and powerful capacity of reason, the rise of integral consciousness likewise brings a similar new capacity that emerges out of its enlarged ability to evaluate internal universe phenomena.

Wilber refers to this emergent capacity as "vision-logic," which he describes as follows:

> Where the formal-mind [modernist consciousness] establishes higher and creative relationships, vision-logic establishes networks of those relationships. The point is to place each proposition alongside numerous others, so as to be able to see, or "to vision," how the truth or falsity of any one proposition would affect the truth or falsity of all the others. Such panoramic or vision-logic apprehends a mass network or ideas, how they influence each other, what their relationships are. It is thus the beginning of a truly higher-order synthesizing capacity, of making connections, relating truths, coordinating ideas, integrating concepts.

According to Wilber, vision-logic represents an integration of intellectual capacity with intuition in a way that brings together the body and the mind so as to produce this new ability to recognize relationships and approach problems with enhanced creativity.

In my experience, this new epistemological capacity of integral consciousness can be best described as "dialectical evaluation," because unlike reason or logic, this new ability is centered in *volition* rather than *cognition*. That is, the new insights provided by "vision-logic" come about through the use of our *will*—it's a process of evaluation informed by head and heart—as opposed to the exercise of reason and logic, which is more analytical and strictly cognitive. The process of integrally informed dialectical evaluation recognizes how conflicting values and worldviews actually work together within a larger evolutionary system, mutually supporting each other in opposition, in a manner that can be compared to the function of a tension strut in an architectural structure. Through dialectical evaluation we can see how the elements of any evolutionary system work together in their mutually supporting roles of thesis-antithesis-synthesis. However, it is only by appropriately *valuing* each element of the system that we can actually correctly perceive its crucial function within the system as a whole. This involves more than simply "weighing the alternatives" and assigning different values to various components; it is a way of understanding and appreciating that requires an intuitive sympathy achieved only by entering into the alternative perspectives that generate the opposing values. When we look at evolutionary processes without this ability, all we can see is conflict; but when we come to recognize the unfolding of larger internal structures through time, we can begin to better appreciate how they fit together within a larger purpose, and this allows us to engage these structures more creatively. Recognizing this, Robert Kegan actually defines integral consciousness as "the capacity to see conflict as a signal of our overidentification with a single system."

As you think about what dialectical evaluation might mean for you, keep in mind that this process is subtle, and that it relies on the expanded vertical perspective provided by integral consciousness. This enhanced epistemological capacity is very real and very powerful, but it does take practice for one to gain an experiential understanding of it. Examples of the use of vision-logic or dialectical evaluation can be found in the upcoming chapters on integral politics and integral spirituality. We'll also discuss this capacity in chapter 7 on "The Founders of Integral Philosophy," where we'll see how Hegel was perhaps the first philosopher to clearly demonstrate this emergent ability. And in chapter 9 on the "Structures of the Human Mind," we'll further discuss the crucial role of *free will* in the growth and development of consciousness at every level.

Integral Consciousness

Perceived life conditions:
conflict between at least 3 previous stages; looming global problems; failure of postmodernism to offer realistic solutions

Worldview and values:
• new insight into the "internal universe"
• confidence in potential of evolutionary philosophy
• personal responsibility for the problems of the world
• renewed appreciation of previous stages' values
• appreciation of conflicting truth and dialectical evaluation
• aspiration for the harmonization of science and religion

Contribution to the spiral:
practical worldcentric morality; compassion for all worldviews; revival of philosophy; seeing spirituality in evolution; overcoming the culture war; renewed insistence on achieving results

Pathology:
elitist; insensitive; aloof; lack of patience

Organizational structure:
world Federalism; any structure appropriate for given life conditions (orgs. from any of the previous levels)

Exemplary leaders:
Albert Einstein; Teilhard de Chardin; Alfred North Whitehead; David Ray Griffin; Ken Wilber

Estimated percent of world population: <1%

Estimated percent of wealth & political power: <1%

Techno-economic mode of production:
global systems economy

Key technologies:
dialectical evaluation; spiral analysis; systems science; spiritual practice

Type of medicine:
integral—scientific, holistic, plus emerging spiritual and subtle energy medicine

The true:
harmonization of science and spirituality; the evolutionary significance of values

The beautiful:
nature; the arts of each level in their emergent phase; the unification of extreme contrasts

The good:
evolution; the prime directive

Average neurological activation:
increasing integration of right and left brain hemispheres

Transition triggers:
need for a greater sense of community; spiritual experience; allures of postintegral culture

Other names for this stage:
authentic consciousness; systems thinking; autonomous; self-actualized; yellow meme

Chart 4-1. Characteristics of integral consciousness.

We will continue to examine the emergent values and capacities of integral consciousness throughout our remaining discussion. But for purposes of comparison with the previous stages of consciousness, Chart 4-1 summarizes the characteristics of the integral worldview as we presently understand it.

Integral Consciousness in the Context of History

Locating integral consciousness within its place along the spiral of development (as illustrated in Figure 4-1, below) reveals the many similarities between the modernist worldview and the integral worldview. However, we can distinguish modernist values from integral values in the way that integral consciousness embraces and includes all the healthy values of postmodernist consciousness (and the other stages) in its evolutionary transcendence. And this transcendent act of inclusion makes the integral worldview significantly different than modernism. But despite the major differences, we can still see many parallels between the emergence of early modernist consciousness during the Enlightenment and the emergence of integral consciousness in our time. Consider the following similarities: modernist consciousness values progress, integral consciousness values evolution; modernist consciousness sees the good life in an abundance of status and material possessions, integral consciousness sees the good life in an

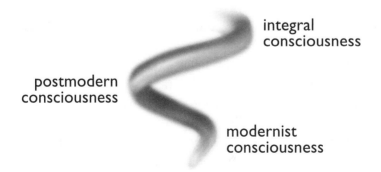

Figure 4-1. The dialectical development of the modernist, postmodern, and integral stages of consciousness.

abundance of consciousness—the abundance that comes from the continuous development of the inner life. Modernists are fascinated by external technologies such as machines and electronics, and similarly, integralists are attracted to internal technologies such as psychospiritual practices. When modernism first appeared, it had a new approach—reason and the scientific method. Now integral consciousness likewise brings a new approach—dialectical evaluation and the compassionate use of the spiral as a method of relating to the good in each level and seeing the bad in appropriate perspective.

As we look for parallels between early modernism and integralism, we can also see how the rise of the modernist worldview in the seventeenth century was catalyzed by what we might refer to as the discovery of the big picture of the *external* universe—the discovery that the earth revolved around the sun. Once Copernicus and Galileo conclusively showed the heliocentric nature of the solar system, the authority of traditional consciousness was undermined, and European intellectuals could never see the world in the old way again. Now in our time we are blessed with a similarly monumental discovery—the discovery of the big picture of the *internal* universe—the systemic structure of the spiral of development. And like the discovery of the solar system, once we recognize the significance of the discovery of the evolving structures of consciousness and culture, we will likewise never be able to see the world in the old way again.

However, as we compare the events of the first Enlightenment with similar developments here in the twenty-first century, the most significant parallel is found in the role of philosophy itself. During the first Enlightenment, the prime mover of cultural evolution was the philosophy of Descartes, Spinoza, Locke, Voltaire, Montesquieu, and Rousseau. This "New Philosophy" (as it was actually called at the time) was born out of the liberating influence of science. Prior to the Enlightenment, "the officially and legally sanctioned philosophy prevailing in universities and academies, and dominating philosophical and scientific discourse and textbooks" was Scholastic Aristotelianism, a philosophical system that had become subservient to the precepts of the Church. But as scientific discoveries began to point to the need for a new philosophy that could accommodate the enlarged picture of the universe these discoveries disclosed, a conflict was inevitable. According to Enlightenment scholar Jonathan Israel:

> It was unquestionably the rise of powerful new philosophical systems, rooted in the scientific advances of the early seventeenth century, and especially in the mechanistic views of Galileo, which chiefly generated a vast *Kulturkampf* [cultural struggle] between traditional, theologically sanctioned ideas about Man, God, and the universe and secular mechanistic conceptions which stood independently of any theological sanction.

While it took over one hundred years for the New Philosophy to finally triumph, by the time of Kant, Enlightenment philosophy had brought to the majority of European intellectuals a new view of the world, a new system of values, and a thirst for progress whose way forward had been illuminated by the liberating insights of this new modernist stage of consciousness. And it was this New Philosophy that catalyzed the democratic revolutions in America and France, and set the stage for the Industrial Revolution.

By the time of the Enlightenment, the ancient philosophy of Scholasticism had become "a senescent structure of pedagogical dogmatism that no longer spoke to the new spirit of the age. Little or nothing fresh was emerging from its confines." Scholasticism had stagnated because it had become the handmaiden of religion. Now in our time we can observe a very similar situation wherein the officially sanctioned philosophy of our age has become stale. But the relative stagnation of contemporary professional academic philosophy, its irrelevance in the lives of most Western intellectuals, has this time resulted from its subservience to the "Newtonian-Cartesian" worldview. Just as Scholasticism had lost its potency by the time of the first Enlightenment as a result of being compromised by religion, now at the beginning of the Second Enlightenment, professional academic philosophy has been similarly compromised by its subordination to science. According to Richard Tarnas, philosophy in the twentieth century had developed to the point where:

the Cartesian critical intellect has reached its furthest point of development, doubting all, applying a systematic skepticism to every possible meaning.... The whole project of the [Western philosophical tradition] to grasp and articulate a foundational reality has been criticized as a futile exercise in linguistic game playing, a sustained but doomed effort to move beyond elaborate fictions of its own creation. More pointedly, such a project has been condemned as inherently alienating and oppressively hierarchical—an intellectually imperious procedure that has produced an existential and cultural impoverishment, and that has led ultimately to the technocratic domination of nature and the social-political domination of others.

So just as in the first Enlightenment, when philosophy was liberated from the static confines of the reigning establishment, leaping forward like a coiled spring, we can now see a similar period of philosophical progress ahead. In the first Enlightenment, philosophy became separated from religion; now philosophy is becoming similarly liberated from the confines of scientific materialism and existentialism as it transcends and includes both science and religion while leaving both institutions secure within their own domains. These historical comparisons are necessarily made in terms of broad generalities, but to my mind the parallels are too significant to ignore.

But how do we really know that integral consciousness is truly a new historical level of civilization? How can we really say that integral consciousness is on the rise? "New paradigms" are a dime a dozen these days. However, the worldview of integral consciousness is not so much a new paradigm as it is an integration and harmonization of all previously existing worldviews within a new and inclusive light. The whole point of integral consciousness is to move beyond the idea of "old paradigm bad, new paradigm good." As we have already discussed, there is significant evidence for the stages of development. And we have seen how the theory of the dialectical spiral "fits the data" and elegantly describes the developmental events of history. But perhaps the most significant evidence that a new level of development is on the rise is the fact that we really need it—that life conditions here at the beginning of the twenty-first century cry out for cultural evolution. So we can have confidence that something very much like the integral worldview will indeed emerge because this is exactly the kind of development that our civilization needs most.

As we look for signs of the emerging cultural structures of integral consciousness, we should remember that modernism required over one hundred years before it became an influential segment of society. Postmodernism likewise took decades after its first identifiable appearance before it could be recognized as a significant subculture. We can thus anticipate that integral culture will similarly take some time before it begins to make a substantial impact. But again, cultural evolution depends on life conditions; the faster things get worse, the faster integral consciousness will develop in response.

Practicing the Integral Lifestyle—Value Metabolism

As we will discuss at length in chapter 6, values such as truth, beauty, and goodness serve as sources of energy for the people who perceive and use them. Values become real—they enact the systems of agreement that build culture—when they are actually used or practiced in a manner that results in the improvement of the human condition. For example, when modernism was originally emerging, its new conception of truth motivated people to pursue scientific research. The naturalists of the Enlightenment were mostly aristocratic amateurs who were drawn to explore nature through the exciting power of the new scientific method. The feelings of excitement that resulted from modernism's new way of seeing things also brought about the sophisticated form of music we now call classical. For instance, if you listen to Vivaldi's *Four Seasons* concertos (written in 1723), you can actually hear the feeling of fresh discovery and the energy of those heady times. However, the values of modernism produced evolution in more than just the fields of science and music; politics also became a central stage for the application of the modernist worldview. Tom Paine, for example, was "practicing modernism" when he penned his famous consciousness-raising document *Common Sense*.

It was activism like this, fueled by the power of new truth and new ideals of liberty and the "rights of man," that would result in modernism's ascendency.

Similarly, we can see how the fresh values of the emerging postmodern worldview provided the energy and inspiration to express a new kind of liberation from what had by then become the tired, materialistic values of modernism. Like the original values of modernism that had emerged two hundred years before, postmodernism's new countercultural values found expression in music, lifestyle, and political activism. Among the first to adopt the outlook of postmodern consciousness were pioneering reformers and social critics such as Woody Guthrie, Margaret Mead, and Eleanor Roosevelt. Then in the 1960s, postmodern consciousness was adopted by the baby boom generation en masse as peace activists, feminists, civil rights leaders, artists, musicians, and the youth movement as a whole championed the values of the postmodern vision. It was also during this time that the peak experiences and spiritual insight provided by Eastern spirituality and psychedelic drugs shifted the consciousness of many into the postmodern worldview. But even after the wave of sixties culture receded in the 1970s, the essential values of postmodern consciousness continued to be adopted by mainstream academia, the entertainment elite, environmentalists, feminists, and those attracted by the various forms of New Age spirituality. These post-sixties adherents of postmodern values were not all aging hippies; as the postmodern worldview matured, its values reflected a diverse but coherent agenda that brought together people from a wide variety of backgrounds. Thus, like the practice of modernism, the practice of the postmodern worldview finds expression in simple things like one's diet and wardrobe, as well as in life-defining choices like one's career.

When it comes to practicing the integral worldview, we have to remember that we are called to actually create this new level of consciousness ourselves. Those of us who can discern the emergence of this new stage of civilization here at its beginnings have the privilege of receiving the creative impulse of the first wave of integral values.

The truths of integral philosophy can be used to produce cultural evolution on many fronts. Wherever we find the culture war—in the workplace, in our schools, and even in our own families—we can skillfully work to raise consciousness by showing how different values apply to different life conditions. As we begin to see how just about every human problem is a problem of consciousness, we can then see how best to raise consciousness by distinguishing between the healthy and pathological values of a given stage, and by translating the values of one stage into terms that can be better appreciated by other stages. Think about all the ways that we can help keep well-meaning postmodern consciousness from literally dissolving the crucial structures of traditional and modernist values upon which our further evolution depends. And conversely, think about all the ways we can communicate the evolutionary necessity of postmodern values to traditionalists and modernists by showing how our civilization's actual survival largely depends on the success of postmodernism.

The values of integralism find expression in the motivation to develop ourselves through spiritual practices such as meditation and worship; by keeping our bodies healthy though good diet and exercise; by involvement with our community; by translating the feeling of integralism into new forms of art; and through lifelong learning and the active life of the mind. However, integral practice is not just a technique of personal development; integral practice also involves our direct participation in the important work of alleviating the growing global problems that seem too hopeless or too remote to most of those who make meaning within earlier worldviews. As we will explore in the forthcoming chapter on "Integral Politics," integral philosophy's new understanding of cultural evolution makes vividly clear what the next steps for civilization must be. Just as the political vision of democracy did much to bring people into the modernist worldview during the Enlightenment, and just as the twin political issues of equal rights and peace in Vietnam served to magnify the worldcentric values of postmodernism and attract many to its worldview, so too does integralism have its own worldview-defining political agenda. And the new politics of integral consciousness provides many exciting opportunities for the kinds of activism that distinguished the heroes of emerging modernism and postmodernism.

During the Enlightenment the rallying cry of "Liberty, equality, fraternity" became the invitation to adopt a new set of values emphasizing self-determination and the political transformation of a nation into a new democratic order of free and equal brothers. Likewise in the sixties, the call for transformation was embodied in the slogan "Turn on, tune in, drop out." And despite its irreverent, semi-humorous quality, Timothy Leary's rallying cry did serve as a potent invitation to reject the pathologies of the modernist worldview and join in a movement that reflected an entirely new set of values. So perhaps there will eventually appear a uniquely integral rallying cry that evokes the longing for a new politics that transcends left and right; a new science that embraces the interior domains as well as the exterior; a new art that reclaims the beautiful and the sublime; and even a new spirituality that recognizes the universal nature of spiritual experience. Perhaps slogans like "Transcend and include," or even "Thesis, antithesis, synthesis" will arise as invitations to become part of this new phase of consciousness. But more than slogans, the integral worldview needs successful applications—demonstrations of its power and purpose by those who will dare to be pioneers in this "new movement in the symphony of human history."

So you may ask: What does it really feel like to have integral consciousness? Well, there is a feeling of amused anticipation, like knowing a big secret that's about to be revealed; there's a feeling of pleasure associated with a sense of wonder—a feeling that must have been felt by the early modernists when they realized just how powerful human reason, the scientific method, and constitutional democracy could be. And with integral consciousness there is a feeling of conviction, a sense of confidence in "the way forward" that arises from the new truths of the integral worldview. This new feeling of confidence is accompanied by a sense of optimism about the inevitability of evolution, and as this feeling of confidence matures, it can be recognized as a form of moral courage. But perhaps the most significant feeling associated with integral consciousness is the way it makes you feel about other people. The practice of integral consciousness definitely results in an increased sense of compassion, sympathy, and respect for those about whom you previously felt consternated. However, accompanying this enlarged feeling of compassion is also a new sense of realism about the inherent limitations of those who dwell in these older worldviews.

I have a direct personal experience of integral consciousness, and thus I know that it is a historically significant new level because I can see how extremely useful it is. Yet integral consciousness is more than just a tool for problem solving; it's an identity-providing platform for cultural allegiance, a worldview that invites our passion and our loyalty. As integral practitioners we have to see ourselves as ambassadors of the future. We have to stand for the righteous values of the spiral as a whole and take responsibility at a very deep level for bringing about integral culture in our homes, in our communities, and across the globe. But when we begin to metabolize integral values, when we begin to use the enhanced vertical perspective on the evolving spectrum of consciousness provided by integral philosophy, we find that we are endowed with the energy and motivation to achieve success. Because "the way forward" in almost every life situation is shown in detail by the map of integral philosophy, and because our opportunities to participate in evolution on a micro and macro level are well illuminated by the integral worldview, we each have a significant part to play in this new wave of evolutionary progress. It's an exciting time to be alive!

Postintegral Consciousness

In our discussion of the evidence for cultural evolution set out in the last chapter, we reviewed the solid research that confirms that consciousness develops in specific stages, and that these stages look something very much like tribal, warrior, traditional, modernist... And in this discussion we also reviewed the good evidence that in America at least, there are three major but distinct subcultures (traditional, modern, and "countercultural") that each hold somewhat different and often conflicting values. So based on this research, and based on a reasonably modest assessment of the current state of our society, it is not irresponsibly speculative to look for and anticipate the emergence of this new integral level of values-based culture. Again, when we look at the evident history of cultural evolution, strong arguments can be made that the next identifiable wave of cultural development is beginning to appear on the horizon of history, and that this wave will be something very much like the integral stage which I have so far described. However, once we move beyond the discussion of this next immediate wave of development, we find ourselves relying on evidence that is far more speculative than what we have so far marshaled for the idea of integral consciousness.

Nevertheless, I don't think there's any doubt that there are higher stages of consciousness, and that many people past and present have achieved these levels in their personal development. But as we have seen, consciousness and culture develop together. So although we can point to evidence of higher stages (such as those achieved by saints, sages, and other spiritual adepts), we cannot point to cultural development in large groups that correspond to these levels. That is, the kind of historically significant worldviews that we've been discussing do not fully come into their own until they exist both in the consciousness of individuals as well as in the cultural structures of societies.

As we've noted, the spiral of development is not a deterministic blueprint that all development is bound to follow. The reality of human free will and creativity must be factored into the equation. The future is largely open to our own choices, so the contours of what can be termed "postintegral culture" cannot yet be described in detail. However, the dialectical trajectory of the spiral pattern does have predictive value. As life conditions change, we can certainly anticipate the eventual rise of levels of culture well beyond the integral. And based on the pattern of the spiral, we can also predict that the next values-based worldview that emerges after the integral worldview will have a communally oriented character that contrasts with the more individualistically oriented nature of the integral stage.

But when we look at the stages of consciousness primarily from a historical rather than a psychological perspective, we can also see how a given stage of consciousness actually depends on the established existence of its previous stage to create the problematic life conditions and pathologies that help define the values of this next given stage. For instance, without the preexisting culture of modernism, postmodern consciousness can arise only in a rather nebulous form. We can perhaps recognize the sensitive values of postmodern consciousness appearing in a premodern society in the example of

Saint Francis of Assisi. But when we compare the values and world-view of Saint Francis with the values and worldview of say, Henry David Thoreau, we can see how Thoreau (who was still well ahead of his time) embodies postmodern consciousness in a more well-defined and identifiable form than Saint Francis. And this is because Thoreau lived after the emergence of modernism, and thus his consciousness could receive the evolution-producing energy created by modernism's specific pathologies.

Nevertheless, just as early forms of postmodernism appeared at the very beginnings of modernism (as evidenced by the Romantic movement), we can likewise expect to see certain early expressions of postintegral culture here at the beginning of the integral stage. Yet we must be cautious of being too certain when labeling anything postintegral at this time in history. Just as much of Romanticism constituted a regression to premodern levels, much of what claims to be postintegral will actually be merely postmodern. In fact, a common tendency of postmodern consciousness is to generally overestimate everyone's level of development, including its own. Even when postmodernists begin to recognize integral consciousness, they often pronounce that it is not merely integral but postintegral.

Other integral theorists have devoted considerable attention to higher stages of consciousness, and these efforts are commendable. But as soon as we go beyond what can be observed culturally, as soon as the only subjects we can research are essentially spiritual teachers, we have gone beyond the confines of public philosophy and entered the realm of spirituality. Spirituality is certainly not a taboo subject for integral philosophy. As we'll explore in the upcoming chapter on "Integral Spirituality," and as we'll discuss further in chapter 8 on "The Integral Reality Frame," this is a rich and important part of the integral worldview. Yet in order for integral philosophy to achieve its mission of helping to bring about the next historically significant stage of culture, it is important for integral philosophy to be described in ways that allow for the inclusion of a variety of different spiritual belief systems. But the more we try to specifically define what higher consciousness actually looks like, the more we find ourselves relying on, or even privileging, the explanations of certain spiritual traditions to the exclusion of others. I have had direct experiences of what might be characterized as higher stages of awareness, and these profound experiences have left me permanently changed for the better. But in my "direct research" into higher consciousness, my experience did not correspond well to the descriptions of higher stages offered by the handful of mystics who have written about the subject. So although the higher and future stages of consciousness are a very interesting subject, these stages are best discussed within the context of spirituality rather than philosophy, because the evidence for these levels is of a different character than what we have explored thus far. The tricky task of defining where the public agreement of integral philosophy ends, and where authoritative spiritual teachings begin, will be taken up in chapter 8, where we'll discuss the metaphysical limits of integral philosophy.

CHAPTER 5

Integral Politics

THE RISE OF EVERY HISTORICALLY SIGNIFICANT NEW WORLDVIEW brings about substantial political evolution. Each emerging world-view's new political vision serves as a showcase for its relatively more evolved values and higher ideals of morality. For example, we noted that emerging modernism rejected the oppressive structures of feudalism and absolute monarchy and championed the new ideals of freedom and equality embodied in the call for democracy. This movement for democracy was, in fact, one of the main themes of the "New Philosophy" that articulated the modernist vision and served to define the character of the Enlightenment. Then again in the twentieth century, emerging postmodernism rejected the ethnocentric morality that condoned racism and the slaughter of innocents abroad and championed the political issues of civil rights, women's rights, and peace in Vietnam. The political issues of the war in Vietnam and the struggle for equality served to bring people together in a common cause. Thus many who adopted the postmodern worldview in the sixties and seventies did so because they had been politicized through their allegiance to these causes.

Just as much of modernism and postmodernism emerged from the crucible of politics, we can expect something similar with the rise of the integral worldview. After considering this carefully for a long time, I've come to the conclusion that the politics of integral consciousness can be expected to engage life conditions in the twenty-first century in two ways: First, integral politics will make common cause with the postmodern political agenda, helping it to be more effective by moderating it and by translating its truths into terms that can be better understood by the modernist majority. And second, integral politics will demonstrate its new ideals by championing a transcendent vision of a more evolved form of human political organization. We'll examine each of these aspects of integral politics in turn.

The Politics of the Spiral

The left-right conception of politics that dominates most political discourse in the developed world is woefully simplistic and generally inadequate as a model of the complex political dynamics of the twenty-first century. For example, we can see in history how the roles of liberal and conservative have actually reversed position several times (the Republicans were the progressives of the nineteenth century), and thus it is likely that some of those who now identify themselves as progressives may in the future find themselves defending the status quo. As we look at the politics of the developed world through the lens of the spiral of development, we can see that most of the current political debates are occurring within the context of modernism; in the United States, the Democratic and Republican Parties are both essentially modernist. We can see the influences of traditionalism and postmodernism tugging on either side of the modernist milieu, but we can also see how the ideologies of these other worldviews are significantly diluted through the compromises that characterize the modernist debate.

When we use the spiral to understand the current political landscape, we must keep in mind that among all the fronts of human evolution to which spiral analysis brings light, politics is the most subtle and complex. When it comes to politics, it is difficult to say anything general enough to be meaningful without being contradicted by numerous exceptions. For example, within each worldview's agenda can be found those who emphasize freedom and those who emphasize order. This often results in activists of decidedly different overall political persuasions finding themselves in temporary alliances with "strange bedfellows." And this is due to the many subcurrents and eddies that occur within the main currents of the spiral's larger dialectical structure. Therefore, although the spiral can be extremely useful in understanding politics and engaging in political activism, its effective use in politics demands a high degree of sophistication and an analysis that is sensitive to the subtleties and nuances of the complex historical dynamics it seeks to describe.

When we examine politics from the perspective of the spiral, we can begin to see the true significance of the worldcentric morality embodied in the politics of postmodernism. From a moral point of view, the higher values that are awakened when people enter the postmodern worldview eclipse the legitimacy of all previous forms of ethnocentric political justification. Postmodernism's deep sympathy for the disadvantaged and oppressed, its righteous outrage over ongoing injustice and hypocrisy, and its own sense of shame about the West's legacy of exploitation are all the result of significant evolution within consciousness. Integral consciousness must thus acknowledge the evolutionary importance and beauty of postmodernism's higher morality, even as it recognizes that this development is currently manifest in an immature form.

The integral perspective rejects the idea that the politics of left and right can be compared to the squabbling of selfish children who refuse to compromise for the greater good. This may be true at the modernist level, but with the rise of postmodernism's unprecedented worldcentric morality, a new era of history is born. Postmodernism represents the beginnings of a new political consciousness that rejects the "Machiavellian realism" of modernism in favor of a worldview that demands real fairness for every living person, regardless of where they live or how much wealth they have. In its most advanced expressions, postmodern politics embodies the spiritual ideals of universal justice and worldwide equality; and these ideals contrast sharply with modernism's historical tolerance of racism, sexism, ultranationalism, and the economic blindness that condones the ongoing destruction of the environment. In solidarity with postmodernism, integral consciousness sees that in the long run, the ethnocentric politics of group selfishness are dead, that the future belongs to those who recognize that all lasting political progress is grounded in morality, and that everybody counts. The integral worldview thus recognizes that civic improvement ultimately depends on the further development of the ethic of fairness within human society and government—integral consciousness can see that the increasing morality of interpersonal relations is the foundation of all real political evolution.

As it makes common cause with postmodern politics, integral consciousness recognizes that postmodernism's biggest political problem is its relative impotence. Since its rise as a political force in the sixties, postmodernism has been influential in the politics of the developed world (achieving considerably more success in Europe than in the U.S.), but there are still many important ways in which its agenda is currently trumped by modernism. Yet from an integral perspective, this is evolutionarily appropriate. Postmodernism may stand for the future of worldcentric political mores, but its policies are not yet mature enough to take charge of the developed world. Integral consciousness can thus make political progress by helping to moderate and restrain postmodernism's radicalism so that its important contributions can be better integrated into the politics of the developed world. Integral politics must therefore concentrate on the two areas where postmodernism needs the most development: moderation of its often staunch antimodern bias, and education regarding the "fragile ecology of markets."

The intense contempt for the achievements of modernism that characterizes many aspects of postmodernism is certainly understandable. The evolutionary impulse that originally called forth the emergence of the postmodern worldview was kindled by the moral failures and selfish excesses that accompanied modernism's historical advance. This power-generating stance of antithesis initially served to create the energy that was required for postmodernism's birth as a new, historically significant worldview. But the anger and shame that is characteristic of much of postmodern politics is now more of a hindrance than a help. Ironically, postmodernism's general disgust for the crimes of modernism is itself a demonstration that modernism resulted in evolutionary progress—modernism's success is evidenced by how it has produced its own transcendence in the form of the postmodern worldview. So although the ongoing hegemony of global modernism continues to stand in need of correction by the higher morality of postmodernism, in order for postmodernism to further increase its credibility and influence, it now needs to better acknowledge all the good that has come from the ascendancy of the Western world. Although there are many aspects of historical modernism that are indeed shameful, when we look at the spiral of development, we can see that modernist consciousness is actually the next unavoidable step for the majority of the world's population. So as modernist consciousness develops in places like China and India, its excesses and inherent pathologies must be moderated by the moral authority of postmodernism and integralism so as to prevent the mistakes of history from being made again. We must work with these newly emerging modernist cultures by helping them develop modernist economies and political structures while simultaneously preventing them from grossly exploiting their workers and destroying the environment. Indeed, moderated modernism represents the world's best hope for cultural evolution. But this will be true only if the future of global modernism is sufficiently tempered by postmodernism's growing influence in the developed world; and this, I am arguing, depends on the success of integral consciousness.

Integral philosophy reduces the anti-Western bias that infects the postmodern worldview by showing how each worldview stage represents the necessary next step for the stage that comes before it. A healthy form of traditional consciousness is what's next for warrior cultures, and a healthy form of modernist consciousness is what's next for traditional cultures. Again, it is not morally imperative that these older cultures evolve—they "have a right to be who they are"—but their children also have a right to education if they choose it. So preserving evolutionary opportunities for everyone means working to foster and preserve healthy expressions of these older worldviews in forms that are sustainable within the larger evolving global civilization.

We can all see the fragility of the remaining tribal cultures that cling to existence in the world's few remaining undeveloped wildernesses. Modernist culture, however, does not appear very fragile here at the beginning of the twenty-first century. Nevertheless, the strength of modernism is in fact bound up with a fragile cultural ecology that needs to be protected; and this brings us to the second main aspect of postmodernism that requires integralism's correcting influence.

Many postmodernists see multinational corporations as global criminals. And this is understandable given the fact that the charters of these organizations require that they maximize shareholder wealth without regard for the social or environmental consequences. Although some multinationals strive to be good global citizens, most are simply profit machines with practically no social conscience. So as I argue in the next section, these organizations need to be brought within a sphere of democratic oversight through the mechanism of effective global law. Yet even as global businesses are made to account for the "externalities" they create, even as they are required to pay for the social and environmental damage they may cause, their value to civilization as a primary source of its wealth must also be acknowledged and protected.

Because it can understand the developmental patterns of history more clearly than ever before, integral consciousness can see that higher levels of civilization actually depend on the prosperity, mobility, connectivity, and economic security provided by healthy market economies. And through its understanding of intersubjective cultural evolution, integral consciousness realizes that healthy market economies are living dynamic systems that exist within a cultural ecology created by the confluence of favorable laws, property security, access to education, loose capital markets, and protection from overreaching bureaucracies. As dynamic systems, modernist economies are similar to ecosystems in the way they can be easily destroyed by too much external pressure. And this is even more true in the case of most individual companies, which exist within a narrow and fragile balance of supply and demand. However, due to the culturally ingrained bias against business held by many postmodernists, it is as difficult for them to see the fragile ecology of markets as it is for traditionalists to see the fragility of the natural environment. When it comes to the environment, traditionalists may acknowledge the need for conservation and respect for "mother nature," but their ability to truly appreciate our current environmental crisis is often lacking. And it is a very similar kind of blindness that keeps many postmodernists from appreciating the vulnerability of market economies and the fragility of modernist culture in general. A complex level of sympathy and care is required to effectively preserve the conditions under which markets can flourish while simultaneously restraining the social and environmental damage that is naturally created by unregulated market forces. And this complexity of consciousness only truly arises from the expanded internal perspective provided by the integral worldview.

At this point in history, we are just beginning to define and experience integral consciousness. Thus the debate about integral politics is first a debate about loyalties. That to which we are loyal is that which provides our cultural identity—our loyalties determine the internal "location" of our consciousness. Once established, loyalties to political institutions are difficult to change, and naturally, those who have strong loyalties to "progressive politics" will defend their own identity when faced with a challenge. However, to the extent that postmodern politics are defined by their strict antithesis to modernism, they are in conflict with integral politics. In order for the majority of the world's population to evolve beyond traditional consciousness, modernism must be healthy and functioning. And for a healthy version of moderated modernism to thrive, individual economic freedom and entrepreneurial opportunities must be preserved. Yet this is not something that leftist governments or state-controlled economies have done well. From an integral perspective, if we want to evolve beyond modernism, we must recognize those aspects of modernism that must be retained, such as fairly regulated market economies. Thus if we want our political consciousness to be truly integral, we must relinquish a certain degree of loyalty to the left's ingrained contempt for the business world.

Integral politics must recognize the moral superiority of the postmodern worldview, but it must also demonstrate respect and loyalty to the foundational morality of modernist and traditional consciousness as well. Integral consciousness is not limited by the choices of only one worldview—it is not constrained by loyalty to only one ideology—so it has access to all the various solutions that have evolved throughout human history to deal with the myriad evolutionary obstacles we face today. To the extent that leftist ideologies fail to acknowledge the legitimacy of the enduring contributions of these previous stages, they must be abandoned by an integral politics. Integral politics must identify with the spiral as a whole—it must be loyal to the prime directive, and this requires that it distinguish itself ideologically from postmodernism, even as it works with it to further the evolution of culture.

However, the task of providing an even more progressive alternative to what is currently called "progressive politics" requires more than the effective integration of what already exists. Integral politics must provide a transcendent vision for the future. It must vividly describe what positive political evolution will look like, and it must show how to get from here to there. And this brings us to what will inevitably become the central political issue of the twenty-first century—the movement for a democratic, federal system of global governance.

Integral Politics and Global Governance

Let's consider the problems of the world. What's your choice for the worst one? Environmental degradation and global warming? Genocide in Africa? Third World hunger and poverty? Terrorism? War and threats of war? Or maybe even unfettered corporate globalization and the increasing homogenization of the world's culture? Many of us are deeply concerned about these problems, but most of us don't really know what we can do personally, or even what the world as a whole can do to solve these global dilemmas. Yet our concerns continue to grow. In fact, the more our consciousness develops, the more our sense of morality—our estimate of the scope of those worthy of moral consideration—expands to encompass the world. Indeed, a worldcentric morality is a clear marker of higher consciousness. But apart from considerations of higher morality, ameliorating global problems is increasingly becoming a matter of self-interest. The globe is more connected and interdependent than ever before, so that what happens in Indonesia or Sudan increasingly effects conditions here in the developed world. Yet with the Republican Party continuing to have such a strong influence on the American government, and with the evident impotency of the United Nations, it seems likely that these global problems are only going to get worse. But what if we had a clear solution to not only one or two of these problems, but a solution to all of them through the same method?

Global governance. This idea usually evokes one of two reactions: either that global governance is an idealistic fantasy best left for another century, or that global governance is the world's worst nightmare, a scenario in which the corporate elite gain complete control, and everything that is currently wrong with the U.S. government becomes writ-large on the world. Most people don't like government and often have an intuitive feeling that the direction of evolution is toward less government, not more. These intuitions arise from the fact that the existing state of consciousness in the world is not yet mature enough to effectively manage and contain the awesome power of a supranational lawmaking authority. And from an integral perspective, a global authority constituted without the benefit of integral thinking would indeed be most undesirable.

A world federation based on postmodern consciousness might embody a worldcentric morality, but as we've discussed, postmodernism's antimodern bias often blinds it to the fragility of economic ecologies and the central importance of modernism in global evolution. Although many postmodernists aspire to "think globally and act locally," their values do not provide the complexity of understanding necessary to create or administer a system of functional global law. Although postmodern values must play an important role in any sustainable form of global governance, integral values will also be crucial. And while global governance based solely on postmodern consciousness may be unrealistic, a world government run by modernists would also be clearly undesirable because the resulting unchecked corporate expansion would only exacerbate terrorism, environmental degradation, the destruction of indigenous culture, and the spread of the generic blight of corporate mediocrity. Modernist consciousness is good at creating democracy at the level of the nation-state, but when it comes to the significant problems that will confront a world federation, the modernist worldview is not evolved enough to satisfy the legitimate concerns of postmodern consciousness while simultaneously dealing with the large populations who make meaning at the traditional level and below. And it goes without saying that a world government based primarily on the values of traditional consciousness would constitute a significant regression in civilization—a totalitarian scenario of Orwellian proportions!

Fortunately, with the rise of integral consciousness, new possibilities appear. These new possibilities become evident when we take an evolutionary perspective on human political organization. According to Robert Wright, in 1500 B.C. there were approximately 600,000 sovereign political groups in the world. Today these groups have been consolidated into just 193 sovereign countries. Although the breakup of colonial empires in the twentieth century created some new nation-states, the overall trend of the century was toward greater interdependence and international consolidation, as evidenced by the creation of the United Nations and the European Union. From the beginnings of human law with the Code of Hammurabi and the Ten Commandments, up to the era of large federations of the United States and the European Union, law and government have continued to evolve over the centuries into larger and larger political configurations. However, although the world enjoys a growing body of international law, these laws are largely unenforceable, and the United Nations and the international system it administers is still based on the underlying principle of unrestricted national sovereignty. So although the recent strengthening of the World Court in the Netherlands is a positive step, the phrase "international law" remains somewhat of an oxymoron because of its implied preservation of "national" power and the "state of nature" that exists between sovereign nations. The significant difference between treaties (and other *inter*-national forms of agreement) and true laws is that in general, treaties apply to countries whereas laws apply to individuals. Law is what replaces the state of nature between "sovereign" individuals or groups. So no matter how much power the U.N. or other international authorities are given, until there is true global law with jurisdiction over individuals, the evolutionary pressures that have produced a world of nation-states will continue to push and pull toward the next developmental level—a world federation.

While we can recognize that the state of the world's consciousness is not yet ready for global governance, we can also see that *globalization* of the world's economy and culture is nevertheless racing ahead. From an integral perspective the world may never be fully *ready* for global governance—by the time consciousness has evolved to the point where everyone is responsible and worldcentric, we may not need government at all. Yet when we make a realistic assessment of the ongoing evolution of global civilization in the twenty-first century, no matter how premature the idea of global governance may seem, the current de facto system of global politics is only going to become increasingly inadequate for a globalized world. As evolutionary pressures continue to mount, we will have two choices: We can either evolve further, or we can collapse back into regression. So if we want to choose the former option, then it is now time to begin discussing what further evolution actually looks like.

The type of global governance envisioned by the integral worldview would consist of a federation of nations united under a constitution of laws guided by the insights and principles of integral philosophy. An integral world federation would be instituted to provide democratic oversight of the global economy, protect the world's environment, establish a universal bill of human rights, preserve cultural diversity, and bring an eventual end to war, disease, and poverty. And even with limited jurisdiction (leaving national legal systems mostly in place), an integral world federation would provide for a system of global justice which would reduce the incentives for terrorism. Such a federation would not need to encompass the globe in one step. It would have to begin with a union of the E.U. and U.S., with other developed nations such as Australia and Japan joining at the beginning. Gradually, other countries could join the federation, but no country would be forced to join, with membership in the federation requiring a supermajority vote of a country's population. An integral global authority would gradually encompass the world through evolutionary methods. National boundaries and local economies would be protected, and full membership in the federation would be granted only to countries that have achieved requisite degrees of freedom and democracy. Just as the E.U. has been gradually expanding, encouraging the political, economic, and cultural evolution of those nations that aspire to join, so too could a world federation be gradually enlarged.

The benefits of effective global governance would be abundant. Democratic control of the global economy would produce greater fairness for individuals and fragile local cultures while at the same time producing greater overall prosperity. An integral world federation would have the authority to protect human rights and the world's environment, inaugurating the kinds of safeguards that are currently impossible in a world of competing nation-states. It will almost always be morally illegitimate for one sovereign country to attack or dominate another sovereign country, regardless of the context. But a democratically controlled global federation will have the moral and political authority to be legitimately coercive over *individual offenders* (rather than entire countries) when it comes to preventing the destruction of people's lives or the environment.

In appendix A, entitled "A Proposal for Integral Global Governance," we'll explore an example of a potential structure that could be used to enact an integrally informed federal system of global governance. However, at this point, rather than going on about the advantages and solutions that could be provided by a world federation, I now need to address the reasonable objection that, even if it were a good idea, at this point global governance is nothing but a "left-wing peacenik fantasy" only dreamed about by "woolly-minded one-worlders."

Is Global Governance an Unrealistic Fantasy?

If a world federation is to come about in the twenty-first century it will have to be based on some kind of union between the European Union and the United States. And among these two giants, the U.S. is clearly the most conservative and can thus be counted on to become the biggest obstacle to the movement for a world authority. However, as the integral worldview begins to emerge, it will have a significant effect on the body politic of America.

We know from Paul Ray's research that about 50 percent of the U.S. population is centered in modernist consciousness. And by looking at the history of cultural evolution, we can anticipate that, even with postmodernism growing, modernist consciousness will continue to be the center of gravity in America for at least the next two or three generations. So an important goal for integral politics will be to convince modernists that global governance is an idea they can endorse. This seemingly unrealistic goal will become far more achievable as it becomes increasingly evident to modernists that without morally legitimate global law, the expanding global economy cannot be sustained. Now more than ever, it is becoming obvious that the health of America's economy can be assured only when the health of the global economy is protected. As the century progresses and the economies of nation-states increasingly become part of a world economic system (diminishing the power of national governments), the need for effective democratic oversight of this system becomes increasingly acute. "To be effective, global markets demand global governance."

During the Industrial Revolution of the nineteenth century, markets were completely unregulated. Although this produced significant economic development, it also resulted in growing poverty, misery, and gross inequality. As dynamic cultural systems, free markets create great wealth, but without democratic oversight these same markets also produce harmful effects on the societies in which they arise. Unless there are laws that prevent companies from effectively enslaving workers or polluting the environment, the companies willing to engage in such behavior will effectively outcompete their rivals. Moreover, as unregulated competitive markets develop, market forces naturally polarize resources—the rich get richer and the poor get poorer. By the end of the nineteenth century, the destructive effects of these unregulated markets had resulted in the rise of the communist and anarchist movements, which became a significant threat to democracy. And it was only through the gradual initiation of government controls, progressive income tax, and the rise of the welfare state that the social damage caused by free markets was brought within acceptable limits. This worked fairly well in developed countries throughout the twentieth century—although free market economies continued to provide obscene riches for the few, and although many remained impoverished, the economies in most developed countries provided sufficient social safety nets and enough upward mobility to prevent the type of widespread social unrest witnessed at the end of the nineteenth century and up through the 1930s.

But now, as free markets continue to grow beyond the borders of nations, as the economies of individual nations become inextricably connected to the global economy, the absence of effective global law is resulting in the same destructive effects witnessed in the past. Although integral consciousness seeks to protect market economies, it also recognizes the need for markets to be fairly and effectively regulated in order to be sustainable. Thus as multinational corporations increasingly operate outside national boundaries, so too must the laws that regulate them not be constrained by national borders. Regulation of the global economy by the WTO and the IMF alone cannot effectively contain the naturally destructive forces of self-serving multinational corporations unless such regulatory bodies are themselves subject to the democratic oversight provided by a world federation. Will multinationals vigorously resist this? Although some responsible multinational corporations will recognize that such global laws will ultimately be for their own good, others will, of course, oppose such laws. But as Alexis de Tocqueville keenly observed, "Can it be believed that the democracy which has overthrown the feudal system and vanquished kings will retreat before tradesmen and capitalists?"

From a strategic perspective, it is not unreasonable to predict that as life conditions begin to threaten the sustainability of the global economy, the self-interested rationalism of the modernist majority in America and Europe will begin to see the wisdom and the necessity of global governance. Similarly, many of those with a postmodern worldview may be persuaded into seeing the wisdom of global governance because of the obvious benefits for human rights, the environment, and other postmodern concerns. But we can, of course, expect that very few of those with a traditionalist worldview will ever be convinced about the desirability of a world federation. Nevertheless, as cultural evolution unfolds in this century, the rise of the integral worldview and its championing of the political issue of global governance can be expected to gradually sway public opinion toward the wisdom of this solution. It is estimated that at the time of the American Revolution, only about 10 percent of America's population made meaning at the modernist level of consciousness. Yet this was enough to bring about the unprecedented rise of constitutional democracy. And similarly, we can anticipate that when integralists comprise approximately 10 percent of the population of the developed world, the integral worldview's political agenda for global governance may become a reality.

There have been many periods in history wherein political changes that once seemed unthinkable came about in very short amounts of time. Consider these examples: In 1750 no one in America could imagine that they would ever go to war with England, but by the 1770s, Americans in large numbers were willing to lay down their lives for the Revolution. Similarly, in 1913 leaders of the suffragette movement thought it too soon to press for a woman's right to vote in national elections; they thought it would take decades before they could hope for such an advance. Yet by 1919 the American Constitution was amended to provide for universal women's suffrage. And in 1980, few of us would have bet that in ten years Soviet communism would be completely defunct, and that in just over twenty years France and Germany would have the same currency.

Is Global Governance Too Dangerous—What are the Safeguards?

The viability and security of a world federation ultimately depends on the success of integral consciousness. As we discussed above, without the requisite integral consciousness, functional global governance is not feasible. But with the emergence of the integral worldview, there appear the values and insights necessary for such an undertaking. This is similar to the relationship between modernism and democracy. Without enough modernist consciousness in a county's population, functional democracy usually cannot be sustained. For example, some Latin American countries have constitutions that are almost identical to the U.S. Constitution, yet these same countries suffer from horrific levels of government corruption and economic stagnation. Democracy continues to have trouble in Latin America because modernist consciousness has not yet been adequately developed within the population through education and the provision of economic opportunity. This is not to say that the U.S. government is free from corruption. But unlike in Latin America, when corruption becomes obvious, America's modernist majority will not long stand for it, as we saw in the case of Richard Nixon. With the modernist worldview comes the values of individual initiative and an expectation of excellence that will not tolerate corruption. And with healthy modernism we see the emergence of a sense of civic duty expressed in John Kennedy's famous admonition to "ask not what your country can do for you, but rather what you can do for your country." It was this same sense of civic duty that baffled European monarchs when George Washington retired from the U.S. presidency after his second term. The traditional worldview could not fathom why Washington did not declare himself "king of America" when he had the chance.

With integral consciousness there is less emphasis on the value of personal status and the accumulation of wealth, so the enticements of corruption are less appealing to those with integral values. And because integralists do not generally depend on social approval for ego validation, they can champion unpopular causes. Also, because those with integral consciousness are psychologically sophisticated, most can see how unethical behavior actually causes more psychic damage to a person than any perceived gains that may accrue from such actions. However, integralists are not saints. The worldview of integral consciousness is only one evolutionary step above the postmodern worldview, and it would be naive to expect that integral values alone would safeguard a world federation from going astray. However, the constitutional structure of an integrally informed world federation will incorporate many legal safeguards designed to eliminate the types of dysfunction that have prevented good government in the past.

You may have heard the joke that the U.S. government was designed by geniuses so it could be safely run by idiots. Well, just as the wisdom of Enlightenment philosophy was used in the design of the separation of powers found in the U.S. Constitution, so too will the new wisdom of integral philosophy be used to design the structure of a world federal constitution. First of all, unlike the U.S. government, which has all but eliminated the autonomy of its states, an integrally informed global authority would be truly federal. The jurisdiction of global law would be limited to matters that required global-level solutions. Nation-states would be left in charge of their own domestic affairs, subject only to the protections of the universal bill of human rights and the restrictions on excessive pollution of the environment. Second, the integral worldview recognizes that while many current problems can be tackled only at the global level, there are also many others that are best solved at the local level. Integral politics thus calls for structures that push power down as well as up, so that decisions can be made as close to the local level as possible. These ideas for the structure of a world federal constitution are discussed further in Appendix A "A Proposal for Integral Global Governance."

In addition to the safeguards afforded by the overall morality of integral consciousness, and the safeguards derived from the application of integral philosophy in the design of the structure of a world federation, other safeguards would be found in the emergence of an integrally informed segment of the media. As the integral worldview develops and finds its application in the movement for world federation, it is inevitable that integralism will also influence the press. Integral consciousness' enlarged understanding of evolution will help journalists see what is actually contributing to evolution and what is retarding it. So just as the world's present democracies are subject to the influence of the media and the effect it has on voters, likewise will a global democracy be subject to the oversight of an integrally informed cadre of journalists.

However, as we consider the safeguards that will ensure that a world federation does not become a threat, we should also consider the threats associated with *failing* to initiate a system of global governance. According to Reinhold Niebuhr, "Man's capacity for justice makes democracy possible; but man's inclination to injustice makes democracy necessary." And this applies as much to the global level as it does to the national. Besides the threats associated with the continuing degradation of the environment, the biggest threat to the developed world is the growing problem of those with warrior consciousness (or pathological versions of traditional consciousness) acquiring and using the powerful technologies created by modernism. Modernist technologies are dangerous enough in the hands of the modernists themselves, but when the power of these technologies is wielded by levels of consciousness that have not earned this power through their own cultural evolution, this has the effect of destabilizing the civilization that originally created the technology. This applies not only to weapons technology, but also to communications technology and the Internet as well. As consciousness continues to evolve, and as the diversity of the different types of consciousness that share our planet increases, this problem of unearned power becomes acute. However, this is exactly the kind of global dilemma that a world federation would be able to effectively address by controlling the production and distribution of weapons and by having better oversight of the global economy.

Again, the world already has a de facto system of global politics. But this existing system cannot really protect us from the host of growing global threats we've discussed. So the right question is not whether a system of global governance would be too dangerous, but whether a more formal and intentional system would be actually less dangerous than the system we currently have.

Global Governance and Integral Consciousness Cocreate Each Other

This vision for a new level of human political organization demonstrates the evolutionary potential of the integral worldview. As we have seen, every new worldview has taken shape around a political issue, and the rise of the integral worldview will be no exception.

Without its championing of the movement for global governance, the integral worldview fails to offer the type of powerful new solutions that the previously arising worldviews have provided. But when the new insights of the integral worldview are applied through this political platform, their power to produce lasting cultural evolution becomes evident. Just as the moral superiority of democracy over feudalism served to convince many to adopt the values of the modernist worldview, so too will the evident moral superiority of global governance over a world of sovereign nations operating in a state of nature eventually convince many that the integral worldview is the way forward.

The mechanism of a world federation is the practical way that integral consciousness can take greater responsibility for the problems of the world. The emotional energy and motivation that accrues to a newly emerging stage of consciousness results from the power of the fresh solutions that a new stage offers. It is often hard to actually see a problem until its solution appears. But as we've seen, the evolutionary potential of a problematic human life condition is unleashed when a way to ameliorate that condition becomes evident. The solutions offered by a system of global governance thus serve to help enact the circuit of value metabolism that gives life to the structures of integral consciousness and culture. These structures made of value agreements are brought more fully into being when the solutions offered by their political agenda directly connect with the real problems of real people. So the more people come to see how integral values can actually cause evolution through visionary proposals such as global governance, the more people will be attracted, and the more people will begin to take part in the value agreements that comprise this growing stage of consciousness.

Because integral consciousness can better see the various "locations" of all the different kinds of consciousness and culture that inhabit the world today, and because it can also better see the directions and methods by which consciousness and culture can actually evolve, it is uniquely qualified to design and administer a world federation. Again, without integral consciousness, global governance is neither desirable nor achievable, but with the rise of the integral worldview, a world federation becomes realistic and even inevitable.

If you have never been exposed to integral philosophy—if you cannot make meaning (even partially) at the integral level of consciousness—then the idea of global governance is just probably not that interesting. However, you know you are beginning to metabolize the values of the integral worldview when the idea of bringing about a world federation within the next fifty years begins to seem very exciting. When we begin to see just how much good a world federation could do, when we begin to see how we could realistically end war, hunger, and the environmental crisis, we begin to feel the energy that gives us the ability to be effective activists.

With integral consciousness comes a new feeling of confidence, conviction, and a strong sense of the moral courage of optimism that provides the emotional power that can actually bring about this kind of evolutionary development—development that seems impossible to less evolved levels of consciousness. The feelings of courage and conviction that once empowered the Enlightenment revolutionaries can now be felt again by the integralists who will dare to become activists for global governance. Is this naive idealism? No, to my mind the naive idealists are those who simply wish for, or even angrily demand, a more caring and sustainable world where everyone cooperates and acts responsibly. However, practical realism can be seen in those who recognize that only *law* can effectively prevent violence, oppression, and environmental destruction, and that law *can* be safely expanded to encompass the world through a democratic global authority guided by the integral value of the prime directive.

This has been just a sample of the power and potential of integral consciousness in the realm of politics. Now we turn to the equally exciting, evolution-producing application of the integral worldview within the realm of spirituality.

CHAPTER 6

Integral Spirituality

As SHOULD NOW BE CLEAR FROM OUR DISCUSSION THUS FAR, THE integral worldview is emerging within an existing system of historical development. This worldview is being shaped by the current life conditions created by the previously arising structures of history that are continuing to influence the present. Thus, while the contours of this new worldview are not completely predetermined by history, the integral worldview is not simply whatever we want it to be. This new phase of cultural evolution is just the next available step in the long road to a higher level of civilization. And if integral consciousness is indeed the next step in our culture's evolution, then we can expect it to produce not only social and political evolution, we can also expect that it will bring about the evolution of our culture's spirituality.

Within postmodern culture there are many who believe that the world is quivering on the brink of a great spiritual awakening. So there is a tendency to project this expectation onto the integral worldview by characterizing it as the beginnings of a spiritual revolution. But while the rise of integral consciousness will definitely result in the evolution of spiritual culture, it is more likely that most of this evolution will involve the refinement, integration, and improvement of existing spiritual forms rather than the creation of entirely new kinds of spirituality. The spiritual evolution produced by the rise of the integral worldview will come about as postmodernism's spiritual excesses and immaturities are overcome, and as the enduring contributions of traditional spirituality are reintegrated into our culture at a higher level.

At the time of this writing, integral spiritual culture is only just beginning to emerge, so it cannot be authoritatively described as if it were fully in existence. However, the cultural agreements that will eventually come to define the characteristics of integral spirituality will be worked out over time by the growing integral community as a whole. And these agreements will naturally arise through the work of integrating the existing forms of premodern, modern, and postmodern spirituality into a transcendent and inclusive new whole.

According to my understanding, spirituality is primarily a matter of direct personal experience. However, one's personal experience of spirit is inevitably guided and enhanced by a belief system that provides a cosmology that defines spirit's role in the universe. And from the perspective of my cosmology, the evolving universe of nature, self, and culture is unfolding within the already-perfect larger spiritual universe. There is thus an aspect of spirit that does not evolve because it is already infinite, eternal, and universal. But not only are we within spirit, spirit is also within us; spirit is our real nature, it is the kernel of true reality at the center of our being that evolves along with us back to its source. Of course, this is just my personal theology; it does not necessarily represent what every integralist believes.

As we survey the current state of nascent integral culture as it is beginning to emerge throughout the developed world, it appears that the enthusiastic pursuit of spiritual experience is usually a central feature in the lives of those who have achieved the complex worldview of integral consciousness. But it also seems that the spirituality of integralists can be inspired by a wide variety of spiritual paths, traditions, and belief systems. These various forms of spirituality define the idea of the sacred differently, so the integral worldview does well not to adopt one univocal definition of spirit. In fact, as I'll argue more fully in chapter 8, if the integral worldview is to emerge as the next historically significant phase of humanity's cultural evolution, then the philosophy that gives rise to this worldview cannot become synonymous with one particular form of spirituality.

In its role as a formal philosophical system, integral philosophy must construct its frame of reality so as to include all the kinds of experience that humans have demonstrated their ability to have—

sensory experience, mental experience, and spiritual experience. And as it tries to adequately account for all these valid experiences (and thus all valid knowledge), integral philosophy must accordingly acknowledge the legitimacy of both science and religion. That is, because integral philosophy affirms that spiritual experience is real, it thus recognizes that religion and spirituality are an indispensable aspect of advanced levels of civilization. However, because the different forms of spirituality practiced by integralists often offer widely varying accounts of spiritual reality, integral philosophy can succeed in enacting a historically significant new worldview only by limiting its own accounts of this spiritual reality so as to preserve a variety of religious forms. In other words, integral philosophy relates to spirituality most effectively by acknowledging the reality of spirit, but not the final authority of any particular explanation thereof. Integral philosophy's new frame of reality—its new agreement about the nature of the evolving universe—will not be broad enough to produce the cultural evolution it promises unless it occupies a philosophical position that honors and encompasses a diversity of spiritual paths.

However, in order to evolve beyond the extreme relativism and indiscriminate pluralism of postmodern spirituality, integral philosophy also needs to perform the role of defending the domains of science and philosophy from the incursions of New Age substitutes for philosophy. That is, as a philosophy, integral philosophy must have the ability to clearly tell when a particular brand of spirituality is claiming that its beliefs about the universe are simply the way things are. And conversely, integral philosophy must also be able to identify where the scientific worldview is asserting essentially metaphysical conclusions that extend beyond what science is qualified to explain. Thus to be effective, integral philosophy must stand in between science and religion, recognizing the basic legitimacy of both of these human endeavors, but also recognizing their inherent limitations. As we discussed in chapter 1, science, philosophy, and religion are the three legs of the stool upon which our civilization rests. At this point in history, we need all three of these institutions, and none of them can be reduced to any of the others. So in chapter 8 we'll return to this subject to explore how integral philosophy can carefully distinguish between the spiritual and the material, and how it can construct its frame of reality with a minimalist metaphysics that effectively *bridges* and *separates* the realms of science and spirituality.

In this chapter, however, rather than discussing the limitations of integral philosophy's metaphysics, we'll focus on the larger cultural aspects of integral spirituality. Just as the culture of modernism now extends far beyond the confines of Enlightenment philosophy, so too will the culture of integralism eventually come to encompass a much greater body of understanding than what is presently recognized as integral theory. So in this chapter's broader exploration of the contours of emerging integral spirituality, we'll see how the integral worldview can transcend and include our society's existing forms of premodern, modern, and postmodern spiritual culture. We'll also see how the integral worldview can create a public commons of universal spiritual experience wherein followers of different spiritual paths can find greater cultural solidarity through agreements about values. Then in the final section of the chapter, we'll consider how the new understanding of evolution provided by the integral worldview reveals the unmistakably spiritual character of evolution itself—that in the common directions of evolution's advance within nature, self, and culture, we can begin to discern the voice of perfection beckoning us home.

The Development of Spiritual Traditions

We have already noted how the different worldviews found within the spiral of development each have their own version of spirituality. Although it is often overshadowed by fear, the tribal stage of consciousness is intensely concerned with its understanding of the spirit world. In the tribal worldview, nature is alive and spirits are everywhere. And the pantheon of gods developed by the tribe is usually carried forward and exalted by the warrior stage of consciousness that grows out of tribal culture. This can be seen, for example, in the warrior culture of the ancient Vikings, whose Norse tribal gods provided a sense of ethnic identity as well as strength and courage for their conquests.

However, as traditional consciousness arises, the older religions rooted in tribal-warrior culture are usually either assimilated or completely destroyed. Almost every one of the world's major traditional worldviews began with the revelation of a great spiritual leader. And as these teachings grew into authoritative traditions, and as they encountered peoples living within tribal and warrior cultures, they naturally asserted their theology and culture as the new and better way. By the time of the emergence of modernism in the seventeenth century, Europe, Asia, Northern Africa, and much of the Americas had become divided among the major blocs of traditional civilization—Judeo-Christian, Muslim, Hindu, Buddhist, and Confucian-Taoist. We can certainly identify other types of traditional consciousness, but the historical record shows that, by the dawn of modernism, traditional consciousness in one form or another had successfully conquered most of the world.

Then with the rise of modernism, we see a partial rejection of religion. Although most early moderns were committed Christians, many others adopted the decidedly less-supernatural religion of Deism, which recognized God in nature and reason, rejecting revealed religion and its authority over humanity. As modernism matured, those who embraced its more extreme versions adopted atheism or existentialism, renouncing religion and spirituality altogether. However, the vast majority of modernists retained their roots in their ethnic traditions by continuing to practice Judaism or Christianity, even as these religions were partially subordinated to the scientific worldview.

With the exception of Japan, which had developed its own native version of modernism with roots in its Buddhist-Shinto traditional culture, by as late as 1950, modernist culture had arisen only in countries with a Judeo-Christian heritage. And it was in the richest and most successful group of these countries that the postmodern revolution began. With postmodern culture came a rediscovery of spirituality—ancient and esoteric spirituality, tribal spirituality, and especially Eastern spirituality. Although not all postmodernists were committed religionists, postmodern culture generally served to reenchant the world with a new spiritual sensibility. Modernism had lost interest in

God; many modernists who were not atheists tended to see religion more as a matter of ethnic tradition than as a source of living faith. Although traditional consciousness remained strong and continued to define the worldview of many within the developed world, its transcendence by modernism rendered it quiescent and contained. But with the rise of the postmodern worldview, religion broke out of its box and took up the leading edge of culture once again.

The variety of vital forms of spirituality evident within the postmodern level of consciousness demonstrates that the world's great wisdom traditions are not stage-specific phenomena, they are not merely the worn-out shells of an earlier time in history; they are living lines of spiritual development that will continue to grow and flourish through many stages of culture on into the future. This is shown by the fact that there are now postmodern versions of all the world's great religions (and many now have integral expressions as well): Postmodern Christianity is seen in New Thought organizations such as the Unity Church, and in many expressions of New Age spirituality. Postmodern Buddhism is seen in much of the Shambhala community of Tibetan Buddhism led by the Dalai Lama, and in the widespread fascination with the mystique of Zen. Postmodern Hinduism is found in the teachings of many popular Indian gurus, in the West's discovery of the wisdom of Vedanta, and in the growing popularity of yoga and other Vedic traditions. Postmodern Taoism is seen in the popularity of tai chi, chi gong, and feng shui, and in the renewed interest in traditional Chinese medicine. Postmodern Judaism can be recognized in the newly revived tradition of the Kabbalah. Even Islam has a postmodern expression in Sufi spirituality and in the popularity of the poetry of Rumi and Hafiz. In addition to the postmodern versions of the major wisdom traditions, we also see within postmodern culture a revival of certain pretraditional religions such as paganism, shamanism, and Native American spirituality. The spiritual fecundity of postmodern consciousness has also produced some entirely new kinds of religion such as ecospirituality, as well as the new forms of spirituality expounded by channelers and contemporary psychedelic mystics.

Now, after listening to this litany of postmodern spirituality, you may have recognized that much of this is not really postmodern at all. Some of these forms of spirituality transcend postmodernism, and many have facilitated peak experiences and altered states that provide glimpses into significantly higher stages. However, much of what has grown out of postmodern culture's spiritual revival constitutes a regression to premodern levels of magical or mythical consciousness. As we have seen, in its reaction to the excesses of modernism, postmodernism sought to reinclude all that had been previously excluded or ignored by modernism's materialistic prejudices. Yet in its inclusionary zeal, postmodern consciousness abandoned Western civilization's standards of excellence; in many cases its value relativism rendered it unable to tell the difference between what Ken Wilber calls the "trans-rational" and the "pre-rational." Although the culture of spirituality had been rescued from death at the hands of atheism, it had reemerged in so many competing and conflicting versions, and in forms often of such low quality, that its potential to produce significant cultural evolution was limited. Overall, however, we can say that these "alternative" forms of spirituality that were embraced by postmodernism did in fact move the center of gravity of our culture forward. Our collective sense of spiritual pluralism and our awareness of the varieties of spirituality has definitely become more sophisticated in the last forty years. But postmodernism's current culture of spirituality is so fragmented and tainted by so many immature expressions that its ability to provide spiritual leadership for our culture in the twenty-first century is clearly in doubt.

So these are the conditions in which the integral worldview now finds itself as it attempts to develop a more evolved relationship to the realm of spiritual experience.

Public Spirituality in the Integral Age

Postmodernism created a kind of public commons wherein interfaith dialogue was encouraged and spiritual diversity was celebrated. And while this was certainly positive, interfaith dialogue tended not to lead anywhere. These kinds of exchanges served to educate religionists about the theology of other traditions, but such dialogue rarely served to actually change anyone's beliefs or practices.

Although there was greater understanding, this did not lead to much of a common culture; most of those who "sought dialogue" simply ended up going back to their insular communities and continuing with spirituality as usual.

The integral worldview is not satisfied with polite spiritual pluralism. Integral consciousness recognizes the opportunity to create a common culture of spiritual experience that honors diverse traditions but also endeavors to discover those aspects of spirituality that all integralists have in common—the aspects of spiritual experience around which new levels of cultural solidarity can arise. In my opinion, this involves two steps: First, we have to transcend and include the spirituality of previous worldviews. This involves identifying the enduring contributions of these older forms of spirituality, and it also involves cleansing the commons by pruning away those aspects of the previous worldviews' spirituality that are clearly wrong—having the courage to reject that which we know is not true. Second, in both what we carry forward and what we discover anew, we have to recognize three ways in which spirituality manifests: 1) as theology or belief system; 2) as empirically verifiable experiential phenomena; and 3) as philosophical spirituality—a common understanding of spiritually significant truths that are neither purely science nor purely religion.

We've seen how each stage of consciousness has a unique relationship to spirituality. And like the other features of these worldviews, each stage has aspects of its spirituality that provide a lasting contribution to the spiral as a whole, and aspects that must be discarded as more complex levels of culture appear. The objectionable aspects of the spirituality of previous worldviews include tribalist descriptions of vengeful gods and evil spirits, traditionalist claims of exclusivity that declare only "one true way," modernist assertions that the universe is a purposeless accident, and postmodern notions that all forms of spirituality are equally valid. These spiritual falsehoods may have served their purposes when the worldviews that propounded them were in their formative periods, but now that we can see these kinds of spiritual propositions from the perspective of history, we can identify them as evolutionary "scaffolding" that may now be removed. We can tell a spiritual falsehood by recognizing the way it narrowly serves the limited purposes of a particular ideology, and by evaluating it in reference to the growing spiritual consensus of the integral worldview. This is not to say that there already exists a general consensus among integralists about most spiritual matters, but there are certain things that I think we can all agree about, such as the falsehoods listed above. Although it can be satisfying, identifying every aspect of the spirituality of previous worldviews that integralism can prune away is beyond the scope of this chapter. Suffice it to say that an important aspect of integral spirituality involves identifying what we can agree to reject.

However, an even more important aspect of integral spirituality involves identifying the everlasting spiritual truths of these previous worldviews that we need to conserve and carry forward into the integral spiritual community. These include tribal spirituality's sense of the enchantment of nature, as well as its childlike innocence in the approach to the spirit world. Even at the integral stage we are all still spiritual children and do well to retain a certain degree of innocence and humility about that which we do not fully understand. When it comes to traditional consciousness, its enduring contributions can be recognized in the world's great wisdom traditions themselves. Although they may have arisen from the teachings of spiritual masters whose development far exceeded traditional consciousness, as they have come down to us, the world's great wisdom traditions are each firmly rooted in the soil of traditional culture. Yet as we have seen, their truths have continued to inform every stage of consciousness that has subsequently appeared. And so the traditionalist birthmarks of these great religions must be honored on their own terms, even as they are stripped of their myths and ethnocentricities. Moreover, traditional consciousness' sense of certainty, its assurance of the ubiquitous presence of invisible spirit, its stalwart faith, and its conviction about the goodness of the universe—these are forms of spiritual practice that integral spirituality would do well to include. We can recognize the enduring contributions of modernist spirituality in its courageous commitment to follow the truth wherever it may lead, and in its recognition of self-evident natural law and the inherent rights of every person. Although these aspects of modernism may seem to be matters of philosophy or politics, the spiritual quality of these ideals is seen in the way they enact a culture of self-examining honesty and integrity, and in the way they stimulate the urge to make things better. These are important motivations that integral spirituality must make use of if it is going to succeed in achieving evolution in the realm of spiritual culture. Then there are the enduring contributions of postmodern spirituality. These include an affirmation of the undeniable reality of the spiritual (by whatever name), as well as an interest in and basic respect for all forms of human spirituality. These important cultural mores serve as a foundation for the development of the "next steps" of integral spirituality.

Integral consciousness understands that worldviews are constructed out of value agreements. And as it works out the agreements that will create the public commons of integral spiritual culture, it discovers the ways that integralists can reach consensus about spirituality. One such agreement involves carrying forward postmodernism's tolerance and respect for all spiritual paths while at the same time being more rigorous in evaluating the relative merit of different spiritual teachings. When we examine the emerging integral spiritual community, we can see that the spiritual orientations of this group include just about every type of spirituality previously discussed under the heading of postmodernism. Moreover, we often see those with integral consciousness adopting more than one spiritual path, holding any apparent conflicts in a kind of dialectical tension. We also find those whose spirituality is completely eclectic, consisting of a smorgasbord of notions about spirit. But regardless of whether someone adheres to one of the great wisdom traditions, or whether they construct their own personal version of spirituality, that which a person knows and believes—that which he holds to be spiritually true—does matter. Every major belief system has certain aspects that can be excessively mythic and dogmatic, but that doesn't mean that all belief systems are merely myths or dogma. Those who characterize all faith-based religions as merely dogmatic fail to recognize one of the most important ways that these traditions actually deliver spiritual experience. I know from my own experience that faith itself is a very powerful spiritual practice that definitely produces a direct experience of spirit. Living faith is not always focused on miracles and myths. As it is practiced in the more developed stages of consciousness, faith in God yields composure, contentment, and supreme joy. Faith in the afterlife is a practice that provides a "million-year view" that encourages one to make investments in this life that may not be enjoyed until the next. And faith that the universe is conceived and upheld by love results in a direct spiritual experience of that love which "surpasses all human understanding."

No matter what spiritual path we may pursue, if our spirituality is living and vital, it will help us feel at home in the universe by providing the kind of orienting explanations of reality that only spirituality can supply. That is, all vital forms of spirituality provide relatively comprehensive explanations of the meaning of life, the purpose of the self, life after death, and the nature of the Ultimate. If a form of spirituality fails to offer such a comprehensive description of the nature of reality, then it doesn't really fulfill the essential role of a vital religion and remains merely a type of philosophy. Again, spiritual teachings about Ultimate realities are not all outmoded myths and premodern relics; they are the indispensable heart of every form of living spirituality, and they need to be preserved and protected if spirituality is going to continue to fulfill its crucial role in human society.

Integral spirituality, therefore, cannot simply dispense with belief systems and recognize spiritual living only in specific exercises or certain prescribed practices. The value agreements that enact the public commons of integral spiritual culture must be sophisticated enough to encompass all the ways that a person can be spiritual.

However, even after we have pruned away the dogma and the myths, the answers to spiritual questions provided by different belief systems are often still found to be in conflict. As an illustration of divergent belief systems, consider the case of Buddhism and Christianity. Any insightful study of these two great traditions will reveal that, although there are many common elements, even the most sophisticated expressions of these religions are still largely pointing in different directions. And this reveals an interesting paradox. We can perhaps see that all significant spiritual paths provide direct and authentic access to spirit, and we can intuit that at higher levels of realization, any apparent conflicts among different teachings about the nature of the universe may eventually be reconciled within a more inclusive "world theology." But even now as we move beyond reason and engage the teachings of various religions with the use of vision-logic and dialectical evaluation, there remain important differences that we cannot simply ignore or gloss over. Indeed, we need to take these contradictions very seriously because much of our culture's future spiritual evolution will be achieved through our exploration and reconciliation of these important differences. However, the task of fully harmonizing the conflicting teachings of the world's great wisdom traditions is an effort that will engage humanity for centuries to come. At this point in history we are just beginning to understand the differences. In fact, there are currently very few people who have a thorough experience of the full spiritual gifts of *both* Buddhism *and* Christianity. So we must acknowledge that our early attempts to reconcile Christian and Buddhist teachings can be only superficial at best. Thus, as emerging integral spirituality faces the seemingly inherent theological incompatibility of the world's great religions, it cannot simply choose sides. If it privileges the teachings of one particular spiritual path over another, it fails at being integral and becomes just another competing religion. But if it merely contents itself with polite spiritual pluralism, it remains at the postmodern level with respect to this issue.

As we will discuss in detail in chapter 8, some have sought to reconcile the conflicting teachings of the various belief systems through an empirical approach to spirituality. This idea first appeared around the turn of the last century in the work of the American pragmatist philosopher William James. James was the first to attempt a rational investigation of religious experience through a method he called *radical empiricism*. James's radical empiricism maintained that spiritual experience could be tested and evaluated in the same manner as the experience of sensory data used by scientists. However, while it seemed promising at first, radical empiricism could not address the fact that there are indeed many aspects of traditional and nontraditional belief systems that can be directly experienced, despite the theological conflicts that those experiences suggest.

For example, on numerous occasions I have had a direct experience of the love of God—a powerful and palpable experience of the direct affection of a personal Deity for me, the child of that Creator. Similarly, I know advanced practitioners of meditation who have had many direct experiences of samadhi, just as it is described by Eastern sages. The point is that spiritual practitioners of all kinds can have direct experiences that correspond exactly to their respective theologies, even while their theologies say different things about the nature of spiritual reality. But as we discussed above, faith can be used as a technique of transrational awareness of that which cannot be touched by the senses or known with the mind; indeed, faith in the realities of spirit can yield direct experiences of the power of those realities, even as they are perceived through the distortions of a given belief system. As paradoxical as this may sound, the spiritual practice of living faith can actually provide an experience of that which is beyond the apprehension of our consciousness, as that consciousness is inevitably situated within an intersubjective worldview. In my experience, "human beings must be known to be loved; but Divine beings must be loved to be known." So there is no doubt that there are many kinds of spiritual experience, and that spiritual experience is a beautiful thing, but it does not always lend itself well to an empirical style of inquiry.

Thus as the integral worldview develops the public commons of integral spirituality in which a significant new level of spiritual culture can arise, it cannot dispense with the conflicting teachings of the great wisdom traditions, and neither can it simply choose to privilege only one or two of these spiritual paths. But what it can do is establish customs, mores, and ethics which help integralists remain conscientious about where integral philosophy ends and where their respective belief systems begin.

In addition to the work of carrying forward the best and negating the worst of the spirituality of previous worldviews, integral spirituality must also develop an agreement around a boundary line that preserves the commons of integral spirituality from attempted colonization by authoritative belief systems. While we can know in our hearts that our particular understanding of spiritual truth is essentially right, we also have to allow that others will have equally sincere convictions, and even direct experiences, that do not match up with our own. We can certainly point to scientifically respectable research that shows how meditation reduces stress and lowers blood pressure, how prayer can be efficacious in healing, and how people with faith live longer. But to the extent that we try to claim an empirical status for what is essentially theological, we are engaging in a form of spiritual imperialism. This does not mean that we must pretend that all theologies say the same thing, or that we must simply agree to disagree—dialogue, debate, and empathetic exchanges among those who are seeking an integral spirituality, but who follow different paths, can be extremely valuable. However, while integral spiritual discussions may achieve greater degrees of harmonization and mutual understanding, a complete cultural unification at the level of theology must await the achievements of higher and future stages of consciousness and culture. In fact, it may come to pass that even as openness and mutual appreciation increases, these different lines of spiritual development will continue to live side by side unreconciled to the end. But regardless of what happens in the future at the level of theology, at this point in history I think it is possible to achieve greater cultural unification through the development of a spiritual philosophy (discussed below) that can include all authentic forms of spirituality while transcending the current limitations of polite spiritual pluralism.

Toward this end, integral philosophy can provide an orienting generalization that can be used in the empirical evaluation of the different spiritual teachings that are welcome within its cultural commons. This method of evaluation is found by looking at the "fruits" of those teachings: Do they vanquish fear and promote compassion? Do they increase morality and loving-kindness? Do they result in evolution? This test of "knowing them by their fruits" can serve as the *Ockham's razor of spirituality;* it provides a simple and rock-solid way of effectively evaluating all forms of spiritual teaching and practice. And this was the conclusion ultimately reached by William James in his famous book *The Varieties of Religious Experience,* wherein he writes that spiritual transformation is ultimately a mystery and that in our evaluation of spiritual experience it is best "to turn our attention to the fruits of the religious condition, no matter in what way they have been produced."

In summary, the culture of integral spirituality is found in the growing agreement about the importance of spiritual experience. Integral spirituality refines its understanding of the nature of spiritual experience by carrying forward the best and carefully pruning away the worst of the spirituality of previous worldviews. Moreover, integral spirituality recognizes the empirical aspects of spiritual experience where it can, but also guards against belief system imperialism by respecting the partially conflicting theological explanations of the world's great wisdom traditions. And in evaluating the merits of different spiritual teachings, integral consciousness generally "knows them by their fruits." But this is not all that integral spirituality can do. Integral spirituality can also bring about the evolution of our culture's overall spirituality through an expanded philosophical understanding of the spiritual nature of the primary values of beauty, truth, and goodness.

Beauty, Truth, and Goodness—Philosophical Spirituality

The idea of "philosophical spirituality" may strike some advanced practitioners as ill-advised. Because any philosophy of spirit is bound to be largely mental, it may seem that this kind of spirituality is completely transcended and left behind by those who have experienced spirit directly and transrationally. It can indeed be quite embarrassing when spirituality becomes overly intellectualized, because this inevitably leads to stagnation and dogmatism. Nevertheless, even while we are aware of these limitations, in our spiritual quest we must continue to labor under the paradox of "making effective use of thought while at the same time discounting the spiritual serviceability of all thinking." Moreover, while philosophy may be of little use in the achievement of the higher levels of personal spiritual progress, it can be very useful in building a functional, pluralistic spiritual community. Thus, those who have achieved spiritual growth for themselves often find that the guidance of spiritual philosophy can be extremely useful in their efforts to give back to their societies as well as in their efforts to coordinate with those on different paths who are also motivated to practice their spirituality by attempting to improve the human condition.

From my perspective, the most potent form of spiritual philosophy is found in the recognition of the spiritual quality of values. Throughout our discussion we have repeatedly seen how values—goals, ideals, desires, intrinsic qualities, standards of perfection—serve to energize consciousness and culture and nourish these internal systems with meaningful sustenance. And although the term "values" does have some baggage due to its adoption by the religious right, this term is too important to concede to those who oppose cultural evolution. Potential alternative expressions of the idea of values could include Paul Tillich's phrase: "matters of ultimate human concern." We can even associate values with the mystical idea of quality itself. However, my own understanding of the idea of values has been most illuminated through the use of the concept of three "primary values"—the beautiful, the true, and the good. These are the three *most intrinsic* values that are recognized as the root qualities from which all values are essentially derived. Just as the millions of colors in the visible spectrum can be fairly represented through the combination of three primary colors, so too can the millions of shades of quality be roughly approximated by reference to beauty, truth, and goodness. If we think about values in terms of beauty, truth, and goodness, it makes the rather abstract notion of values more specific while retaining the level of generality we need to really understand values as a category of human experience.

So now we'll spend some time discussing how the triad of beauty, truth, and goodness can become an organizing principle of the emerging spiritual culture of integral consciousness. First, we'll discuss the significant history of the triad of beauty, truth, and goodness, and explore why so many of the world's greatest leaders and thinkers have acknowledged these three as primary. Next, we'll examine the primary values in relation to the spiral of development to see how these values have both a relative and local quality that is shaped by the worldview from which they are perceived, as well as a universal quality that is seen in the way these values define the ever-advancing trajectory of all internal evolution. Then in the following section we'll discuss how these values serve as content for spiritual experience, how they can be recognized as important forms of "spiritual nutrition," and how these conceptual categories actually lend themselves to specific practices that can bring about evolution in both individual consciousness and collective culture.

The fundamental values of beauty, truth, and goodness have been recognized since antiquity as the intrinsic qualities from which all values are essentially derived. Plato was the first writer to associate the beautiful, the true, and the good together, and to exalt these three as primary. And since Plato in the fourth century B.C., this triad of terms has continued to impress itself upon the minds of philosophers and mystics. This is not to say that all the proponents of beauty, truth, and goodness have been followers of Plato; some have discovered the significance of this triad through decidedly nonphilosophical methods. But whether they are arrived at through intuitive inspiration or rational deduction, these three terms keep showing up in the writing of a wide variety of notable luminaries. However, these exact terms are not always mentioned directly. For example, Immanuel Kant clearly recognized three essential modes of mental function; they formed the subject matter of his three great philosophical works: *The Critique of Pure Reason* (which is about truth), *The Critique of Practical Reason* (which is about morality or goodness), and *The Critique of Judgment* (which is about aesthetics or beauty). Since the Enlightenment, the idea of the primary values has continued to be discussed by thinkers as diverse as Freud, Gandhi, and Einstein. Even the *Encyclopedia Britannica* has acknowledged the significance of this ubiquitous trio, stating that: "Truth, goodness, and beauty form a triad of terms which have been discussed together throughout the tradition of Western thought. They have been called 'transcendental' on the ground that everything which is, is in some measure or manner subject to denomination as true or false, good or evil, beautiful, or ugly."

Many mystics and spiritual teachers such as Rudolf Steiner, Sri Aurobindo, Thich Nhat Hanh, and Osho Rajneesh have also championed the idea of these three essential "windows on the divine." For example, Sri Aurobindo describes what he calls "three dynamic images" through which one makes contact with "supreme Reality."

These are: 1) the way of the intellect, or of knowledge—the way of truth; 2) the way of the heart, or of emotion—the way of beauty; and 3) the way of the will, or of action—the way of goodness. Aurobindo comments further that "these three ways, combined and followed concurrently, have a most powerful effect."

Among the founders of integral philosophy itself, the triad of beauty, truth, and goodness has also enjoyed considerable attention. Alfred North Whitehead devotes a significant portion of his book *Adventures of Ideas* to the discussion of the primary values, which he calls the "eternal forms." But unlike Plato, who saw beauty and truth as being derived from goodness, Whitehead recognized beauty as paramount. According to Whitehead: "The teleology of the Universe is directed to the production of Beauty." Following Whitehead, philosopher David Ray Griffin cites "cosmic support for truth, beauty, and goodness" as one of the main benefits of a nonmaterialistic view of evolution. According to Griffin: "The eternal forms are the material of the divine persuasion...." Likewise does Ken Wilber acknowledge the priority of the beautiful, the true, and the good by connecting them with the three main "cultural value spheres" of art, science, and morals, which he further equates with the subjective, objective, and intersubjective domains, respectively.

The idea of any kind of "primary values," of course, drives deconstructionist postmodern academics crazy. For them, values are arbitrary interpretations imposed by establishment power structures, so the proposition that there are three fundamental values is the height of idealistic pretense. After all, beauty, truth, and goodness are just conceptual categories, just abstract words that point to nebulous ideals that perhaps everyone can agree about, that is, until you actually get specific. There is certainly no "hard proof" that all human values can be captured and expansively described using these three concepts. But as we have seen, there is a large degree of "consensus evidence" about the special significance of beauty, truth, and goodness. So why is this? Why not exalt "wisdom, compassion, and humility," or any other group of lofty ideals? Well, I think the reason that beauty, truth, and goodness have received continuous veneration is because they correspond to some very deep intuitions about the way the universe works. As I describe at length in chapter 10 on "The Directions of Evolution," the primary values are essential descriptions of the primordial influences at the heart of all evolution. And if this is true, then there are some very good reasons for the remarkable agreement about this specific triad of values.

So far, I have tried to avoid defining beauty, truth, or goodness. But there have certainly been many attempts by philosophers to provide concise definitions. Thomas Aquinas defined beauty as "unity, proportion, and clarity." Whitehead defined truth as "the conformation of appearance to reality." And Kant defined goodness by reference to the "categorical imperative," which says: "Act according to those maxims that you could will to be universal law." However, like spirit itself, the values of beauty, truth, and goodness cannot be easily defined in abstract terms apart from the situations in which we experience them, and so far, academic approaches have not proved entirely satisfactory. This is especially evident when we consider the primary values from the perspective of the spiral of development. As we have discussed, each stage of consciousness constructs its worldview out of agreements about values. These value agreements generally arise out of the struggle to find solutions to the problematic life conditions faced by those who participate in a given worldview. Each stage of culture thus develops a discrete set of values that are tailored to its location along the timeline of history. This is one reason why values are "location specific"—as life conditions change with the progress of cultural evolution, that which is most valuable for producing further evolution likewise changes.

But notice that even though exactly what is beautiful, true, or good, is defined specifically (and often conflictingly) by each successive stage of development, the overall valuation of the general directions of the beautiful, the true, and the good remains a common feature of each level. In other words, the values of beauty, truth, and goodness act as compass headings for the improvement of the human condition, regardless of the assessor's psychic location. Even though each stage of development has its own version of what is valuable, we can see that the spiral as a whole acts to define the overall trajectory of internal evolution for both the individual and the culture. So regardless of the location of a person's consciousness, we can identify something that is beautiful, something that is true, and something that is good from their perspective. Within the consciousness of every level, the general directions of evolution tend toward more pleasurable feelings, truer thoughts, and decisions that consider the welfare of larger and larger communities.

Thus we can begin to see how beauty, truth, and goodness are relative and subjective, but also universal. Beauty, truth, and goodness are relative because they are always working to contact consciousness where it is, and then move it into increasingly advanced states. This is what the structures of consciousness and culture actually do—they act as dynamic systems of value that take these universal directions of improvement and translate them, down-step them, so that they can be applied to a given set of life conditions—so that they can be used to make things better "on the ground," if you will.

However, this aspect of the local relativity of all estimates of value points back to the universal nature of values. According to Plato and Whitehead, we can observe within the universe a certain "Eros," which has been defined as "the urge towards the realization of ideal perfection." In our consciousness, this Eros of evolution—this hunger for greater perfection—is stimulated by the eternal images of the beautiful, the true, and the good, which, as we've seen, spur us onward and upward and inward into increasingly more evolved states.

When we look out at the external world around us, we describe its most exquisite features as "beautiful"; spirit appears to us in the objective world as delicate loveliness, bold drama, and sublime elegance, all of which are forms of beauty. In the internal realm of thoughts and ideas, those which exhibit the most quality are the ones that are the most accurate, the most descriptive of reality, and the most useful at providing solutions; when we look for spirit in the subjective realm, it most often looks like truth. And in the intersubjective realm of human relations, spirit is revealed through kindness, compassion, fairness, forgiveness, mercy, and justice—actions guided by the value of goodness. So it is from this perspective that we can begin to see how these primary values, these glimmers of relative and fleeting perfection, are truly *the comprehensible elements of Deity*—the most direct ways that we can experience spirit.

Beauty, truth, and goodness are only ideas and ideals, but as we can see throughout history, it is often "just ideas" that end up changing the world. In my own life, the pursuit of these simple ideas has contributed significantly to my spiritual growth. Hopefully, my description of this spiritual philosophy, here and in the sections below, will testify to how much light these concepts can bring. This triad of values is a *conceptual cathedral*, a form of philosophical high technology, and as I explain in chapter 10, a key to the "physics of the internal universe." The ideals of beauty, truth, and goodness represent philosophy's finest hour—these are the concepts by which philosophy makes contact with the spiritual and helps to define the way forward from a middle ground in between science and religion. Indeed, it is in the pursuit of beauty, truth, and goodness that we find the pinnacle of human life. Beauty, truth, and goodness are truly sacred in the way they name and describe the "eternal forms" by which the persuasive influences of evolution enact the universe's essential motion of consciousness seeking its source.

And now, for some concrete examples of how consciousness can seek its source, we turn to our discussion of the practice of the primary values.

The Practice of Beauty, Truth, and Goodness

Just as our physical health is maintained by taking in good nutrition and by using this energy through exercise, we can likewise see how the vitality of our consciousness can be enhanced and maintained in a similar way. As we've discussed, values serve to energize consciousness by providing input and throughput for its systemic metabolism. So we can perhaps begin to see how the energy-like quality of value needs to flow through us in a *circuit*, being both taken in and given out, in order for our consciousness to be whole and healthy. The values of beauty, truth, and goodness can each be "taken in and given out" through the natural practice activities by which these values are lived. That is, we metabolize truth by the practice of *learning* and *teaching*, we metabolize beauty through *appreciation* and *expression*, and as we'll explore below, we can fully experience the spiritual nutrition of goodness through the practices of *service* and *stillness*.

The integral practice of truth involves the discernment of that which is most real in what we experience. The spiritual quality of truth can be seen in the way that it illuminates the potential for progress by giving us the power to see how things really are, and thereby to improve any situation by making contact with *actual conditions*. Truth thus becomes *spiritual* when it results in the power to create evolution—to improve the human condition, even in the smallest ways. We take in truth by reading or watching, by admiring the actions of others, or by following prescribed practices. "Learning," in this context, refers to all the ways that we receive truth and its related values of meaning. Likewise, the concept of "teaching" here describes all the ways that we can give out the wisdom of what we've learned. Teaching in this sense includes not only writing and speaking, but also teaching by demonstration—teaching by living. The spiritual experience of learning real truth naturally provides the energy and the motivation to teach or apply the value of a given lesson to others. The fact that learning and teaching are connected in a circuit can be seen in the way that we never really learn something until we teach it, until we share it with another or live it out in some way. We can see this flowing circuit of truth in action by recalling that when we have a vivid truth experience—when we learn something of real value that we are enthusiastic about—it fills us with a desire to relate this truth to someone else.

The integral practice of beauty involves feeling the pleasure and delicious satisfaction that results when our emotions become entrained to the vibrations of universal unity found in nature and in certain forms of human art. Beauty provides a fleeting glimpse of relative actual perfection. The pleasure we receive from a beauty experience thus comes from the temporary respite or relief from the *relentless pressure* of evolutionary development. With beauty, the background tension caused by the subtle compulsion of the incomplete is released as the need to improve things is briefly satisfied. According to Whitehead, "beauty is the final contentment of the Eros of the universe."

Like the complementary and mutually supporting practices of learning and teaching truth, the experience of beauty is had through the natural activities of appreciation and expression. Like truth, beauty is experienced on the "way in" as it is appreciated, and on the "way out" as it is expressed. And both these modes of experience are enlarged and enhanced when they are connected in a circuit of practice. That is, our ability to perceive beauty—to really see it in the world, in more variety and with greater intensity—is partially dependent on our ability to use it, to express it. When we have an outlet for the expression of beauty, whether it involves creating images or music, or simply beautifying our homes, we find that the act of expressing beauty opens the aperture of our minds to receive the light of more beauty of every kind.

We all practice some form of beauty and truth every day. But the *philosophical* appreciation of the significance of these qualities provides us with the mindfulness that helps elevate many of our regular activities to the level of spiritual practice. This integral understanding of beauty and truth helps us have the spiritual experience that is already all around us—this enlarged understanding of the nature of values points us to the spiritual heart of these ordinary activities. In fact, one of the common characteristics of all saints and sages is their ability to find beauty and meaning in the familiar features of everyday living. However, the spiritual practice of beauty and truth not only makes the ordinary more extraordinary, it also helps us see the highest expression of these values with new spiritual eyes. As we are instructed by the truth that truth itself is a window on the divine, we become filled with fresh enthusiasm for the many vehicles of truth by which we can be transported—scientific, philosophical, and religious truth. All of these can literally raise our consciousness by attracting us to new locations—higher elevations—in the topography of consciousness and culture that forms the internal universe.

Like the practice of truth and beauty, the practice of goodness can also be understood through the giving and receiving rhythm of service nurtured by stillness. Goodness is transmitted—it is expressed or taught—in the form of service. Service is a way of communicating goodness to another person. When it comes to our physical health, we know that it's hard to stay healthy without some kind of physical exercise; we need to use the energy that we take in as food. And it is likewise important for our spiritual health that we give out the energy of value in the form of service. That is, it's hard to stay spiritually healthy without rendering some form of service to another. But understanding the kinship of beauty, truth, and goodness helps us better recognize our service opportunities. Service doesn't have to be about volunteering at the soup kitchen; the spiritual practice of service also includes all the ways that we can teach truth and express beauty. Goodness is the inner principle of beauty and truth; goodness actually helps to define truth and beauty through the test of their service value—what they are good for. Real truth is something we can live and use to improve our lives. Even the rarefied beauty of fine art provides the service of pleasure and inspiration. However, the idea of a service of goodness embraces all acts of kindness and consideration—all the ways that one human being can give to another. Just as there are many ways to give out the value of goodness, there are also many ways to receive its spiritual nutrition. The service of goodness can be received from others through their teachings of truth or their expressions of beauty. And as we receive goodness from others, we can return goodness through the value channels of admiration, loyalty, and gratitude. Yet we can also receive goodness directly from its source through the spiritual experiences provided by contemplation, meditation, prayer, and worship; practices that might be collectively characterized as forms of *stillness*.

Figure 6-1 below illustrates the giving and receiving practices that are directly associated with the spiritual experiences of the primary values.

Like electricity, values are not static or absolute; values are "alive, free, thrilling, and always moving." And like electricity, values are captured and harnessed by making a circuit through which they can pass. The circuit of values is thus engaged, and spiritual practice is made most real, when there is a connection established between the subjective and intersubjective domains through objective communications of beauty, truth, or goodness. When we see how our personal practices are energized by their extension into the realm of culture, we are moved to be of greater service. We come to understand spiritual practice not just in terms of our own enlightenment, but also

Figure 6–1. The practice activities of the primary values.

in terms of our duty to others. And this is one of the important ways that integral spirituality creates community. That is, this cultural agreement about the importance of the spiritual practice of values enlarges our conception of the common community of spiritual practice so as to include every kind of integral activism that these value practices suggest. Spiritual practice becomes extended to include the expression of art, the creation of new works of literature, philosophy, and science, and the work of improving the morality of human organizations, locally and globally.

When our spirituality is informed by this cultural agreement about the primary significance and sacred nature of beauty, truth, and goodness, it also provides a way for us to "go public" with our spiritual discourse. Understanding the spiritual significance of the beautiful, the true, and the good helps us share our spiritual experiences in terms that do not rely on the parlance of a particular belief system. The primary values provide us with a common spiritual language that helps enact the public commons of integral spirituality. And when we practice talking about our spirituality in these terms, we often find that it helps us to discern the essence of what is truly spiritual about our practice experiences.

So these are just some of the ways that the philosophy of beauty, truth, and goodness can become an organizing principle of the emerging spiritual culture of integral consciousness. Obviously, there is much about the subject of integral spirituality that we have not discussed. But as the integral worldview emerges, I'm sure that this subject will receive a great deal of attention. However, before we close our discussion of integral spirituality, I'd like to spend just a few more pages considering the spiritual significance of evolution itself.

The Revelation of Evolution

Since the discovery of the Big Bang in the early 1960s, physicists have made significant progress in their understanding of the evolutionary nature of the physical universe. And when this emerging understanding of cosmic evolution is connected to the increasingly sophisticated neo-Darwinian accounts of biological evolution, this scientific story of human origins begins to appear comprehensive.

Yet from an integral perspective, although the scientific story of evolution is beautiful and inspiring, it is only the external story. Integral consciousness can see that evolution is unfolding not only in the external universe of matter and life, but also in the internal universe of consciousness and culture. And as integralists come to better appreciate the evolving nature of consciousness in the universe, evolution's spiritual character becomes increasingly evident. That is, when understood in the light of the integral worldview, the methods, directions, and historical unfolding of the epic of evolution come to be recognized as forms of spiritual truth. In fact, we can anticipate that the magnificent display of creativity and unfathomable genius of design exhibited by evolution at every scale will provide a teaching that will edify humanity for millennia to come. Even now, the power and profundity of our growing understanding of evolution—both external and internal—is one of the primary forces that is giving rise to integral philosophy itself.

Because of these origins, integral philosophy naturally seeks to find connections between the scientific truths of evolution and the unmistakable spiritual realities to which evolution points. Indeed, the goal of harmonizing science and religion has been the elusive pursuit of many of humanity's best thinkers for over a century now, and many excellent books have already been written on the subject. However, the building of agreements between science and spirituality is an endeavor that will occupy integral philosophy throughout the course of its development, and I doubt that this is a task that will ever be declared complete. Nevertheless, integral philosophy can contribute much to this important field by further opening up the internal universe and thereby showing how evolution is fully active in the realm of consciousness and culture. As it works to harmonize science and spirituality, integral consciousness focuses on the subject of evolution because it recognizes that, among the numerous subjects addressed by the community of scholars engaged in the field of "science and religion," evolution is the subject whose study has the greatest potential to yield meaningful results.

The work of finding agreement between science and spirituality is so important because it is through these efforts that we can better learn how to raise consciousness all over the world in sustainable ways. When we begin to take personal responsibility for the growing global-level problems that confront us, and when we then recognize that the solution to every one of these problems calls for the evolution of consciousness in one form or another, we realize that evolution is not a subject we can leave solely in the hands of the scientific community.

The subject of evolution originally found popularity among nineteenth century intellectuals because it seemingly provided a justification for their atheistic metaphysics. And as a result of the "desacralizing" of humanity's story of origins, today in America the subject of evolution has become a battleground in the war between the most orthodox elements of both traditional and modernist consciousness. But beginning with the postmodern worldview, and continuing with greater intensity within the integral worldview, evolution comes to be seen more as a narrative story with a sacred meaning.

There is in fact a strong movement within postmodern culture to recognize the spiritual nature of what is now being called "the Universe Story." According to cosmologist Brian Swimme, one of the ablest proponents of this view, the whole story can be told in one line: "You take hydrogen gas, and you leave it alone, and it turns into rosebushes, giraffes, and humans. ...The point is that if humans are spiritual, then hydrogen's spiritual." This recognition of spiritual significance within the story of evolution has served as a guiding principle of the "deep ecology" movement, which seeks to preserve the environment, not only because humanity depends on it, but also because it is sacred in itself.

The power of evolution's "Great Story" has been heralded by a variety of writers. Some atheistic scientists have naively suggested that this story will eventually become a substitute for religion. Others, such as Thomas Berry, have hailed it as "a meta-religious contribution that can enrich...the full diversity of religious expression...[an] over-arching narrative that includes and uplifts all sacred stories." And there's no doubt that this new story of the evolving universe is indeed a sacred and significant contribution by science to spirituality. Integral philosophy thus does well to include these insights within its own understanding of the nature of evolution. However, as the story has been told so far, it is still basically science. And no matter how much beauty they point to, and no matter how much literary language we use to describe them, facts about the physical universe by themselves cannot engage consciousness at a deep emotional level. We may find awe and wonder in science's story, but this is a story that up till now has focused primarily on *nature* to the relative exclusion of *self* and *culture*.

The strength of the "Great Story" is that it is founded squarely on the discoveries of science, and thus its power compels agreement. But because it relies so heavily on science, it naturally suffers from the material limitations of contemporary science. Abundant meaning and spiritual truth can indeed be found by looking deeply into nature. But as we look for deep meanings within the natural universe, we can easily fall into some version of the *naturalistic fallacy*. That is, spirituality in its fullness inevitably involves considerations of human kindness and goodness. And the requirements of human goodness often transcend what's merely natural.

However, when integral consciousness looks to evolution to learn its spiritual lessons, it sees the glories of evolution at work in both the external and the internal universe—it sees how evolution is working in all three realms of nature, self, and culture. And when we begin to recognize the influences of evolution within consciousness and culture, we can more clearly see how evolution is affecting us right now. The story of evolution is not just something that happened in deep time; the forces that turned rocks into rosebushes are just as intense as ever, in fact, more intense now that they can engage the will of human consciousness and enlist its cooperation in the evolutionary adventure.

When we open up the internal universe and begin to see the forces of evolution that are active therein, we encounter the evolutionary significance of values. We begin to see evolution as Whitehead saw it, as a gentle persuasion through love, seducing us into progressive development through the allure of the eternal forms of the Eros of evolution—the splendor of the beautiful, the true, and the good. That is, as we have seen throughout this book, consciousness and culture evolve primarily through the influence of values; values such as beauty, truth, and goodness provide both the lure and the sustenance for every advancing stage of consciousness and culture. And when we understand the role of values within the evolution of the internal universe, we begin to see how values partake of perfection.

Understood from an evolutionary perspective, the beautiful, the true, and the good show themselves to be *the directions of perfection*. It's by creating and increasing beauty, truth, and goodness whenever and wherever we can that we make the world relatively more perfect. Thus the revelation of evolution, when viewed from the perspective of integral consciousness, is seen as a progressive teaching about perfection that unfolds by stages, one after another. These "lessons of perfection" are taught to each stage of consciousness through the distinct octave of values that are the heritage of that stage. A worldview's values can thus be understood as the way that it connects the decidedly imperfect human conditions that it finds here on earth with universal ideals—ideals that are translated and down-stepped into useful goals by every worldview's particular set of values.

In the realm of consciousness and culture, evolution is a two-way street. Its persuasive influences move us not only to pursue our own ascension, to improve ourselves, but also to try to make things better here on earth during our brief sojourn in this world. That is, not only are we called to rise to higher stages, but we are also called to bring the wisdom of these higher stages down to the levels that need assistance. Our world is full of trouble and suffering, and those who have attained elevated states of consciousness have a sacred duty to use this light to make a difference. And now, through the insights of integral philosophy, we have more detailed instructions on how we can actually bring more beauty, truth, and goodness into the world. Thus it seems to me that the role of human consciousness in the evolving universe, our place within the cosmic economy, is to gradually perfect ourselves by *bringing perfection down to us*. In this way we directly participate in the creative act of evolution by which the universe is brought forth. We become partners with spirit in the grand pageant of development wherein our personal evolution is directly linked with our participation in social evolution.

The integral worldview's search for the full revelation of evolution is only just beginning. And although not all forms of spiritual truth can be found through the study of evolution, there is certainly a wealth of insight still waiting to be discovered. But even now, as we come to better understand the spiritual significance of evolution, we can begin to see clearly how personal spiritual growth is almost always accompanied by an experience of the call to make things better—an inner voice exhorting us to become agents of evolution by working to improve the human condition wherever we are gifted with the opportunity to do so. So just as we began this book's Main Narrative by observing that when we follow a spiritual path, we naturally want to make the world a better place, we now end with this same observation. Yet perhaps, after considering the evolutionary future of integral consciousness, we now have a better idea of just how some of this progress might actually come about.

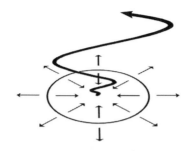

PART II
A DEEPER DISCUSSION

Introduction to Part II

My intent in Part I was to describe integral philosophy in a concise and usable form. The contents of Part I were chosen to present the most practical aspects of the integral worldview within an overall structure designed to actually produce integral consciousness. Whether this has worked or not will be partially measured by your interest in Part II. That is, once you have tasted integral consciousness, once you have surveyed the panoramic view that is to be had from this new location in the internal cultural landscape, it is inevitable that you will crave to learn more. Part II is thus intended to solidify your hold on the integral worldview by filling in some important pieces not covered in Part I, and by providing additional knowledge that will be useful in employing the power of integral philosophy.

We begin Part II with chapter 7 on "The Founders of Integral Philosophy." In this chapter we'll become familiar with the origins and development of what can now be recognized as the *integral canon*. Knowledge of these origins is important because seeing where integral philosophy has come from helps us recognize where integral philosophy is going, and how it is part of a developing stream of thought that has included some of humanity's most gifted thinkers. Then in chapter 8, "The Integral Reality Frame," we examine the philosophical agreements (and disagreements) that are beginning to define the distinct integral worldview. Chapter 8, which extends the discussion begun in chapter 2 on "The Internal Universe," examines how integral philosophy justifies and defends its perspectives relative to our culture's previously existing worldviews. This chapter explores the relationship between integral philosophy and human spirituality, and it concludes by considering some possible critiques of the integral frame of reality. Although chapter 8 is the most intellectually demanding in the book, it is also the most rewarding in the way it shows why integral consciousness is indeed a historically significant new worldview that represents the next crucial step in humanity's cultural evolution. Once we have grounded our understanding of the integral worldview through a deeper appreciation of its agreement frame, we then turn to chapter 9's description of the "Structures of the Human Mind." This chapter, which extends our discussion of the "Stages of Consciousness and Culture" begun in chapter 3, provides the foundation and justification for integral consciousness' most useful method: the ability to see consciousness and culture through the lens of the spiral of development. Chapter 9 explains how the structure of the spiral influences the mind, and how the various lines of development within consciousness find unity within the self as a whole. Then in the final chapter, entitled "The Directions of Evolution," which extends the discussion of "Integral Spirituality" begun in chapter 6, we'll look more closely at the external and internal patterns of overall evolutionary development to discern where evolution is actually taking us. With the new access to the internal universe provided by integral consciousness, it is now becoming possible to actually see the directions of evolution as never before. And this new understanding of the deep patterns of universe development provides a pragmatic method for improving the human condition in both large and small ways.

Although I have tried to keep the discussion grounded and accessible, admittedly, Part II addresses philosophical and psychological subject matter that is generally more difficult than the material covered in Part I. However, I invite you to approach Part II as a kind of "truth practice," recognizing that integral consciousness is a form of psychic strength that requires a certain amount of exercise for its development. And even if you don't entirely agree with the arguments in Part II, the effort required to digest these ideas will give you a better understanding of how your own view of reality is inevitably framed by your philosophical conclusions.

Just as modernist consciousness arose during the Enlightenment through the power of a New Philosophy, the rise of integral consciousness is likewise being brought about by a popular philosophical revival wherein the power of philosophy is being reclaimed by ordinary people who are using it to see things more clearly and to make life better in tangible ways. Thus, although Part II is decidedly philosophical, it is designed to be of use to any thinking person—no previous reading or philosophical familiarity is required. And I have done my best to avoid tediously extending my arguments so as to satisfy every potential criticism or to try to address every possible objection.

Integral consciousness represents the future of cultural evolution, and this worldview of the future is becoming available now to those who would use integral philosophy to illuminate their minds and hearts with the light of integral values. However, in my experience, not only are the concepts of integral philosophy extremely useful, they are also beautiful in themselves. According to Pythagoras, "philosophy is the highest music." So I hope that you will approach the philosophical discussions that follow not only for their usefulness, but also for their beauty. And perhaps, somewhere in between integral philosophy's goodness and beauty, you may come to appreciate its truth.

CHAPTER 7

The Founders of Integral Philosophy

IF THE THESIS OF THIS BOOK IS CORRECT, THEN IT IS TOO EARLY FOR anyone to write an intellectual history of integral philosophy. That is, if integral consciousness is truly a new, historically significant level of consciousness and culture that is now emerging, then it will be decades before anyone can get an objective view of the full expression of integral philosophy. Moreover, if the integral worldview is truly a self-organizing dynamic system of values that is arising within the internal universe of consciousness and culture, then the philosophy that is catalyzing this emergent system must be recognized as merely a contributing element of the system, and not the system itself. Just as the modernist worldview now extends far beyond the confines of Enlightenment philosophy, so too will the integral worldview eventually define an entire era of human history encompassing more knowledge and wisdom than even integral philosophy can contain.

Nevertheless, it is important, even at this early stage of its evolution, to attempt to describe the various streams of thought whose confluence forms the emerging canon of integral philosophy. Most of the essential elements of integral philosophy have been around for a long time. As we will explore in this chapter, the influential German philosopher Georg Hegel recognized the dialectical progression of human history at the beginning of the nineteenth century. Then at the beginning of the twentieth century, the French philosopher Henri Bergson described the spiritual nature of the evolutionary process. It was also around this time that the American developmental psychologist James Mark Baldwin discovered the stage-wise progression of the development of human consciousness. Then in the 1920s, the British mathematician and philosopher Alfred North Whitehead showed how reality could best be understood as a process wherein matter and consciousness are connected at every level of universe development. Writing in the 1930s, the French paleontologist and evolutionary philosopher Pierre Teilhard de Chardin advanced the idea of the internal universe and described the unity of internal and external evolution. In the late 1940s, the Swiss cultural philosopher Jean Gebser wrote about the impending emergence of the integral stage of consciousness. And in the 1970s, the German thinker and social philosopher Jürgen Habermas argued that in modern society, moral judgments can be justified through a culture's intersubjective agreements.

However, it is only since the 1990s that integral philosophy has emerged in its current form. And this has come about largely through the work of the American philosopher Ken Wilber. As we will explore in this chapter and the next, Wilber's achievements in framing the synthesis of integral philosophy in its current form are enormous. One could even argue that integral philosophy did not exist before Wilber. So in any discussion of integral philosophy, Wilber must occupy a central place. However, from my perspective, Wilber's ideas can be challenging and occasionally problematic. So before we begin our discussion of the other brilliant thinkers who have contributed to the growing body of integral philosophy, it will be helpful to understand the context in which Wilber's thinking can best be appreciated.

Ken Wilber in Context

Ken Wilber (born 1949) is known in progressive circles worldwide as a founder of transpersonal psychology and as an innovative evolutionary thinker. Although Wilber's first book, *The Spectrum of Consciousness*, was published in 1977, his mature philosophy did not appear until the publication of his 1995 masterpiece, *Sex, Ecology, Spirituality*, wherein he describes the contours of what I'll call integral philosophy's twenty-first century synthesis. Wilber's strength is found in the way he integrates the work of hundreds of theorists from a wide range of disciplines. Using his entertaining writing style, Wilber brings together science, philosophy, and spirituality in an impressive synthesis that demonstrates the unmistakable reality of the internal universe. Wilber thus carries forward the canon of integral philosophy and reinvigorates it by effectively integrating the latest research and thinking.

However, among Wilber's weaknesses is the fact that he sometimes plays fast and loose with a lot of serious scholarship, using it in ways that the authors he cites would be unlikely to agree with. Moreover, his synthetic philosophy does not adequately address the basics (such as causation or being) in the analytical and methodical way that the philosophical profession generally requires. But as we will discuss below, many of these same criticisms were leveled against pioneering philosophers such as Henri Bergson and Pierre Teilhard de Chardin. Bergson was said to lack analysis, and Teilhard was accused of being a romantic mystic and a poor philosopher. Nevertheless, these thinkers did make meaningful contributions to human understanding in general, and to integral philosophy in particular, and the world is now a better place because they were here. Thus I think Wilber will be remembered by history, like Bergson and Teilhard, as one of the primary founders of integral philosophy.

But in addition to his occasionally questionable scholarship, Wilber's work can also be challenging because he is a spiritual teacher as well as a philosopher. Although he rejects the "guru" label, he does make authoritative proclamations about the nature of spiritual reality, he does advance his personal belief system as though it were an empirical matter of fact, and he is an enthusiastic evangel of his Vedanta/Vajrayana religion. Yet I do not mean to criticize him for any of this. Many great philosophers have professed their spiritual beliefs as part of their philosophy. And the spiritual teachings that Wilber espouses are part of a venerable lineage that has edified humanity for thousands of years. Wilber has made some significant contributions to this lineage, and his spiritual teachings have positively influenced the lives of thousands of people. However, for those of us who are not Hindus or Buddhists, Wilber's spiritual teaching does not always speak to our experiences of spirit. Thus another problematic aspect of Wilber's work is that it is often difficult to separate his philosophy from his religion. And this is perhaps the main reason why his work has been largely ignored by academia.

As we discussed in Part I, philosophy serves humanity best when it retains a certain degree of independence from both science and religion, while at the same time being informed by both of these disciplines. Philosophy differs from religion in the way that it argues for its conclusions, and in the way that it attempts to describe "public truths" whose validity claims are not based on the authority of a particular spiritual teacher or revelation. And by this definition, much of Wilber's work is fully philosophical. However, because Wilber often seamlessly grafts his spiritual teaching onto his more public philosophy, unless we are willing to accept his specific belief system, reading and understanding his work requires us to be particularly vigilant in our discernment.

Although I have been a keen student of thinkers such as Teilhard de Chardin for over thirty years, much of my initial understanding of integral philosophy came through the writing of Wilber. Wilber's synthesis helped me to appreciate the significance of intersubjectivity and developmental psychology, two of the essential areas of understanding that make the current form of integral philosophy so powerful. However, after adopting and practicing the integral worldview for over ten years now, and after reading most of Wilber's sources for myself, I can see that integral consciousness is a self-organizing dynamic system with a "life" of its own. Integral philosophy is more than simply "Ken Wilber's philosophy," and at the end of this chapter I'll describe where I differ from Wilber and what I add to integral philosophy.

I've met with Wilber on several occasions in the past and found him to be friendly, extremely funny, firmly self-possessed, and of course, brilliant. Wilber has been subject to a lot of vicious and unfair criticism, so it is my intention to generally support him and stand as his ally in the movement for integral consciousness. However, although I share his commitment to spirit, I do not share his religion, nor do I agree with all of his philosophical and psychological conclusions. Nevertheless, I must acknowledge my debt to him and my gratitude for his significant contribution to human philosophy in general and to integral philosophy in particular. Because Wilber has reinvigorated interest in evolutionary philosophy and advanced it in the marketplace of ideas, he has made it possible for others like myself to write about the subject. Indeed, philosophy needs creative mavericks like Wilber who can help it make progress in ways that are otherwise blocked by the limitations of cautious and conventional academia. But rarely do such mavericks find credibility in the eyes of the professionals who guard the gates of academic legitimacy. However, as we discussed in the Part I, because the integral vision effectively transcends the modern and postmodern status quo, we cannot expect those who are invested in defending this status quo to validate our transcendence of their way of thinking.

We will return to our discussion of Wilber's work toward the end of this chapter. But now we turn to the roots of integral philosophy and the work of some of the other great thinkers who have contributed to its formation. The numerous contributors to integral philosophy can be compared to a large mountain range; just as there are hundreds of mountains in a large range, over the past two hundred years there have been hundreds of significant contributors to the growing body of integral philosophy. In this chapter, however, I will only be describing the highest peaks, so to speak. Although I do not wish to perpetuate the "great man" theory of history, I do believe it is worthwhile to examine the thinking of integral philosophy's most prominent luminaries and to specifically recognize these particular writers as "the founders of integral philosophy."

In this description of integral philosophy's founders I won't try to summarize the overall philosophy of these thinkers. I'll rather be focusing more directly on their specific contributions to the integral worldview. Moreover, I must acknowledge that a thorough and complete description of the evolution of integral philosophy could occupy the entire careers of many scholars, and so this chapter is merely intended as an introductory overview of the canon of integral philosophy as it has evolved so far.

The Evolution of Philosophy as a Human Endeavor

The deepest root of integral philosophy runs all the way down to the beginnings of philosophy itself, which can be traced to the pre-Socratic philosophers of ancient Greece. Prior to Greek philosophy, religion dominated all institutions of human knowledge. But as the earliest forms of modernist consciousness began to appear among the Greeks, philosophy emerged as a distinct system of human inquiry about the universe. With this newly appearing modernist level of consciousness came the expanded epistemological capacity of *reason*, an emergent human ability which craves philosophy and science. Unlike other early forms of philosophy, such as those systems of philosophical thought expounded by ancient Hindu, Buddhist, and Chinese thinkers, Greek philosophy exhibited modernist consciousness more distinctly in the way that it embodied a kind of *proto-science*. Because ancient Greek philosophy achieved a relatively complete separation of reason-based philosophy from faith-based religion (together with the appearance of the first recognizable forms of science within that philosophy), we can recognize it as a marker of the true beginning of the modernist worldview. And as we will explore next in our discussion of Hegel, whenever the note of modernism is sounded, we can also hear the faint harmonic of integralism.

As we've discussed, the precocious modernism of the ancient Greeks could not be sustained, and the proto-science that had emerged within Greek philosophy became frozen in the writing of Aristotle and Ptolemy, showing little progress for over a thousand years. It was not until the Enlightenment that philosophy and science became separated from their religious confines once again. But during most of the Enlightenment, science was still considered to be part of philosophy. It was not until the nineteenth century that science finally became fully separated from philosophy, as its various branches such as physics and biology became identified as distinct fields of inquiry. Then in the second half of the nineteenth century, social sciences such as psychology, sociology, and anthropology began to emerge. Modernism's scientific approach to human consciousness and culture through the sensory-empirical orientation of the social sciences initially produced progress. But as the limits of what could be understood through the investigation of the exterior aspects of consciousness and culture began to be reached, the bright promise of the social sciences began to dim. As these disciplines became increasingly frustrated in their ability to provide answers and explanations due to the constraints of scientific materialism, they began to develop "physics envy"—they yearned for the certainty and respectability of the "hard" sciences—and this tended to make the social sciences even more materialistically oriented. Indeed, even much of philosophy itself succumbed to physics envy during the twentieth century as many philosophers became seduced by scientism.

But now as philosophy displays new signs of evolutionary development in the form of integralism, it is beginning to partially reclaim the domains of the social sciences for itself. While integral philosophy recognizes that science still has much to contribute to our understanding of consciousness and culture, it also recognizes that the exterior approach of science alone cannot provide the kind of enlarged understanding of consciousness and culture that our civilization now needs. Integral philosophy thus makes use of the social sciences, but it does not defer to these academic disciplines as the sole authority in their respective fields. The integral worldview's expanded reality frame, its new ability to understand the evolution of consciousness and culture achieved through its fresh recognition of the evolving structures of the internal universe, allows it to reclaim the domains of the social sciences as a proper subject of its own inquiry. And this reinclusion, this practice of taking what has been previously separated or differentiated, and reintegrating it at a higher level, is a general description of the overall project of the Second Enlightenment. Thus, integral philosophy seeks not only the aforementioned reintegration of philosophy and the social sciences, it also seeks the larger reintegration of science and spirituality in general. This does not signal a return to the premodern fusion of science and religion, but rather a transcendent new level of harmonization wherein the pathological dissociations of modernism can now be healed through the integral worldview's integrating vision.

However, at this point we are getting ahead of ourselves. In order for us to see how the integral worldview developed this new integrative ability, we need to trace the history of its founding pioneers. And this begins with perhaps the first truly integral philosopher, Georg Wilhelm Friedrich Hegel.

Georg W. F. Hegel

Hegel—the First Integral Philosopher

It is difficult to overestimate the contributions of Hegel (1770–1831) to the evolution of human consciousness and culture. Hegel's thought permanently altered the reality frame of Western philosophy by showing how reason and order can be discovered in human history, in spite of the contradictions and chaos apparent in the historical record. By revealing how history unfolds in a dialectical process wherein conflict makes possible the transformation to a higher state, Hegel laid the foundation for the evolutionary understanding of the universe that has since become central to all scientific and philosophical thought. Although professional philosophy has now largely abandoned Hegel's metaphysics, as we look back at Hegel from the perspective of current integral philosophy, we can appreciate his system in a new light. Even though integral philosophy is not "strictly Hegelian," even though it rejects certain aspects of his thinking, it nevertheless recognizes the foundational contributions of his powerful philosophy.

In the Main Narrative we examined the critical role that philosophy had played in the awakening of modernist consciousness in Europe. The Enlightenment philosophy that had begun with Descartes found its culmination in Kant's three great *Critiques* of reason and judgment. Then after Kant, at the beginning of the nineteenth century, a school of German philosophers arose, known as the *Idealists*, who sought to "complete Kant's system." The Idealists included a number of talented philosophers who made general progress in their attempts to go beyond Kant. Idealism, however, truly broke new ground with the 1807 publication of Hegel's first book, and arguably his greatest work, *The Phenomenology of Spirit*.

Hegel rejected Kant's conception of the timeless categories of knowledge and insisted that knowledge, as well as consciousness itself, is part of an overarching developmental process. Hegel was the first to fully recognize that consciousness develops through a series of distinct stages, and that the conscious self is "constructed" through its interaction with society. In Hegel's philosophy, "Consciousness grows. It develops new concepts and categories. It finds itself torn between one 'form of consciousness' and another, and it learns to reconcile them or, in any case, move beyond them. Consciousness and knowledge are dynamic. They are a *dialectic*. They grow through confrontation and conflict, not by way of mere observation and understanding."[1] Hegel recognized that the developmental process of consciousness mirrored the larger dialectical developmental of spirit as a whole, which he called the "absolute"—a synthesis of humanity, nature, and God. He was thus among the first to understand how this process of development or "becoming" is the central motif of the universe. According to Hegel, "every era's world view was both a valid truth unto itself and also an imperfect stage in the larger process of absolute truth's self-unfolding."[2] Although Hegel did not adopt an evolutionary view of the origin of species (as did his contemporary Jean-Baptiste Lamarck), his philosophy was thoroughly evolutionary in its understanding of consciousness and the universe as a whole.

After Hegel's death in 1831, his philosophy continued to have a profound influence. "When this was all set forth in the early nineteenth century, and for several decades afterward, Hegel's great structure of thought was regarded by many as the most satisfying and indeed ultimate philosophical conception in the history of the Western mind, the culmination of philosophy's long development since the Greeks."[3]

And now from the perspective of current integral philosophy we can begin to see how many of Hegel's breakthroughs resulted from the fact that he had developed an early form of integral consciousness. In fact, it is arguable that what Plato is to modernist consciousness, Hegel is to integral consciousness. Hegel's integral consciousness is clearly demonstrated by his use of the emergent capacity of dialectical evaluation, or what Ken Wilber calls *vision-logic*. It was through dialectical evaluation that Hegel recognized the developing nature of consciousness and human history. He used this capacity to see how the conflicts inherent in all dualistic perceptions are simultaneously preserved and negated in the synthetic process of growth. In other words, as we will explore more fully in chapter 10, developmental processes achieve new levels of synthetic progress by resolving the conflict inherent in a thesis and its antithesis such that both sides are partially preserved. The synthesis retains part of the conflict as "the identity of identity and difference," negating only those aspects of the conflicting elements which are mutually exclusive relative to each other. Hegel thus glimpsed the whole-part "holarchic" structure and the dynamic, systemic nature of the universe's master evolutionary method of transcendence and inclusion.

Hegel was quite aware of the fact that he was using a new epistemological capacity to uncover the truths of his philosophy. He distinguished this capacity (which he termed *Vernuft*, or mature reason) from the more simple form of rationality found in modernist consciousness (which he called *Verstand*, or mere understanding). By transcending Kant, and thus by transcending the limitations of modernist consciousness, Hegel's was one of the first minds to venture into the "virgin territory" of the integral worldview. And today we can recognize many of the essential elements of integral philosophy (albeit not fully developed) in Hegel's thinking. However, like the modernist consciousness of ancient Greece, Hegelian integralism was similarly unstable and premature, so it could not be sustained. Although Hegel described many applications of his dialectical philosophy, in practice his Idealism did not always "reach all the way down to the ground." That is, the most useful aspects of integral philosophy—knowledge of the details of the dynamics of the spiral of development, recognition of the systemic nature of the structures of consciousness and culture, or the political vision of a world federation—did not yet exist at the beginning of the nineteenth century, and so Hegel's grand system (although remarkably integral for its day) did not incorporate the essential features that make contemporary integral philosophy so practical and compelling. Thus, Hegel's

Idealism would eventually lose much of its influence. According to historian Richard Tarnas:

> Hegel had spoken with the autocratic confidence of one who has experienced a vision of reality whose absolute truth transcended the skepticism and demands for detailed empirical tests that other systems might require. To his critics, Hegel's philosophy was unfounded, fantastic. The modern mind did indeed incorporate much of Hegel, above all his grasp of dialectic and his recognition of the pervasiveness of evolution and the power of history. But as an entirety, the Hegelian synthesis was not sustained by the modern mind. In fulfillment, as it were, of its own theory, Hegelianism was eventually submerged by the very reaction it helped provoke—irrationalism and existentialism (Schopenhauer and Kierkegaard), dialectical materialism (Marx and Engels), pluralistic pragmatism (James and Dewey), logical positivism (Russell and Carnap), and linguistic analysis (Moore and Wittgenstein), all movements increasingly more reflective of the general tenor of the modern experience [modernism]. With Hegel's decline there passed from the modern intellectual arena the last culturally powerful metaphysical system claiming the existence of a universal order accessible to human awareness.[4]

As Tarnas makes clear in the above quote, the decline of Hegelian Idealism resulted from a number of factors. But although Hegel's critics included spiritually oriented thinkers such as Soren Kierkegaard, it was generally the tide of atheistic ideology that arose in the second half of the nineteenth century that caused many Western intellectuals to reject Idealism. And much of this atheistic enthusiasm was stimulated by the publication of Charles Darwin's *The Origin of Species* in 1859, the impact of which has, of course, changed the world forever. Although materialistic philosophies could be traced to the ancient Greeks, and although materialism had emerged strongly even before Kant and Hegel in the writing of empiricists such as Thomas Hobbes, David Hume, and Denis Diderot, it was not until the nineteenth century that the Enlightenment's secular progression would culminate in the positivism of Auguste Comte and the enthusiastically atheistic philosophy of Ludwig Feuerbach, Karl Marx, and Friedrich Nietzsche. While *The Origin of Species* did not deny the existence of God, it did seem to provide a way to explain the phenomenon of humanity in fully naturalistic terms. And this greatly encouraged those who were hostile toward spirituality and who sought to replace religion with science.

Darwin has received much of the credit for the discovery of evolution. But Darwin was part of a larger "evolutionism movement" that had begun when Lamarck first published his views on evolution in 1801. In 1861, Darwin credited Lamarck as the first to recognize the evolving character of nature, writing that "he first did the eminent service of arousing attention to the probability of all changes in the organic, as well as in the inorganic world, being the result of law, and not of miraculous interposition."[5] In addition to Lamarck, Darwin, and Alfred Russel Wallace (who recognized the process of natural selection at the same time as Darwin), another giant of nineteenth-century evolutionism was Herbert Spencer. Spencer had written about evolution prior to Darwin, publishing his seminal *The Development Hypothesis* in 1852. Although Darwin and Wallace had focused exclusively on biology, Spencer recognized that the forces of evolution were also at work in human societies. In 1862, Spencer published the first volume of his *Synthetic Philosophy*, wherein he proposed the following formal definition of evolution: "Evolution is a change from an indefinite, incoherent homogeneity, to a definite, coherent heterogeneity; through continuous differentiations and integrations."[6] Spencer was thus the first to provide a scientific description of evolution's essential method of transcendence and inclusion.

However, even though Spencer had incorporated many of the elements of what would become integral theory within his Synthetic Philosophy, he generally failed to produce an integral philosophy because he could not recognize the essentially spiritual character of evolution. Spencer's atheism led to his advocacy of a rather twisted conception of cultural evolution, which came to be known as "Social Darwinism." Spencer coined the phrase "survival of the fittest" and used this concept of evolution to justify his ultralibertarian politics. The dark character of this atheistic philosophy of cultural evolution would later be demonstrated in the twentieth century when Social Darwinism was used by the Nazis as a justification for their eugenics and conquests.

With the fading of Idealism and the rise of atheistic scientism in the second half of the nineteenth century, the living root of integral philosophy had been cut back, and it lay dormant until the beginning of the twentieth century when a bold new shoot of integralism appeared in the form of the optimistically spiritual philosophy of Henri-Louis Bergson.

Henri-Louis Bergson

Bergson—the First Post-Darwinian Integral Philosopher

Bergson (1859–1941) was born in the year that Darwin had published *The Origin of Species*, and he was initially attracted to Spencer's Synthetic Philosophy. Bergson, however, would eventually come to recognize Spencer's philosophy as "the diametric opposite of his own theory of a creative evolution: a materialistic, mechanistic, reductive and deterministic picture"[7] which Bergson thoroughly rejected. Bergson was thus the first to propose a spiritual interpretation of the discoveries of evolutionary science. According to the eminent historian of philosophy, Frederick Copleston, by proposing an alternative, nonatheistic account of evolution, Bergson's philosophy:

> exercised a liberating influence on many minds. For it offered a positive and to many people appealing interpretation of the world, an interpretation which was neither confined to criticism of and attack on other views nor a return to past ways of thought. It did not seem to be a philosophy thought out by someone fighting a rear guard action but rather the expression of an outlook for the future. It was capable of arousing excite-

ment and enthusiasm, as something new and inspiring, and as putting the theory of evolution in a fresh light.[8]

Bergson emphasized the importance of intuition, or unmediated knowledge of the inner nature of things. He recognized the practicality of analytical thinking, but maintained that when we use our intellects to recognize distinct points in time or separate objects in space, we create a fiction which blinds us to the true nature of reality, which is a continuously flowing process of becoming. Bergson's conception of reality as a creative process led to the recognition of what he called the *élan vital*, which has been translated as "vital impulse" or "life force" within evolution. "Bergson believed that the mechanical processes of random selection are inadequate to explain what occurs. There seems to be some sort of persistent drive toward greater individuality and yet at the same time greater complexity, in spite of the fact that these always mean increased vulnerability and risk."[9] According to integral theorist Allan Combs, the essential nature of Bergson's concept of élan vital was consciousness itself, which Bergson associated with an organism's power of choice. Bergson maintained that humans can have a direct experience of the nondeterministic and spiritually creative nature of the process of evolution through an intuition of their own personal freedom of choice. Like consciousness itself, "the universe is not made, but is being made continuously."[10] Our own freedom and creative liberty thus provides an exemplary experience of the evolutionary becoming of the universe.

Bergson's greatest work, *Creative Evolution*, was published in 1907, exactly one hundred years after the publication of Hegel's *Phenomenology of Spirit*. However, while Hegel's writing was ponderous and difficult, Bergson's style was poetic and exciting, demonstrating his preference for intuition over analysis. Although Hegel and Bergson have both made important contributions to integral philosophy, their respective philosophies are significantly different and cannot be counted as being part of the same formal line of thought. Integral philosophy thus incorporates the work of both of these great philosophers while acknowledging their many dissimilarities. Historians of philosophy Robert Solomon and Kathleen Higgins provide an elegant description of Bergson's approach:

The alternative to analysis, according to Bergson, is to "seize from within," to grasp things as a whole by intuition. Here he leaves Hegel and instead joins with the romantics and their idea of the inexpressible, all-embracing intuition. Through intuition, we see things in their wholeness and in time. We see how they embody oppositions and justify opposing viewpoints. We get beyond the frozen moment and appreciate the life, the vital force of things. Nowhere is this intuition of life more immediate and more important than in our intuition of our selves as pure duration. We are [quoting Bergson] "the continuous progress of the past which grows into the future, swelling as it advances. Our desires and actions are not momentary; they carry with them our entire past. Through ourselves, we recognize the truth about the world. The world is duration. The world is evolution. We extend ourselves infinitely, and we transcend ourselves." What we call "matter" is nothing but the repetition of experience. To ask *what* it is that changes, that develops, is to miss the point. Indeed, the whole aim of Bergson's philosophy is to get away from such questions, with their bias in favor of stasis and substance.[11]

While Bergson's emphasis on intuition can be distinguished from Hegel's clear use of dialectical evaluation, Bergson's recognition of the need to go beyond modernist reason in the approach to a more complete understanding of truth can be seen as an early form of integral consciousness. And Bergson's own creation of a stunning new philosophy of evolution is a powerful demonstration of the fruits of his own nascent integral consciousness. Bergson is important to integral philosophy because he carried forward the enterprise of showing the fallacy of the materialist metaphysics of scientism, and because he is truly the father of what would later be called *process thinking*. He was the first to recognize in the theory of evolution itself a spiritual philosophy of love and freedom. Bergson can thus be numbered among the founders of integral philosophy because of the achievements of his philosophy and because of his significant influence on Whitehead, Teilhard, and Sri Aurobindo, who we will discuss below.

Despite the tremendous popularity that Bergson's *Creative Evolution* enjoyed upon its initial publication, Bergson's sway on mainstream philosophy would eventually be eclipsed by the rise in phenomenology and existentialism later in the twentieth century. Bergson's philosophy, however, would live on through the work of Alfred North Whitehead, who developed Bergson's ideas further and who used his own considerable genius to produce the enduring institution of process philosophy.

Alfred North Whitehead

Whitehead—Spiritual Philosopher for the Ages

Alfred North Whitehead (1861–1947) demonstrated a powerful new use of the emergent capacities of integral consciousness by propounding a spiritual philosophy of consciousness that now forms the basis of much of integral philosophy's reality frame. Unlike the work of Bergson or Hegel, Whitehead's philosophy is a living philosophy that has been carried on by some extremely talented successors and which continues to influence science and spirituality to this day. After his death in the 1940s, Whitehead's philosophy was expanded and carried forward by the American philosopher Charles Hartshorne (1897–2000). And today, Whitehead's vision continues to be applied and expanded by American philosopher and theologian David Ray Griffin (born 1939). Thus, because "Whitehead's living philosophy" (known as *process philosophy*) can now be more properly understood as the philosophy of Whitehead-Hartshorne-Griffin (even though both Hartshorne and Griffin acknowledge Whitehead as the master), our discussion will focus on the most recent articulations of process philosophy.

From an integral perspective, process philosophy's most significant contribution is the way it serves to harmonize and integrate science and spirituality. According to Griffin:

[Whitehead] believed that the apparent conflicts between science and religion have been due about equally to inherited religious ideas and to the worldview with which science has recently been associated (which he called "scientific materialism"). And he believed that the needed modifications on both sides could only be achieved by means of philosophy, with "philosophy" understood primarily as metaphysical cosmology, the attempt to create an all-inclusive worldview in which scientific facts and inescapable religious intuitions can be harmonized. Like those who speak of mutual independence of religious and scientific beliefs, Whitehead recognized that they originate in very different types of experience. [quoting Whitehead] "The dogmas of religion are the attempts to formulate in precise terms the truths disclosed in the religious experience of mankind. In exactly the same way the dogmas of physical science are the attempts to formulate in precise terms the truths disclosed in the sense-perception of mankind." Whereas scientific beliefs are based primarily on sensory perceptions, religious beliefs are based primarily on nonsensory perceptions. Unlike advocates of the independence thesis, however, Whitehead did not believe that the different roots of scientific and religious beliefs meant that they could remain unreconciled.[12]

Process philosophy thus attempts to reconcile science and religion by incorporating William James's method of *radical empiricism* (discussed in chapter 6), which recognizes the validity of nonsensory experience in the philosophical enterprise. By recognizing the authenticity of spiritual experience, process philosophy thus limits its inquiries to that which can be experienced while still being able to address spiritual realities. Process philosophy can talk philosophically about "the soul of the universe" because, according to Griffin, "we directly experience this soul's power by virtue of experiencing cognitive, aesthetic, and moral forms, through which we feel the call of Truth, Beauty, and Goodness as normative ideals."[13] Process philosophy's "metaphysical cosmology" is thus based on direct experience.

Process philosophy overcomes dualism, materialism, determinism, and reductionism by advancing a plausible solution to the mind/body problem. This solution is achieved by Whitehead's conception of consciousness not as something that emerges only in the higher animals, but as an aspect of the cosmos that can be found inside every naturally occurring universe structure, no matter how small. Whitehead's hypothesis is that the essential "stuff" of nature is creative, experiential events, or "occasions of experience," rather than simply particles of matter. Thus, according to process philosophy, all outsides have an inside. In other words, every naturally arising universe structure, from atoms, to cells, to mammals, to humans, has both a subjective mode and an objective mode. These internal and external aspects of reality arise together from the beginning, interact naturally and nondualistically, and pervade the universe at every level of its organization. This is not to say that atoms, for example, are actually conscious in the same way humans are conscious, but that they do possess a primitive form of awareness, which Whitehead called "prehension." That is, every atom demonstrates rudimentary awareness in the way it interacts with other atoms. If an atom's orbital shell is empty, this state of being serves as a signal to other atoms that their electrons may enter the empty shell, and this basic form of proto-communication reveals the primordial nature of "prehensive" awareness.

Whitehead's doctrine, which characterizes reality as an aggregation of processes, or events of experience, is now known as *panexperientialism*. In summarizing Hartshorne's elaboration of this doctrine, Griffin writes:

> One advantage of panexperientialism is that it gives us some idea of what matter is in itself. Modern philosophy has left the nature of matter wholly mysterious, saying that we cannot know what it is in itself, only how it appears to us. But, Hartshorne says, we should take advantage of the fact that in ourselves we have an individual piece of nature that we know from within as well as without. If we are naturalists, and hence regard our own experience as fully natural, not as a supernatural something added to nature, should we not assume that all natural unities have two sides? The fact that it is only ourselves whose inside we know directly does not prevent us from assuming that other people have insides, that is, experiences. And most of us assume that other animals have

experience of some sort. Why should we not assume that all natural entities, all the way down to subatomic events, have inside experience as well as outer behavior? We realize that a purely behavioristic approach is inadequate for human beings, and other higher animals. By generalizing this insight to all levels of nature, we can have some slight intuition into what things are in themselves. What we call matter is then the outer appearance of something that is, from within, analogous to our own experience.[14]

Whitehead's recognition of the pervasiveness of *interiority*, as elaborated and clarified by Griffin in the quote above, provides a critical foundation for integral philosophy's understanding of the internal universe. While we can see an inkling of these ideas in the work of certain philosophers before Whitehead, and while Teilhard did arrive at many similar conclusions on his own, the idea that there is an internal universe that is contiguous with the external universe, and that these two dimensions are united in a continuous process of becoming, finds its initial expression in Whitehead. Although the philosophical concept of the internal universe originates from a variety of sources, when we look for the beginnings of the metaphysics of interiority, we find much in Whitehead that is completely new and original. Whitehead, however, conceived his philosophy before the emergence of postmodernism, so his primary focus was on overcoming the metaphysics of scientific materialism. Because he wrote in the early part of the twentieth century, Whitehead encountered neither the problems nor the opportunities of postmodernism, so his evolutionary metaphysics did not include the essential insights of intersubjectivity, which have since come to form such a significant part of integral philosophy's twenty-first-century synthesis.

However, from my perspective, the most significant aspect of Whitehead's work is his recognition of the spiritual nature of evolution, which he characterized as "gentle persuasion through love." That is, according to Whitehead, divine influence in the universe does not predetermine the course of future events; consciousness is partially self-determining and relatively free to make choices and participate in the creative acts through which the universe is manifest. Divine influence does, however, direct the evolutionary process by sharing with all forms of consciousness divinity's appetite for increasing perfection. And it is through this insight that Whitehead derives his criterion for evolutionary progress, which is measured as *an increase in the capacity to experience what is intrinsically valuable.*

Overall, process philosophy is *an* integral philosophy, but it is not exactly *the* integral philosophy I'm describing in this book. Despite its power to harmonize science and spirituality, as it has developed so far, it still lacks an understanding of intersubjectivity and the spiral of development, and thus it fails to provide many of the important insights and applications that make the present form of integral philosophy (described by Wilber and myself) so powerful. Nevertheless, as integral philosophy develops and gains recognition, process philosophy will continue to inform the larger integral worldview, and accordingly, the enduring significance of Alfred North Whitehead will be increasingly appreciated.

Pierre Teilhard de Chardin

Teilhard de Chardin—Master of the Internal Universe

Both Bergson and Whitehead developed philosophies that recognized the inherent spirituality of the evolutionary process, but Pierre Teilhard de Chardin (1881–1955) went even further in that he was both *more scientific* and yet also *more spiritual* than either of these other two great thinkers. Because Teilhard was both an accomplished scientist (a prominent paleontologist) and a deeply religious man (a Jesuit priest), he used this range of vision to develop a unique worldview that was at once fully evolutionary and also fully spiritual. And, like Whitehead, Teilhard's evolutionary worldview now forms an important foundation for integral consciousness.

Because of the inherent conflict between his controversial views on evolution and his loyalty to the Jesuit order, the Catholic Church prevented Teilhard from publishing his philosophy during his lifetime. But upon his death in 1955, the publication of his seminal work *The Phenomenon of Man* caused a great deal of excitement. Teilhard was significantly influenced by Bergson's *Creative Evolution*, and much of Teilhard's philosophy was formulated with the intent of carrying forward Bergson's understanding of the spiritual significance of evolution. Teilhard, however, was apparently not aware of the work of Whitehead, and this is remarkable given the many affinities between Teilhard's and Whitehead's thought (including their mutual recognition of panexperientialism).

Central to Teilhard's philosophy was his conception of the development of evolutionary thresholds—successive enveloping spheres representing different kinds of evolutionary activity. In Teilhard's scheme of cosmogenesis, the first sphere of evolutionary development to appear on earth was the *physiosphere* or geosphere, which contains all evolution prior to life (including the development of the lithosphere, hydrosphere, atmosphere, and stratosphere). Then in the early years of planetary development, inorganic evolution within the physiosphere reached a critical threshold wherein a new kind of evolution appeared. According to Teilhard, the emergence of life marked the distinct beginning of a new evolutionary layer, which we recognize as the *biosphere*. Development in the biosphere then proceeded for billions of years until a new evolutionary threshold was reached—the emergence of what Teilhard called the *noosphere*, or psychosocial layer of evolution. And just as the biosphere eventually came to envelop and transform the physiosphere which preceded it, the noosphere has recently come to envelop and transform the biosphere.

According to Teilhard, the crossing of the critical threshold of the noosphere resulted in the emergence of a qualitative distinction or change of state between conscious life and self-conscious humanity. As we noted in chapter 2, Teilhard recognized that the primary difference between humans and animals is *within*—the higher animals may be able to know, but man knows that he knows, and this self-reflective ability signals the beginning of a new realm of evolutionary possibilities. "From *without* the human zoological group represents just one other biological species, but from *within* the human phylum represented, for Teilhard, the continuation of the spiritualization of the cosmos."[15] Teilhard explains:

> Man is an embarrassment to science only because it hesitates to accept him at his full significance, that is to say as the appearance, at the goal of continuous transformation, of an absolutely new state of life. Let us recognize frankly, once and for all, that in any realistic picture of world history, the coming to power of thought is as real, specific, and great an event as the first condensation of matter or the first appearance of life: and we shall perhaps see, instead of the disorder we feared, a more perfect harmony pervading our picture of the universe.[16]

More than any philosopher before him, Teilhard recognized in the story of evolution a profound spiritual teaching about humanity's place in the universe. He could see that the facts of evolution themselves reveal that the development of the cosmos has order, direction, and purpose. And Teilhard could also see that this spiritual understanding of evolution orients us to our natural task of improving the human condition by participating in the evolution of the noosphere. Teilhard also recognized the essential spiritual quality of evolution in the trend of its general progress toward greater levels of unity and perfection, positing that the next great evolutionary threshold would be the achievement of what he called the "Omega Point," the realization of the Brotherhood of Man on earth. Teilhard conceived of the Omega Point as a kind of "utopian attractor," whose existence as a potentiality produces a kind of evolutionary gravity that influences the development of the noosphere. However, although Teilhard saw the potentiality of the Omega Point as preexistent, his views were not completely deterministic; he did recognize the reality and importance of human free will.

As a scientist, Teilhard had set out to develop a scientific knowledge of the internal universe. He thus brought forward aspects of integralism that we don't see in Hegel, Bergson, or Whitehead. For example, Teilhard advanced his "law of complexity-consciousness" which holds that consciousness develops in direct proportion to an organism's organizational complexity. According to Teilhard, "complexification due to the growth of consciousness, or consciousness the outcome of complexity: experimentally the two terms are inseparable."[17] Teilhard's recognition of the systemic nature of evolution, its "development by envelopment" and its transformations triggered at critical thresholds (even before this was described by systems science), combined with his clear understanding of the direct developmental connection between the inside and outside of all evolving entities, secures his place as an important founder of integral philosophy.

Although Bergson had received criticism from the materialists for his teachings about the spiritual nature of evolution, Teilhard's scientific credentials and the general framing of *The Phenomenon of Man* as a work of science raised the ire of scientism more than perhaps any other work of the twentieth century. However, although much of the criticism was scathing, there were others in the scientific community who were greatly inspired by Teilhard's spiritual philosophy of evolution. The influence of Teilhard's thought, however, has extended far beyond philosophy and the evolutionary sciences, making an impact on fields as diverse as law, business, and medicine.

We will return to our exploration of the important insights of Teilhard de Chardin in the last chapter, *The Directions of Evolution*. But now we turn to our discussion of perhaps the most prophetic thinker to be numbered among the founders of integral philosophy, the Swiss philosopher and sociologist Jean Gebser.

Jean Gebser

Gebser—Prophet of Integral Consciousness

Although Hegel, Bergson, Whitehead, and Teilhard are not all part of the same "philosophical school," although they do not always agree with each other on every point, the winding developmental line that connects these thought leaders does trace the emerging canon of integral philosophy up through the first half of the twentieth century. However, in addition to their status as founders of integral philosophy, these geniuses have already been recognized by academia as significant contributors to human knowledge in general. But when we come to Jean Gebser (1905–73), we have a thinker of a different character. Unlike the famous philosophers we have discussed, Gebser is relatively obscure. And this is perhaps because his writing can sometimes seem excessively cryptic, eccentric, and dogmatic. While Gebser's writing is amazingly insightful and prophetic in its description of integral consciousness, his work has not had the significant impact on the field of philosophy that has been achieved by the other founders we have discussed. Nevertheless, when we now look back at Gebser from the perspective of twenty-first-century integral philosophy, we can see that he definitely deserves a place among the primary founders of the integral canon.

Beginning in the late 1930s, Gebser had a clear intuition that human history would soon produce an emergent new structure of consciousness and culture, which he termed *integral consciousness*. As he investigated this intuition, he was led to the recognition that human history had unfolded through a series of discontinuous mutations, with each mutation resulting in an entirely new pattern of experience and a new perception of space and time. Gebser recognized that each new mutation in consciousness produced an expanded type of perspective. According to Gebser, the emergence of such a new perspective was particularly evident in the rise of modernist consciousness, which he called the *mental-rational structure*. To illustrate this point, he cited the example of the appearance of three-dimensional perspective in painting during the Renaissance, which marked the beginning of the then newly emerging mental-rational structure with its distinct form of *mental-perspectival awareness*. Gebser, however, attacked mental-perspectival consciousness as being centered in the ego, and he thus blamed this way of seeing as the primary cause of the pathology of modern society. Against the rational-perspectival outlook of the mental structure, Gebser advocated the superiority of what he saw as the newly emerging mutation of the integral structure, with its distinct form of *integral-aperspectival awareness*. According to Gebser, aperspectival awareness is ego-free; it is "not transfixed in partial viewpoints," its perspective is not bound to the ego of one individual or one type of consciousness, but is rather able to adopt multiple perspectives. Through aperspectival consciousness, the previous structures of consciousness become transparent and "diaphanous," and this results in an increasing intensity of consciousness that integrates all previous structures. In Gebser's seminal work *The Ever-Present Origin*, first published in 1953, he writes:

> In order to achieve the requisite basis for the transformation to which we have alluded, we wish to present as a working hypothesis the four, respectively five, structures we have designated the archaic, magical, mythical, mental, and integral. *We must first of all remain cognizant that these structures are not merely past, but are in fact still present in more or less latent and acute form in each one of us.* Only an explication and its attendant awareness in us of the hitherto more or less ignored evidence will enable us to achieve an integral mode of understanding in contrast to the practice of, say, Hegel and Comte. We are therefore not just proposing our consciousness mutation theory in opposition to the theory of evolution. In our reflections on the presentation of the past (thus making it present to consciousness), we shall include the future as latently existent and already present in us. We not only leave open the possibility of a new consciousness mutation toward integral awareness of the aperspectival world, but also bring it closer to us, that is, effect its presentation.[18]

Hegel had described the evolution of human history as the unfolding of a series of stages of consciousness, but Gebser went further by defining these stages more distinctly and by describing how recognition of these discrete stages of historical development actually causes the emergence of the next stage. In other words, Gebser's posited mutation into integral consciousness is achieved as *the viewpoint of each previous stage becomes transparent to aperspectival awareness*, and this is what actually gives rise to a new structure—a new philosophy, a new epistemological capacity, and a new values-based worldview.

Gebser's emphasis on the new and distinct epistemological capacity that arises with each stage of consciousness is one of his most important contributions to integral philosophy. We have already explored how the emergence of modernist consciousness endows those who adopt the modernist worldview with an expanded rational ability—a new capacity for reason and logic. Gebser, however, recognized in modernist consciousness both an *efficient* form of reason—"balanced directional thought" (such as that used by Plato)—and a *deficient* form of rationalism, which he characterized as excessively analytical, divisive and dualistic. According to Gebser, rational perspectivity's highly crystallized form of "ego-consciousness" is overcome by the integral structure through the use of what he called "verition," a way of seeing things as they really are—a perception of truth that *sees through* things. He argued that it is the achievement of this aperspectivity of awareness that renders reality transparent and diaphanous, allowing us to literally see through previous perspectives and recognize the ever-present origin behind all appearances. Gebser claimed that this "aperspectival verition" results in a category-free perception that is reminiscent of German philosopher Martin Heidegger's phenomenology of being. Although Gebser criticized Heidegger's secularized "Theology without God," he also praised Heidegger's work as an expression of "diaphaneity in recent philosophy" whose "renunciation of the demand for conceptualization...permits the mutation from the three-dimensional mentality into four-dimensional integrality of the whole."[19]

Although Gebser likened the category-free method of phenomenology to aperspectivity, he also distinguished the *efficient* form of integral-aperspectival awareness, which involves the transcendence of ego, from the *deficient* form of integralism, which according to Allan Combs's assessment of Gebser, "refers to ordinary emptiness, the void of the existentialists, and to the relativism of multifaceted perspectives, literal or figurative, that are not translucent to the origin, but are simply complex."[20] And it is in this kind of distinction that we can see Gebser struggling to tease apart the differences between postmodern consciousness and integral consciousness.

Gebser's prescient intuition of the emerging contours of the integral canon can be seen in his affinity for Teilhard and for the Indian mystic philosopher and spiritual teacher Sri Aurobindo (1872–1950). In his preface to the second edition of *The Ever-Present Origin*, written in 1966, Gebser referred to the appearance since the first edition of certain "encouraging events" whose "spiritual potency" needed to be mentioned:

> Among these achievements, the writings of Sri Aurobindo and Pierre Teilhard de Chardin are pre-eminent. ...Both develop in their own way the conception of a newly emergent consciousness which Sri Aurobindo has designated as the "supramental." ... Although both authors have a human-universal orientation, Sri Aurobindo—integrating Western thought—proceeds from a reformed Hindu, Teilhard de Chardin from a Catholic position, whereas the present work is written from a general and Occidental standpoint. But this does not preclude the one exposition from not merely supporting and complementing, but also corroborating the others.[21]

Like Teilhard, Sri Aurobindo had attempted to show how the facts of evolution could be harmonized with a spiritual conception of the universe. In his masterpiece, *The Life Divine*, Aurobindo undertook the task of combining premodern Hinduism with the scientific and philosophical insights of Western modernism to achieve an early form of integral spirituality.

There is no doubt that Sri Aurobindo is a significant pioneer of integral consciousness, and he must be recognized as a prominent founder of the integral worldview. In my opinion, his masterful integration of evolution and spirituality in *The Life Divine* represents one of the twentieth century's most profound religious works. Although I do not follow a spiritual path rooted in Hinduism, Aurobindo is nevertheless a personal spiritual hero of mine. However, his work is far more religious than it is philosophical. Although he dealt with philosophical subject matter, he presented himself more as a spiritual teacher in the Hindu tradition than as a philosopher in the Western tradition. Aurobindo accordingly wrote with the autocratic authority of an omniscient spiritual master, proclaiming universal truth as an all-knowing guru. He did not see the need to thoroughly argue for his conclusions, nor to explain how he came to know the fantastic truths he proclaimed. Moreover, Aurobindo did not acknowledge his debt to Hegel or to most of the other Western philosophers whose work he clearly relied on. Furthermore, although Aurobindo was devoted to an enlarged understanding of the evolution of consciousness through stages, he failed to adequately recognize the direct connection between the evolution of consciousness and the evolution of culture.

Nevertheless, Aurobindo's genius has made a significant contribution to the rise of the integral worldview, and this can be seen in the fact that many of the integral movement's most prominent leaders follow spiritual paths that are rooted in Hinduism and inspired by Aurobindo's teachings. However, I will not describe his work at length here because I believe it is primarily a form of integral spirituality rather than mainline integral philosophy. In fact, according to official Aurobindo biographer M. P. Pandit, Sri Aurobindo's evolutionary philosophy, which first appeared in his journal *Arya*, and which later became the foundation for *The Life Divine*, was produced through a kind of automatic writing. According to Pandit, "This corpus of knowledge, it may be noted, was not a product of his brain—brilliant though it was. The whole of the *Arya*, he recalls, was transmitted directly into his pen."[22]

As I explain at length in the next chapter, it is very important for integral philosophy to be understood as a way of seeing the world that can include and accommodate a wide variety of spiritual paths and perspectives. Therefore, to include the spiritual teachings of Sri Aurobindo among this description of the primary founders of integral philosophy, without discussing all the other spiritual teachers, East and West, who have also had a profound impact on integral philosophy, would run the risk of unfairly associating integral philosophy with one particular spiritual tradition.

Aurobindo is often credited as the first to use the term "integral" in connection with evolutionary philosophy. However, Harvard sociologist Pitirim Sorokin also began using the phrases "integral philosophy" and "integralist" in this connection at around the same time as Aurobindo.[23] In fact, it appears that Sorokin, Aurobindo, and Gebser each originally adopted the term "integral" independently without knowledge of its use by others. While these three writers were not all referring to exactly the same thing, we can see how they all had a similar vision of what was to come.

But returning to our discussion of Gebser, as viewed from our current perspective, although *The Ever-Present Origin* does anticipate many of the elements of integral philosophy, although it is tantalizingly almost-complete in many important ways, it ultimately fails at being an adequate manifesto of usable integral philosophy because it does not fully distinguish integralism from postmodernism. Although much of Gebser's description of the integral structure fits well with our current understanding of integral consciousness, there is just as much, if not more, that can better be attributed to the postmodern stage. So even though Gebser called his anticipated new structure of consciousness *integral*, his prophetic vision of an emerging mutation in consciousness was actually more prescient of postmodernism than of later appearing integralism.

Nevertheless, we can certainly forgive Gebser for these shortcomings given the fact that a complete understanding of the difference between postmodern consciousness and integral consciousness was not fully recognized by integral theorists until the insights of Clare Graves were integrated into integral philosophy in the late 1990s. But as we have seen, Gebser's overall understanding of the discrete stages of consciousness, together with his emphasis on how the integral structure uses its new recognition of these stages to actually construct its worldview, secures his place as a founder of integral philosophy.

However, it is worth mentioning in this regard that although Gebser was remarkably prophetic in his early recognition of the stages of consciousness, it is rather odd that even though *The Ever-Present Origin* cites the work of hundreds of philosophers, scientists, and artists, there is no mention of developmental psychologists such as James Mark Baldwin or Gebser's fellow Swiss thinker Jean Piaget. And this is especially curious given the fact that by the time of the second edition of *The Ever-Present Origin*, the work of Piaget was well known in intellectual circles. Gebser's omission of developmental psychology can thus be recognized as a major shortcoming of his research, because today we can clearly see how the line of developmental psychology that begins with Baldwin and culminates in Graves has now become a major part of the integral worldview. So it is to a discussion of the evolution of this line of thinking that we now turn.

Developmental Psychology and the Mapping of the Internal Universe

In addition to its roots within Western philosophy, the canon of integral theory is also grounded in the social sciences, and particularly in developmental psychology, which we briefly explored at the beginning of chapter 3. So in this section of the present chapter we return to the beginning of the twentieth century to trace the evolution of developmental psychology, which is a strand of thought that now forms an essential part of integral philosophy's twenty-first-century synthesis.

The field of psychology in general has never been integrated or coordinated in a coherent way. It emerged from philosophy as a distinct discipline in the late nineteenth century. And characteristic of this period, early psychologists thought of themselves as scientists who were founding a science of the mind that would demystify consciousness once and for all. However, due to the inherent limitations of a material approach to a nonmaterial subject, the field was marked by divergent and competing theories, each vying to assert their empirical authority in a domain wherein empirical certainty remained elusive.

It was in this formative period that the branch of psychology that we now label "developmental" had its beginnings. It was Hegel, however, who was really the first to describe how consciousness develops in distinct stages. Indeed, we can now recognize the entire corpus of integral theory within Hegel's philosophy, albeit in an early, undeveloped form. Unlike most of the other branches of psychology that had their beginnings in the late nineteenth century, developmental psychology carried forward the insights of moral philosophers such as Kant and Hegel. But despite the affinity of developmental psychology with evolutionary philosophy, neither Bergson, Whitehead, nor Teilhard recognized the significance that developmental psychology had for their theories; they did not fully understand the significance of the correspondence between the evolution of culture and the evolution of consciousness.

Unlike the other founders we have discussed so far, Gebser is again a special case. Writing in the late forties and early fifties, Gebser developed his own independent understanding of the stages of consciousness and culture without the benefit of the significant body of empirical research that developmental psychology had amassed even as of the time of his writing. So like the rest of Gebser's thinking, his insights about the evolution of consciousness remained relatively isolated until his "rediscovery" by integral theorists in the 1980s. It was not until the 1970s that mainstream philosopher Jürgen Habermas began to recognize the significance of developmental psychology to evolutionary philosophy. And it was not until the 1980s that these two fields would begin to find a comprehensive integration through the work of Ken Wilber.

James Mark Baldwin

But despite the fact that evolutionary philosophy and developmental psychology developed independently, both of these fields originally arose from insights achieved through the use of vision-logic, or what I'm calling dialectical evaluation—the emergent epistemological capacity of integral consciousness. We discussed above how the enlarged epistemological capacity provided by integral consciousness was employed by Hegel, Bergson, Whitehead, Teilhard, and Gebser to produce their respective philosophies. But in addition to these renowned philosophical geniuses, there was another early genius who would use the power of integral consciousness to discover essential features of the internal universe that have now become central to integral philosophy. This genius was James Mark Baldwin (1861–1934), and his great contribution was the discovery that consciousness evolves through universal, cross-cultural stages of development. As we briefly explored in chapter 3, Baldwin's work provided the foundation from which the entire field of developmental psychology has subsequently arisen.

Baldwin was originally motivated by a desire to overcome the dualisms inherent in the worldview of modernist consciousness. He was at first attracted to the panexperiential philosophy of Spinoza, but he was also greatly influenced by the thought of Kant and the Idealists, such as Fichte and Hegel. Indeed, the development of Baldwin's intellectual career reads like a microcosm of the development of integral philosophy itself. Although he wrote over 150 academic books and articles, the mature expression of his thought appeared in his seminal work *Thought and Things: A Study of the Development and Meaning of Thought, Genetic Logic* (completed in 1911), which described the dialectical development of human consciousness through the following distinct stages: "pre-logical, quasi-logical, logical, extra-logical, and hyper-logical."

In addition to his early discovery of the stages of development in consciousness, Baldwin also recognized separate but related lines of development arising within those stages, which he associated with the Kantian categories of feeling, thought, and will, or aesthetics, science, and morality. And like Whitehead, Baldwin recognized the aesthetic line of development as primary. But despite his early prominence as a recognized founder of the field of psychology, as a result of his Idealistic orientation, Baldwin's contributions would later be dismissed by an academic psychology obsessed with sensory-empiricism and the metaphysical constraints of scientism. Nevertheless, Baldwin's insights were recognized and carried forward by another developmentalist whose empirical research would place the question of developmental stages beyond any reasonable doubt. This famous researcher was, of course, Jean Piaget (1896–1980), and his empirical confirmation of the universal, cross-cultural, developmental stages of consciousness, each with its own worldview, has now been validated and revalidated by literally hundreds of scientific studies. Piaget's theory of the cognitive line of development has served as an inspiration and a template for the research of a long line of subsequent developmental psychologists who have since investigated other developmental lines (such as moral reasoning or the sense of self), and who have consistently found that the development of consciousness proceeds through these distinct, universal, cross-cultural stages, with these same stages being evident regardless of the particular line being traced.

However, unlike Baldwin's clear demonstration of early integral consciousness, Piaget and most of his successors in the field of developmental psychology were academic social scientists operating largely within the modernist worldview. The constraints of modernist ideology thus kept these researchers from connecting their theories to the larger philosophical understanding of evolution to which their findings pointed. Although we can trace the line of succession in mainstream developmental psychology from Baldwin to Piaget and then from Piaget to the many prominent stage theorists that he inspired—including Kohlberg, Loevinger, Gilligan, Gardner, and Kegan—what we now recognize as developmental psychology has also incorporated the insights of humanistic and transpersonal psychology, which did not emerge from the work of Baldwin and Piaget.

Although he is now almost always included among the list of prominent developmental psychologists, Abraham Maslow (1908–70), like Gebser, was apparently unaware of the work of Baldwin or Piaget when he formulated his famous stage theory of human needs, first published in his 1954 masterwork *Motivation and Personality*. Unlike the Piagetian developmentalists of the time, Maslow's consciousness evinced a unique combination of modernism, postmodernism, and nascent integralism. As an atheist, Maslow was attracted to the existentialism of the 1950s, and his attempted unification of existentialist philosophy and scientific psychology gave rise to "humanistic psychology," which he described as the "third force" apart from the Freudian and Behaviorist schools of psychology that were dominant at the time. Maslow's influence on the field of academic psychology as a whole was enormous, but in the late 1960s he grew disenchanted with the limitations of humanistic psychology, and as a result of the influence of postmodern counterculturalists, he became one of the founders of transpersonal psychology, which he characterized as the "fourth force." And interestingly, it was in the field of transpersonal psychology that Ken Wilber began his career. Wilber, however, would later distance himself from this area of psychology as it became increasingly mired in postmodernism's New Age spirituality.

Clare W. Graves

But as viewed from the vantage point of integral philosophy's twenty-first-century synthesis, Maslow's greatest legacy is arguably his influence on Clare W. Graves (1914–86), whom we discussed extensively in the Main Narrative. Although Graves was also influenced by Piaget, his research program on the "ideal human," which began in the late 1950s and which eventually led to his discovery of the spiral of development, was originally designed to verify and confirm the stages of development postulated by Maslow. Maslow's significant influence on Graves can be seen in Graves's designation of the integral stages and beyond as "being levels," with his idea of "being values" derived from Maslow's description of the values and orientation of self-actualized people. Graves's research, however, revealed problems in Maslow's stage theory, which Maslow later acknowledged.

As we discussed in chapter 3, among all the developmental psychologists who have followed Baldwin, Graves is the most significant to integral philosophy because of his clear recognition of the systemic nature of the spiral of development. Although Graves's research was more extensive and more empirical than Maslow's, it did have significant limitations and was not as scientifically impressive as Piaget's. What makes Graves so important is not the data he accumulated, but his *interpretation* of the data. Graves achieved an unprecedented understanding of the interdependence of life conditions and the distinct values-based worldviews that arise in response to these conditions. His insights into the cocreative relationship between the stages, the "bio-psycho-social" character of human development, and the recurring, spiraling nature of the dialectic evolution of consciousness also represent significant contributions to our understanding of the internal universe. Graves's unrivaled grasp of the systemic structures of consciousness and culture, taken together with his reputation among the academic psychologists of his day as a curmudgeonly maverick who rejected the received wisdom of humanistic psychology, are clear evidence of his own achievement of integral consciousness.

Before he adopted the *Spiral Dynamics* model advanced by Graves's popularizers Beck and Cowan, Wilber's developmental philosophy rested on a combination of the stages of consciousness described by Piaget and his followers and the stages of culture described by Gebser. It was only after adopting the more advanced understanding provided by Graves that Wilber developed a clearer recognition of the difference between postmodern and integral consciousness, which led to Wilber's book on postmodern pathology entitled *Boomeritis*.

We will return to our discussion of developmental psychology in chapter 9, on the *Structures of the Human Mind*. But as we continue our exploration of the evolution of integral philosophy as a whole, we now return to the field of mainstream Western philosophy to examine the work of Jürgen Habermas.

Jürgen Habermas

Habermas—Architect of Integral Foundations

German social philosopher Jürgen Habermas (born 1929) must be recognized as a de facto founder of integral philosophy because several important features of integral philosophy's twenty-first-century synthesis find origin or amplification in his writing. However, unlike the spiritually oriented philosophers of evolution we have discussed so far, Habermas is an atheist and a neo-Marxist and he is thus not a true "integral philosopher" after the manner of Whitehead or Teilhard.

Nevertheless, because of Habermas's skill in defending the dignities of modernity against the antimodern onslaughts of Europe's most ardent deconstructionist postmodernists; because of his insights into the correlation between the evolution of consciousness and the evolution of culture; because of his recognition of dialectically evolving stages that he sees emerging within objective, subjective, and intersubjective "worlds"; and because of the credibility he brings to these arguments as a result of his stature as one of the world's most respected living professional philosophers, his ideas serve as a foundation for many of the essential tenets of current integral philosophy.

Habermas's impact on integral philosophy has been made almost exclusively through his influence on Ken Wilber, who regards Habermas as "the world's foremost living philosopher and social theorist."[24] So although Habermas would undoubtedly reject many important elements of integral philosophy in its current form (if he were to take notice of it), his significant contributions to the integral reality frame cannot be overlooked.

Habermas inherited the mantle of the famous "Frankfurt school" of philosophy, which was known in the early twentieth century for its postmodern rendition of Marxism. Today it seems that Habermas's Marxism is largely ceremonial, but he nevertheless remains committed to a "methodological atheism." As a "public intellectual" in the European tradition, Habermas has been chameleon-like in his worldview, appearing at the same time as both a leftist social critic and as a partisan of modernity and avid supporter of the European Union.

Habermas's social philosophy combines the stage theory of Piaget and Kohlberg with Marx's historical materialism in arguing for the recognition of a loose correspondence between the evolution of human consciousness and the evolution of human culture. He sees human history evolving across three broad worldview stages—mythical, religious-metaphysical, and modern—which he correlates with Kohlberg's stages of moral development in the individual. These are the same stages that Kohlberg labeled preconventional, conventional, and postconventional. Habermas recognizes the superiority of the modern/postconventional stage of evolution in the way that its worldview has differentiated the "value spheres" of science, morality, and aesthetics, separating them from their premodern fusion in religion, and resulting in a clearer understanding of objective standards of morality.

In his defense of the Enlightenment ideals of universal rationality, Habermas has sought to avoid transcendental and idealistic (i.e, spiritual) justifications of morality by grounding his moral theory in the ethical validity of intersubjective agreements. That is, Habermas argues that a legal norm is morally justified for a community only if it is agreed upon as a result of a free, rational discussion. And the criteria he uses to determine whether such an agreement is "free and rational" (and therefore objectively justified in its enforcement of a norm) is whether the participants in the agreement all possess postconventional morality, or modernist consciousness. In seeking to avoid extreme postmodern relativism on one side and a morality based on ecclesiastical tradition on the other, Habermas has sought to preserve a conception of reason and objective morality that enables the evaluation of social norms without resort to religious authority. Thus for Habermas, the evident reality of intersubjective agreements serves as the foundation of his moral and social theories.

Habermas also connects his concept of the three primary value spheres (which are derived from Kant's three "instances of reason") with his idea of the "lifeworld," which according to Habermas encompasses the *objective* world, the *social* or *intersubjective* world, and the *subjective* world. By focusing on what he calls the "worlds" evidenced by the actual content of human language, Habermas shows that in addition to objective propositions of factual truth, human language is also clearly concerned with "normative rightness" and "subjective truthfulness." According to Habermas, if we are to recognize the objective "world" of facts we must also postulate "a world not only for what is 'objective,' which appears to us in the attitude of the third person, but also one for what is normative, to which we feel obligated in the attitude of addresses [relations], as well as one for what is subjective, which we either disclose or conceal in the attitude of the first person. With any speech act, the speaker takes up a relation to something in the objective world, something in a common social world, and something in his own subjective world."[25] It is thus through an analysis of "speech acts" that Habermas arrives at an independent, but nevertheless integral, recognition of the objective, subjective, and intersubjective domains of the lifeworld. But Habermas also goes further by distinguishing the difference between the natural lifeworld perceived by individuals and the realm of the artificial systems of capitalist society, which he criticizes for their "technicizing of the lifeworld" and their tendency to degrade the morality of human society to the level of mere instrumental efficiency. Thus in addition to his recognition of objective, subjective, and intersubjective realities, Habermas also insightfully incorporates the separate domain of artifacts and man-made systems into his philosophical framework.

As we will explore further in chapter 8, it is rather ironic that Habermas has made such a significant contribution in outlining the integral worldview's objective-subjective-intersubjective metaphysical reality frame, while at the same time claiming that his philosophy is strictly "postmetaphysical." In his use of the term postmetaphysical, Habermas is generally referring to the late modernist worldview's political and social transcendence of religious or metaphysical authority. And he is also signaling his acknowldgement of Martin Heidegger's critique of traditional metaphysical philosophy that has become accepted wisdom in most European universities. However, because he is constrained by the limitations of a materialist philosophy, following his chameleon-like strategy, he does not adequately explain how his notions of the dialectic teleology of history are postmetaphysical, nor does he explain why his ideas about subjective or intersubjective "worlds" do not have ontological implications beyond the realm of language.

But despite his general hostility toward spirituality and the opportunistic political maneuvering in some of his writing, Habermas has demonstrated a remarkable grasp of some of the highest truths that philosophy has yet uncovered. His extraordinary understanding of most of the essential tenets of integral philosophy, which he comes to from a completely different angle than the other integral philosophers we have discussed, is suggestive of a powerful intuition for the truth. We will return to Habermas and discuss his philosophy in greater detail in the next chapter. But as we now conclude our survey of the founders of integral philosophy, we finally turn to the work of Ken Wilber.

Ken Wilber

Wilber—Framer of Integral Philosophy's Twenty-First-Century Synthesis

As we discussed at the beginning of this chapter, Wilber's work has carried forward and expanded the canon of integral philosophy in a number of important areas. I refer to Wilber's contribution as "integral philosophy's twenty-first-century synthesis" because Wilber has effectively updated evolutionary philosophy by skillfully incorporating many of the significant advances in science and philosophy that emerged during the last quarter of the twentieth century. Moreover, not only has Wilber expanded the content and contemporary relevance of integral philosophy, he has also enlarged the frame of integral philosophy's reference. That is, Wilber has developed a model of evolving reality that reveals the internal universe in new and important ways. As we will discuss in the next chapter, Wilber's four-quadrant model reveals aspects of reality that heretofore have not been fully recognized or understood, and so in certain respects this new frame of reality does for the *internal universe* what Descartes' philosophy did for the *external universe* during the Enlightenment. Wilber's twenty-first-century integral synthesis provides the beginnings of the expanded reality frame that is serving to enact the next historically significant worldview to arise in humanity's cultural evolution.

Although Wilber has attempted to include and integrate the work of hundreds of thinkers and theorists, his most significant additions to evolutionary philosophy involve his incorporation of the recent insights of systems science, developmental psychology, and postmodern philosophy. Teilhard and Whitehead had glimpsed the systemic nature of internal evolution, but they did not have the benefit of the scientific breakthroughs that significantly expanded systems science in the 1970s. These breakthroughs included Ilya Prigogine's Nobel prize winning discovery of self-organizing dynamic systems, and Francisco Varela and Humberto Maturana's recognition of *autopoiesis*—the mechanism through which evolutionary systems maintain their organization and overcome entropy. Wilber recognized the significance of these discoveries for evolutionary philosophy and incorporated them into his theory by using the concept of *holons*, or whole-part systems. As we will discuss in the next chapter, the theory of holons effectively shows the similarities between the evolutionary structures found in the external realms of biology and cosmology, and the evolutionary structures found in the internal realms of human consciousness and culture. Moreover, this recognition of the universal whole-part structure of all evolutionary development reveals how systems manage to maintain their integrity in the face of increasing complexity.

In his formulation of integral philosophy's twenty-first-century synthesis, Wilber also skillfully illuminated the connection between developmental psychology and evolutionary philosophy. Although Hegel, Gebser, and Habermas had each in their own way recognized how consciousness and culture develops through distinct stages, Wilber demonstrated more clearly how these stages have shaped the historical evolution of human culture and how they are now defining the problems and opportunities of contemporary society. Although Wilber had grasped the significance of developmental psychology from the beginning of his work, he was also quick to recognize the expanded understanding provided by the work of Clare Graves when Graves's findings were brought to light through the work of Beck and Cowan in the late 1990s.

With respect to postmodernism, as we will explore in detail in the next chapter, Habermas had already described the limitations of postmodern philosophy and had attempted to overcome them with a "post-postmodern" approach that sought to rehabilitate the legitimacy of theoretical reason and morality. Wilber, however, was able to go beyond Habermas's insights about postmodernism by following Graves in showing how the postmodern way of seeing actually arises from a distinct worldview that occupies a position in between modernism and integralism. As a result of his enlarged understanding of postmodernism as a historically significant stage of consciousness, Wilber has been able to transcend postmodernism more thoroughly than Habermas by clearly recognizing postmodernism's enduring contributions as well as its debilitating falsehoods. And it is through this thorough transcendence of postmodernism, in both its cultural and philosophical expressions, that Wilber has shown how and why the integral worldview is indeed the next stage of humanity's development.

However, the most important contribution of Wilber's twenty-first-century synthesis to integral philosophy overall is his willingness to attempt a description of "the big picture." This is seen in both his general recognition of what he calls "the Great Nest"—matter, mind, and spirit—and in his framing of the evolving universe with his four-quadrant model of evolution (reproduced in chapter 8, on page 222-23). Using this four-quadrant map of universal development, Wilber shows how the evolution of culture is intimately connected with the evolution of biology, the evolution of individual consciousness, and the evolution of the external structures of human society. Wilber locates each of these distinct aspects of evolution within a separate *quadrant* of his model, which attempts to map the inside and the outside of both the individual and collective aspects of evolution. Connecting the quadrants are the *levels* of evolution that extend across all four domains simultaneously, and within each quadrant are various *lines* of development through which evolution unfolds. And in addition to quadrants, levels, and lines, Wilber's model also recognizes the various transitory *states* and nonhierarchical *types* of consciousness that inhabit the internal universe. Thus, by recognizing *quadrants, levels, lines, states,* and *types,* Wilber attempts to provide a complete picture of all discernible aspects of evolutionary development. But Wilber's philosophy also attempts to integrate *spirit* into the big picture in the way that it connects evolution and spirituality, in the way that incorporates the wisdom of a wide variety of the spiritual traditions, and in the way that it makes spiritual growth the centerpiece of its orientation.

Wilber has been able to bring all these various aspects of reality together by using what he calls "orienting generalizations" that reveal a "pattern that connects." Describing his motivation for the creation of this new integral synthesis, Wilber writes:

> I therefore sought to outline a philosophy of universal integralism. Put differently, I sought a world philosophy—an *integral* philosophy—that would believably weave together the many pluralistic contexts of science, morals, aesthetics, Eastern as well as Western philosophy, and the world's great wisdom traditions. Not on the level of details—that is finitely impossible; but on the level of *orienting generalizations:* a way to suggest that the world really is one, undivided, whole, and related to itself in every way: a holistic philosophy for a holistic Kosmos, a plausible Theory of Everything.[26]

We'll focus more closely on the merits of some of Wilber's ideas in the next two chapters. However, although I have adopted and restated much of Wilber's twenty-first-century integral synthesis in this book, I have also tried to advance integral philosophy in some new and original ways. While I certainly acknowledge Wilber's historically significant contribution to humanity's understanding of evolution, it is clear to me that the emerging worldview of integral consciousness is providing the creative impulse for a host of new philosophers. And it is thus my privilege to be one of them. So we conclude this chapter with a brief summary of what I am attempting to contribute to the canon of integral philosophy.

What I Add to Integral Philosophy

As a result of the feedback received on previous drafts of this book, it became apparent that I needed to be more explicit in describing what I add and why I am not merely trying to restate or popularize the work of others. Accordingly, this section serves as a kind of overview or summary of the elements of my work that are original or otherwise novel. This overview is offered with the caveat that these ideas require a more thorough explanation than the brief description in this summary in order for them to be properly understood and appreciated. The discussion below therefore references the respective sections of this book wherein these broader explanations can be found.

First, in the area of *integral spirituality*, my contribution includes the contention that within the integral worldview the disciplines of science, philosophy, and spirituality should be afforded a degree of separation from each other. As I explained in chapter 1, philosophy serves humanity best when its view extends beyond the materialistic constraints of science. But in its quest for meaning in the universe, philosophy must also be careful not to become a specific form of spiritual teaching. At this time in history, integral philosophy promises to fulfill the critically important role of helping to establish a new values-based worldview. Yet to the extent that it becomes largely synonymous with a particular religion or spiritual teaching, it will not be able to produce the broad agreement that such a worldview will require—the integral worldview will only reach critical mass if it can successfully accommodate a wide variety of different perspectives on spiritual growth.

As we noted at the beginning of this chapter, Wilber does not really distinguish his philosophy from his religion, but rather asserts that both of these areas of his thought are substantially matters of fact established through the method of broad empiricism. By contrast, I think that integral philosophy should recognize spirit in general, but should limit its attempts to explain this Ultimate Reality, thereby preserving spirituality as a distinct category of human experience apart from philosophy. These concerns are discussed in chapter 8, and especially in the section entitled "Integral Philosophy and Human Spirituality."

Also in the area of integral spirituality is my exploration of the evolutionary significance of values. Here my contribution includes an expanded conception of the significance of the primary values of beauty, truth, and goodness. While other integral philosophers have acknowledged the central significance of this value triad, I attempt to show, first in chapter 6 and then more fully in chapter 10, how these primary values are essentially descriptions of the primordial influences at the heart of all evolution. This enlarged philosophical recognition of the significance of beauty, truth, and goodness: 1) helps define spiritual experience and enact a public commons of integral spirituality wherein practitioners of different traditions can find solidarity; 2) suggests pragmatic forms of spiritual practice that can help focus our efforts to improve the human condition; and 3) helps us better understand the methods and directions of evolutionary development by revealing perfection's "threefold influence" on the evolving universe. Chapter 10 concludes with an exploration of how the "value attractors" of beauty, truth, and goodness actually shape the unfolding of evolution in its three essential domains of nature, self, and culture.

The second area of integral philosophy where I contribute new thinking concerns the contours of the *integral reality frame* itself. This discussion begins in chapter 8 wherein I clarify the "minimal metaphysics" that are necessary for the integrity of the integral worldview. This includes the recognition that evolution is subject to some kind of transcendental causation or morphogenetic pull, and that it is a purposeful phenomenon of growth that proceeds in a generally positive direction. In this context I also describe how integral philosophy effectively transcends postmodern philosophy's prejudice against all "reality frames" by acknowledging the worldview-specific limitations of the integral reality frame, including the anticipation of its own eventual transcendence by the inevitably antithetical metaphysics of the "postintegral reality frame."

In addition to these considerations of integral metaphysics, I have also tried to enhance our overall understanding of the integral reality frame through my critique of Wilber's four-quadrant model of evolution. Beginning in chapter 8 and then continuing with greater depth in Appendix B, I argue that by trying to honor and include the work of social systems theorists, Wilber has committed a kind of category error that compounds the mistakes of "subtle reductionism" and confuses the role of human-made artifacts in the evolution of culture. This discussion helps clarify and simplify the integral reality frame by sharpening the focus on the intersubjective domain of human agreements and relationships.

The third area in which I contribute original analysis to integral philosophy centers on the *importance of the spiral of development* and the significance of the "values line" or "worldview line" of development found within evolving consciousness and culture. This analysis is contrary to the recent writing of Wilber, who uses a model called the psychograph to describe the multiple kinds of intelligence exhibited by humans as strictly independent lines of development. While I agree that the different types of human intelligence, such as cognitive ability or emotional intelligence, can develop relatively independently, I hold that these various lines of development are organized within a larger holarchic structure wherein three primary lines of development encompass the rest. And it is through the recognition of this holarchy of developmental lines that we begin to see why the "worldview line" seems to have the most significant overall influence on a person's consciousness. These considerations are presented in chapter 9, "Structures of the Human Mind."

Finally, although others have connected the integral worldview with the *evolutionary goal of global governance*, I have argued that this goal will become a central focus of the integral political agenda as it emerges throughout the twenty-first-century. My original contribution in this area consists in the description of why an integrally informed world federation is desirable, achievable, and inevitable, as well as in my express conviction that integral consciousness and global governance are as inseparable as modernist consciousness and democracy. These arguments are set out in chapter 5 on "Integral Politics" and elaborated further in Appendix A.

There are certainly other insights and observations in this book that have not been described before, but the foregoing provides a general overview of the main areas in which I attempt to make an original contribution to integral philosophy.

CHAPTER 8

The Integral Reality Frame

In chapter 2 on "The Internal Universe" we briefly explored how the worldview of modernism initially took shape around the expanded frame of reality provided by the philosophy of Rene Descartes. In fact, most historians and philosophers now generally agree that Descartes' "subject-object metaphysics" played a significant role in the birth of science and the rise of the modernist worldview in the seventeenth century. But because this is regarded as an established historical fact, we often tend to overlook just how amazing was Descartes' accomplishment. Although other geniuses, such as Galileo, obviously played significant roles in the birth of modernism, Descartes' philosophy took the scientific way of seeing things and elevated it to a new level, showing how this new understanding of subjects and objects actually provided a transcendent personal identity for those who could adopt this new way of seeing and thinking. In essence, Descartes wrote a philosophy book that, more than any other single influence, produced one of the most spectacular events of cultural evolution in human history. And if integral philosophy is correct, then this historical event is extremely relevant to our time in history. Because if we can duplicate Descartes' achievement in this century, if we can use philosophy to enact a new historically significant worldview that provides a transcendent personal identity for those who can adopt this new way of seeing and thinking, then we can help bring about the cultural evolution that our world so sorely needs.

Now, of course, historically significant new worldviews do not simply arise from insightful philosophy books. Integral philosophy's understanding of cultural evolution makes clear that new worldview systems emerge only when the previous worldview has become successful enough to create the distinct type of problematic life conditions that the next successive worldview requires for its emergence. In other words, it is only when the time is right that philosophy can help trigger the birth of a new phase of human history by creating a new vantage point, a new "internal location" from which new aspects of reality can be seen. But assuming that the time is indeed becoming right for such a transcendence, then our attempts to duplicate Descartes' philosophical achievement could prove to be extremely fruitful. As we will explore in this chapter, the integral worldview is now taking shape around an enlarged understanding of reality that provides solutions to many contemporary problems by revealing the internal universe as never before. The integral worldview does this by reframing reality in a way that makes the evolution of consciousness and culture more evident. This new way of seeing gives birth to what might loosely be understood as the "science of the internal universe." Just as Descartes' reframed reality in a way that allowed people to see things more *objectively*, integral philosophy provides a similarly expanded new frame of reality that allows us to see things more *intersubjectively*. That is, integral philosophy reveals the significance of the intersubjective dimension of cultural evolution. And by doing so it makes it possible for us to better guide and cultivate positive cultural evolution on every front.

So in this chapter we will take a closer look at the substance of the integral reality frame. We'll examine how all historically significant worldviews are framed by metaphysical conclusions about reality, and we'll see how integral philosophy departs from the metaphysics of modernism and postmodernism. We'll examine where this new integral frame of reality comes from and how it is justified and defended. Then after discussing the contours of integral philosophy's frame of reality, we'll explore the current struggle to define integral philosophy's relation to spirituality. But in this chapter, not only will we discuss the sophisticated metaphysics of integral philosophy, we will also explore some critiques of this metaphysics—critiques that naturally arise whenever we attempt to frame reality in terms that humans can understand.

Metaphysics and the Evolution of Reality Frames

The term "metaphysics" is exceedingly problematic. Nowadays, many philosophers regard the subject of metaphysics as a relic of the philosophies of the past. Moreover, many ordinary people associate the term with New Age or occult belief systems. However, if you look up the term metaphysics in the dictionary, you'll find a definition like this: "Metaphysics is the branch of philosophy that examines the nature of reality, including the relationship between mind and matter, substance and attribute, fact and value." The word was originally coined by the followers of Aristotle, who generally regarded it as "that which comes after physics"—that which is beyond science. That is, in between the hard facts of science and the revealed truths of religion, there are to be found questions about the nature of reality that seek answers within the realm of reason. Metaphysics can thus be understood as philosophy's attempt to discern that which is beyond the external, material realm without resorting to explanations that rely solely on the unquestioned authority of spiritual teachers or sacred texts.

In modern societies, issues of justice, economics, education, social relations, freedom, and morality (to name only a few) are ultimately decided with reference to a society's reality frame, and that reality frame is largely constructed from the metaphysics of philosophy. For example, the founding documents of the United States government are filled with reality-framing metaphysics and "self-evident truths." In fact, almost every law rests on the highly metaphysical idea that people are responsible for their actions. In premodern societies, the metaphysics that supported the social order were supplied largely by religion. But with the rise of modernity, as the institutions of society became increasingly differentiated from the dominance of a monolithic religion, the need for a reality frame that could accommodate the truths of both science and a plurality of religions became acute. And as we discussed above, it was Descartes' success at providing such a metaphysical reality frame that really helped modernity to become permanently established.

However, it was not long after Descartes' subject-object metaphysics had become accepted that the effort to transcend it had begun. And in many ways, this is where professional philosophy now remains, engaged in a variety of attempts to overcome what has come to be known as the "philosophy of the subject," the world-changing metaphysical reality frame that began with Descartes' famous starting point: "I think, therefore, I am."

In chapter 2 we noted how Descartes' early modern reality frame posited the existence of two kinds of substance: *matter*, which was objective and natural, and *mind*, which was subjective and supernatural. This explanation worked very well at first because it enacted what has been called the "enchanted circle of objectivism." It provided a "place" for an objective observer to "stand," so to speak. This objective standpoint provided the worldview that was necessary for the emergence of the scientific method and perspective. But it was this same scientific perspective that began to notice that Descartes' supernatural subjectivism was untenable. If consciousness was a kind of substance that was entirely different than the material brain that it inhabited, how did it make contact with the brain? How could the natural and the supernatural interact? Was there really a "ghost in the machine"? It was not long before the scientific philosophy of the Enlightenment sought to reject the supernatural side of Descartes' dualistic metaphysics by simply collapsing the subjective into the objective. And in this we can now recognize the first attempt to overcome Cartesian dualism through a materialistic philosophy that attempted to banish metaphysics by simply declaring that there was nothing beyond physics. Despite the well-reasoned critiques of Kant, and the visionary alternatives of the Idealists, materialism has persisted as a strong form of antimetaphysical metaphysics that continues to dominate many critical fields of human knowledge into the twenty-first century.

By the beginning of the twentieth century, the stunning success of science had given the metaphysics of materialism an essential credibility that helped it retain its ongoing stature as a respectable philosophy despite a glaring problem: Materialism could not adequately explain the rich inner life that every person could directly experience. The philosophy of materialism was really undone by the undeniable reality of subjectivity. Yet materialism stubbornly persisted even as it was demonstrated that a reality frame claiming that the universe was nothing more than "matter in motion" was just as extra-scientific as any other kind of metaphysics. As the materialists continued to struggle with the mind/body problem, as they continued to ask: "How can conscious experience arise from the electrical activity of the brain?"—they couldn't quite see that starting their inquiry with the false certainties of physical matter was still a thoroughly metaphysical starting place. This dilemma arises from what Whitehead famously identified as "the fallacy of misplaced concreteness."[1]

However, as modernism matured, its philosophical problems became far worse than those created by scientism's naive reductionism. As philosophers struggled with the problems of the "philosophy of the subject" upon which the Enlightenment had been founded, they began to question the legitimacy of the entire Enlightenment project. As the religious forces of social integration grew weaker, this put more pressure on the legitimizing role of reason, which Enlightenment philosophers had advanced as a replacement for the unifying power of religion. Yet the metaphysics of reason also had its limits. And these shortcomings were dramatically exposed in the reactionary philosophy of Friedrich Nietzsche, the first of a long line of philosophers who would question and attack the validity of subject-centered reason and open the path into postmodernity. Nietzsche's radical critique of reason would be further advanced by Martin Heidegger who sought to transcend the metaphysics of reason altogether by arguing that all of philosophy since Plato had been mistakenly preoccupied with mere concepts of being, facsimiles of the real that actually blinded philosophers from seeing the authentic nature of being as it was in itself. Heidegger declared the "end of philosophy" and proposed an entirely new kind of nonconceptual thinking that would replace the focus on, as well as the need for, any kind of metaphysics.

Heidegger's postmetaphysical program of undermining Western rationalism would later be carried forward by French "poststructuralists" such as Michel Foucault and Jacques Derrida, who argued that all claims of truth were merely social constructions and that philosophy as a whole was nothing more than a pretentious literary fiction. These postmodern "professional philosophers" attempted to pull down the rational reality frame of modernism while simultaneously doing their best to keep anything else from taking its place. Yet, as we discussed in chapter 3, the cultural worldview of postmodernism would nevertheless take shape around a kind of inverted and scattered metaphysics that found the good in that which modernity had rejected or neglected. Postmodernity seized the ground of pure antithesis and constructed its worldview around the frayed edges of the Enlightenment. According to prominent Habermas scholar, Thomas McCarthy, "The critique of subject-centered reason [was] thus a prologue to the critique of a bankrupt culture."[2]

But despite professional postmodern philosophy's attempt to deconstruct itself, its antimodern worldview did serve to indirectly nurture healthy reform movements such as feminism, environmentalism, and multiculturalism.[3] Moreover, as the deconstructionists achieved academic legitimacy and professional philosophy accordingly became increasingly irrelevant to all but specialists, this also served to indirectly encourage the rise of New Age alternatives to philosophy. By disempowering the philosophy of modernity, the postmodernists created an opening wherein the countercultural spiritual revival could flourish in an environment in which the gates of metaphysical legitimacy had been blown open by the French subversives. This freedom from the now delegitimized rigors of Enlightenment philosophy gave the postmodern West a new appreciation of myth and helped it to discover and incorporate the spiritual wisdom of the East. But as postmodern culture began to mature in the 1990s, it increasingly found that its worldview was still constructed by a form of metaphysics, albeit a metaphysics that lacked any kind of systemized expression and contented itself with unrestrained subjective relativism.

In response to the dilemmas that arose with the success of postmodern philosophy, beginning in the 1970s, we find the work of the "post-postmodern" philosopher Jürgen Habermas, who has made a valiant attempt to reconstruct the legitimacy of reason through an "intersubjectivist paradigm of communicative action." By focusing on the inherent reason found in the intersubjective domain of human relations and mutual understanding, rather than on the reason that

Descartes had situated exclusively in the subject, Habermas sought to rehabilitate the philosophical discourse of modernity. Habermas generally agreed with the critiques of reason leveled by the post-structuralists, but he rejected the "totalization" of these critiques. In other words, according to Thomas McCarthy:

> Habermas agrees with the radical critiques of Enlighten-
> ment that the paradigm of consciousness is exhausted. Like
> them, he views reason as inescapably situated, as concretized
> in history, society, body, and language. Unlike them, how-
> ever, he holds that the defects of Enlightenment can only be
> made good by further enlightenment. The totalized critique
> of reason undercuts the capacity of reason to be critical. It
> refuses to acknowledge that modernization bears develop-
> ments as well as distortions of reason.[4]

By acknowledging the valid critiques of the postmodernists while simultaneously attempting to transcend the "dead end" implications of their deconstructions, Habermas has tried to define a middle ground between metaphysical conceptions of reason and radical deconstruc-tions of reason. And he has tried to do this exclusively through an examination of language. That is, Habermas, committed to a "meth-odological atheism," has tried to avoid all metaphysics by limiting his inquiry to the analysis of speech acts. He uses a method that he calls "reconstructive science" to discover the "deep structures" of rea-son within language. According to Habermas, reconstructive science working within the narrow philosophy of language reveals "three validity dimensions" of intersubjective reason—theoretical truth, subjective truthfulness, and normative rightness. These linguistically situated validity dimensions, arrived at without resorting to transcen-dental ontological categories, are said to provide a postmetaphysical foundation for reason, allowing reason to be rehabilitated and thus used to judge and justify the institutions of human society.

And if this all sounds rather narrow and implausible, it's because it is. No matter how hard we try, we cannot find the fullness of truth within the confines of language. Linguistic philosophy origi-nally arose as a response to the breakdown of Cartesian dualism; it provided an avenue of retreat from the metaphysical problems of modernism. By focusing on the philosophy of language, professional philosophers could avoid committing to any particular abstract conceptions of reality. Language thus became the place where philosophy could carry on in the face of scientism and (later) postmodernism while avoiding metaphysics and spirituality altogether. In fact, what all of the major philosophical movements of the twentieth century have in common—logical positivism, existentialism and phenomenology, and linguistic analysis—is that they have all made progress through a staunch antithesis to the philosophy of the subject, so they all naturally share and support the postmodern worldview's metaphysical agreement that there are no transcendent ontological categories. According to Richard Tarnas, "Despite the incongruence of aims and predispositions among the various schools of twentieth-century philosophy, there was general agreement on one crucial point: the impossibility of apprehending an objective cosmic order with the human intelligence."[5] Habermas's philosophy thus provides an example of really the best one can do with the charred remains of the Enlightenment in a postmodern world.

As we've discussed, philosophy had its birth in the partial emergence of the modernist worldview during the golden age of ancient Greece. Then, when modernism was reborn during the Enlightenment, it was ushered in through a revival of philosophy. But in the course of cultural evolution the modernist worldview was eventually transcended by its postmodern antithesis. And with this transcendence came the "death of philosophy" as a distinctly modernist enterprise. Habermas has tried to resurrect philosophy while essentially remaining within the worldview of the postmodernists, but the results have been less than inspiring. That is, just as the postmodernists recognized the exhaustion of modernism, Habermas has, in turn, recognized the exhaustion of postmodernism as a philosophical endeavor. Yet by failing to reject the postmodernists' insistence that there can be no reality frame, no metaphysical descriptions of the universe, Habermas ultimately fails at using philosophy to enact the framework of the next emergent worldview in humanity's cultural evolution.

However, once we recognize, by examining history, that culture in fact evolves through successive worldview stages, and once we admit that all worldviews are fallible human constructs that are partial and destined to eventually be transcended, we don't have to look for the ultimate, final worldview—our new worldview does not have to satisfy every possible objection. So we do not have to remain stuck in the postmodern worldview's insistence that there can be no valid worldview, no reality framing metaphysics that can mediate between science and religion.

Postmodernism's critiques make clear that modernism is no longer the leading edge of cultural evolution. But postmodernism is not the end of history. Through integral philosophy we can now begin to see that postmodern philosophy is itself part of a historically significant worldview framed by its own antimetaphysical metaphysics. And as the *Encyclopedia Britannica* puts it: "To seek to overthrow a metaphysical theory...is itself to engage in metaphysics—not very interesting metaphysics, perhaps, but metaphysics all the same."[6] For example, when Habermas states that his philosophy must be "disburdened of all religious and metaphysical mortgages," he is clearly stating a worldview-defining metaphysics of his own. In other words, if we understand metaphysics as the aspect of philosophy that is in between science and religion, then we can see how Habermas's foundational philosophical position, which flatly states that his postmetaphysical philosophy cannot connect to, or associate with, religion, is indeed an antimetaphysical metaphysics that is ultimately an expression of a specific, values-based worldview. As he tries to come to terms with meaning and value, Habermas's worldview requires that he remain disconnected from anything spiritual, despite the inconvenient fact that humanity has almost always connected meaning and value with spirituality. Habermas's ontological allergy thus results from a distinct brand of linguistically bound metaphysics, albeit a rather implausible one.

However, as we are increasingly confronted with the growing problems of the world, we begin to realize that the solutions to these problems require large-scale cultural evolution. And when we examine the past historical instances of such large-scale cultural evolution, we can see that this most often comes in the form of new, values-based worldviews—new reality frames enacted through enlarged understandings of reality explained through new forms of metaphysics. Thus, as we try to bring about cultural evolution, we can see that the time has come to advance a new philosophical synthesis in the form of a new reality frame, one that does not attempt a still-born synthesis that continues to exist within the confines of postmodernism (as Habermas has done), but rather a synthesis that moves far enough beyond postmodernism so as to achieve a usable, inspiring, and worldview-enacting philosophy that transcends and includes the premodern, the modern, and the postmodern.

Now, we can predict that from the postmodern perspective, integralism will appear to be just modernism in disguise. As integral philosophy gains ground, postmodernists will inevitably level the same attacks against it as they did against modernism—they will attack the frame of the integral worldview and the metaphysics that enact it. So in order for the metaphysics of integralism to survive these attacks, they will have to demonstrate their own transcendence of modernism and thus secure their liberation from the deconstructed worldview of postmodernism, where little progress can now be made.

On the other hand, despite their destructive effects, it must be said that the devastating critiques of postmodernism also provide a kind of propellant force for further evolution. The very success of postmodern philosophy has created the life conditions necessary for the emergence of the next historically significant philosophical worldview. And no one has harnessed the forces of postmodernism's problems more effectively than Ken Wilber. Wilber has gone beyond Habermas by boldly transcending the limitations of postmodernism through the framing of integral philosophy's twenty-first-century synthesis. Wilber's four-quadrant reality frame effectively enacts the initial metaphysics of a historically significant new worldview. Like Habermas, it takes notice of the valid critiques of postmodernism without falling victim to their totalization; but unlike Habermas, it completes the transcendence of postmodernism's antimetaphysical metaphysics by showing how it is possible to gain useful knowledge of the internal universe beyond the confines of language alone. The power of the integral reality frame comes from the way it describes the evolving systems and structures of consciousness and culture in richly ontological terms—it shows how these dynamic systems of consciousness and culture *actually exist*. This new ontological grasp of the structures of the internal universe provides new opportunities to heal the wounds of the past and make significant progress toward a better future. And Wilber has defended this reality frame through a variety of arguments.

As noted earlier, one such argument makes use of what Wilber calls *broad empiricism*. This is similar to William James's concept of radical empiricism, which we briefly discussed in chapter 6—the doctrine that the empirical methods of science can be extended to include not only the direct experiences delivered by the physical senses, but also mental experiences and (to a certain extent) spiritual experiences. Wilber's idea of broad empiricism incorporates James's concept by arguing that any kind of direct experience (including spiritual experience) can be subjected to an empirical test of demonstrable falsifiability. In response to the attacks that have been leveled against Enlightenment and Idealist philosophy—attacks that pointed out how these philosophical systems had no means of verification, and that there could thus be no experiential confirmation or rejection of their metaphysical explanations—Wilber has argued that his descriptions of the interior dimensions of reality are indeed subject to direct reproducible experience and therefore can in fact be counted as valid knowledge. Wilber's broad empiricism brings to the internal universe the same three-step method that has been used so successfully by science in the external universe. This three-step method includes: 1) an instrumental injunction ("If you want to know this, do this"); 2) a direct apprehension (receipt of the experience); and 3) a communal confirmation (acknowledgment of authenticity by a "community of the adequate"). Wilber concludes that the method of broad empiricism provides a way to verify the ontology of the internal universe described by integral philosophy.

Overall, I think broad empiricism is an adequate defense against arguments that the integral reality frame is not subject to verification. However, despite the sufficiency of this argument, Wilber has recently advanced some additional arguments claiming that integral philosophy is now free from all metaphysics.

Wilber's initial position on the metaphysics of integral philosophy was stated in 1995 in *Sex, Ecology, Spirituality*, where he writes: "I suppose many readers will insist on calling what I'm doing 'metaphysics,' but if 'metaphysics' means thought without evidence, there is not a metaphysical sentence in this entire book."[7] But since *Sex, Ecology, Spirituality* was published, Wilber has expanded his rejection of the metaphysical label by claiming that the integral philosophy he is expounding is strictly postmetaphysical after the manner of Habermas. Wilber's "postmetaphysical turn" can be seen, like broad empiricism, as a way of trying to overcome postmodernism's critiques. According to Wilber, his philosophy is postmetaphysical because first, it "replaces perceptions with perspectives," and second, because it rejects any pregiven levels or preexisting invisible planes of reality, recognizing that existing evolutionary levels are really just "Kosmic habits" that originally emerged in creative novelty but which have now become ingrained as more concrete levels through repetition over time.

Let's briefly examine these claims, starting with the idea of "postmetaphysical perspectives." According to Wilber:

> there are no perceptions anywhere in the real world; there are only perspectives. A subject perceiving an object is *always already* in a relationship of first-person, second-person, and third-person when it comes to the perceived occasions. ... Moving from perceptions to perspectives is the first radical step in the move from metaphysics to post-metaphysics. Subjects don't prehend objects anywhere in the universe; rather, first persons prehend second persons or third persons: perceptions are always within actual perspectives. "Subject perceiving object" (or "bare attention to dharmas") is not a raw given but a low-order abstraction that already tears the fabric of the Kosmos in ways that cannot easily be repaired.[8]

This position thus rejects Cartesian conceptions of objective reality as being simply pregiven by incorporating postmodernism's important insights about contexts and interpretations. However, while I agree that nothing can be simply perceived as it is "objectively," while I agree that all perceptions are always already perspectives, I cannot agree that this understanding somehow completely negates the ontology of the objective dimension of reality, or otherwise eliminates metaphysics from our worldview. Even though we cannot achieve perspective-free perceptions, this does not mean that there is nothing to perceive but perspectives. If we limit our ontology only to perspectives, if we maintain that only perspectives are real, this has the inevitable effect of collapsing the universe into the subjective dimension, and I'm sure that this is not what Wilber intends. Indeed, as we've discussed, the value of integral philosophy is found in the way that it clearly identifies the evolving systems of the internal universe—integral philosophy derives its power from its recognition of the relative *actuality* of these internal systems. So if we want to effectively transcend and include the worldviews of modernism and postmodernism while simultaneously realizing a new worldview that can do the needed work of producing cultural evolution, we have to try to steer between the extremes of both naive realism and relativistic contextualism by avoiding both the Myth of the Given (which ignores the interpretive and participatory nature of reality) and what Karl Popper calls the "Myth of the Framework," under which reality is seen as essentially illusory or arbitrarily constructed by the observer.[9] Although every perception is always already a perspective, although humans can never perceive things *as they really are*, a given perspective can be relatively more or less powerful depending on the degree of reality that it apprehends. And one test of the relative degree of a given perception's grasp of reality is its ability to improve the human condition.

As we think about the boundaries of our reality frame, it is important to keep in mind that as integral philosophy tries to develop a post-postmodern conception about the nature of "what is," it actually achieves cultural evolution by delivering an expanded ontology of the internal universe and by enlarging what we can see of reality. Thus, unlike Habermas's postmetaphysics, which limits its ontological descriptions strictly to language, integral philosophy situates its "perspectives" of the internal and external universe within reality as a whole. And it is this very expanded grasp of the ontology of

the evolving universe—this enlarged recognition of the evolutionary systems found within the interrelated domains of nature, self,
and culture—that allows integral theory to make new philosophical progress by transcending postmodernism's prejudice against all
ontological descriptions of reality.

Now, regarding the second part of Wilber's postmetaphysical
turn, namely, that there are no pregiven ontological levels, only accumulating Kosmic habits, Wilber seems to be of two minds. On the
one hand, he is adamant that his system contains "No metaphysical
baggage—no archetypes, no ontological planes of reality, no independent levels of being that are lying around waiting to be seen by
humans …"[10] But on the other hand, in an endnote to the long article in which he articulates his new postmetaphysical position, Wilber brings back the thoroughly metaphysical idea of "involutionary
givens." In answer to the question of whether anything existed prior
to the Big Bang, Wilber writes that: "Among the few theorists who
have thought clearly about this issue, the consensus seems to be yes."
Wilber then offers the following explanation:

> As Spirit throws itself outward (that's called *involution*) to
> create this particular universe with this particular Big Bang,
> it leaves traces or echoes of its Kosmic exhalation. These trac-
> es constitute little in the way of actual contents or forms or
> entities or levels, but rather a vast morphogenetic field that
> exerts a gentle pull (or *Agape*) toward higher, wider, deeper
> occasions, a pull that shows up in manifest or actual occa-
> sions as the *Eros* in the agency of all holons. (We can think
> of this "pull" as the pull of all things back to Spirit; White-
> head called it "love" as "the gentle persuasion of God" toward
> unity; this love reaching down from the higher to the lower
> is called Agape, and when reaching up from the lower to the
> higher is called Eros: two sides of the same pull). This vast
> morphogenetic pull connects the potentials of the lowest
> holons (materially asleep) with the potentials of the high-
> est (spiritually awakened). The involutionary given of this
> morphogenetic field is a gradient of potentials, not actuals,
> so that Agape works throughout the universe as a love of

gentle persuasion, pulling the lower manifest forms of spirit toward higher manifest forms of spirit—a potential gradient that humans, once they emerged, would often conceptualize as matter to body to mind to soul to spirit. "Spirit" (capital "S"), of course, was (and is) the ever-present ground of all of those manifest waves, equally and fully present in each, but "spirit" (small "s") is also a general stage or wave of evolution: spirit is the transpersonal stage(s) at which Spirit as ground can be permanently realized.[11]

After spending a considerable amount of time trying to fathom Wilber's postmetaphysical arguments, I was greatly relieved to find this passage and to learn that Wilber had not entirely abandoned the historical canon of integral philosophy. As the above quote makes clear, although he has tried to make them as sparingly lean as possible, to his credit, Wilber's spiritual metaphysics are still firmly in place. And in my opinion, this metaphysical recognition of spirit's role in evolution is integral philosophy's most important foundational truth.

However, I can understand why Wilber has chosen to reject the term "metaphysics," and I can certainly agree that integral philosophy has transcended the metaphysics of the premodern and modernist worldviews. But I cannot agree that integral philosophy is strictly postmetaphysical in the manner that thinkers like Habermas require. Indeed, it is through its unique brand of minimal, broadly empirical metaphysics that integral philosophy effectively transcends the flattened, antimetaphysical metaphysics of postmodern philosophy.

It is thus clear that integral philosophy's reality frame is inescapably metaphysical—not in the bad, unevidenced sense, but in the way that it definitely recognizes the objective, subjective, and intersubjective categories of evolution. These categories are used to frame reality because they enact a vantage point from which the evolving entities of consciousness and culture can be more easily recognized, contacted, and improved. These categories are thus an indelible part of the metaphysics of the integral worldview. But in addition to its recognition of the distinct but overlapping categories of nature, self, and culture, as stated in Wilber's quote above (and as we'll explore more fully in chapter 10), the metaphysics of the integral reality frame also recognizes how all categories of evolution are influenced (persuaded) by what Wilber (after Rupert Sheldrake) calls a *morphogenetic pull*, a kind of *Eros* that draws evolution forward from the future, so to speak. This is not an argument for teleology as that idea has been traditionally understood, but it is a foundational recognition that the universe is not a purposeless accident and that evolution is definitely going somewhere.

But how do we know this? How can integral philosophy maintain that evolution is somehow being pulled forward or attracted by some force or influence? Well, as we've discussed, integral philosophy constructs its worldview so as to include all the kinds of experience that humans have demonstrated their ability to have—sensory experience, mental experience, and spiritual experience. And as it tries to adequately account for all these valid experiences, integral philosophy situates itself in between science and religion, attempting to honor and connect with both of these human institutions.

Staying connected with science is fairly straightforward; integral philosophy does this by maintaining that when there is a direct conflict between science and anything else, science (but not scientism) wins. In other words, science is the final authority on matters of the external universe. However, while it may be simple to honor the conclusions of science, adequately honoring religion and spirituality is far more complex. As we'll discuss in the section after next, there is currently disagreement among integralists about just how integral philosophy should relate to spirituality. As I see it, integral philosophy relates to spirituality most effectively by acknowledging the reality of spirit, but not the final authority of any explanation thereof. But regardless of the specifics of how integral philosophy relates to spirituality, we must insist on this: If it is going to honor spirituality at all, then it must acknowledge that the evolving universe is not a purposeless accident. There is really no way to include spirituality in your philosophy without recognizing that there is some kind of *point* to the universe. Although what this "point" exactly is can be defined in various ways by different spiritual traditions, all forms of authentic spirituality recognize meaning in the universe. Even people who believe that life is meaningless, nevertheless act daily as if it is—*we all presuppose in practice* that life has a point. And if you agree that there's a point, then you have already agreed that there is some kind of purpose. In fact, the attempt to deny that the universe has a purpose is a clear denial of spirituality, by almost any definition. The idea that the universe is completely random and meaningless is an affront to spirituality. So if integral philosophy is going to adequately honor the reality of spiritual experience, if it is going to maintain that spirit by whatever name really exists, then it must include the metaphysics of universe purpose in its reality frame. And if the universe has a purpose, then evolution, the all-encompassing activity of the universe, also has a purpose, and this leads to inescapable recognition of some kind of transcendental causation or morphogenetic pull that exerts a subtle influence on all forms of evolution. This does not necessarily mean that biological evolution is the product of "intelligent design" or supernatural intervention, but it does mean that evolution is a purposeful phenomenon of growth that proceeds in a generally positive direction.

Thus by starting with experience, and by recognizing that human experience includes the three essential categories of physical, mental, and spiritual experience—none of which can be reduced to any other—integral philosophy finds that it indeed has a metaphysics that is an inescapable part of its worldview.

As integral philosophers, we can never get away from metaphysics completely. No matter how much experiential evidence we can point to, when we ask questions about the nature of reality, the answers will always be of a metaphysical character. Even if we maintain that there can be no philosophical questions or answers about the "nature of reality," this is still a thoroughly metaphysical position. So it is through this understanding that integral philosophy is guided to strive for a "minimalist metaphysics." This minimalist position recognizes that evolution is indeed occurring within the distinct but interacting categories of nature, self, and culture, and it situates these domains of evolution within a larger frame of reality. Moreover, this minimalist position also recognizes the reality of spirit. But rather than directly addressing the nature of spiritual reality, integral philosophy does well to leave these questions to be answered by the various kinds of religion and spirituality encompassed by the integral worldview. It is thus by preserving religion as a distinct area of human experience, one that is largely beyond the inquiries of philosophy, that integral philosophy can keep its metaphysics to a minimum while simultaneously recognizing the spiritual nature of the universe.

But even as it advances this expanded understanding of nature, self, and culture, integral philosophy also recognizes that every historically significant worldview evolves within the dialectical system of the spiral of development, and that while we must rely on these successively evolving worldviews to provide the steps of our progress, we must now also see that every worldview is partial and incomplete—every worldview will eventually be transcended in the course of continuing cultural evolution. Thus, the metaphysical reality frame that forms the container of every worldview is always just a scaffolding that is destined to be taken down as the building of civilization becomes more complete. This is not to say that the objective, subjective, and intersubjective categories are arbitrary or completely fabricated. But it is to say that these categories constitute a frame of reality that, because of its very usefulness for this next stage of evolution, because of its worldview-specific nature, is necessarily partial and destined by definition to eventually be transcended. And this transcendence will come through the emergence of the inevitably antithetical metaphysics of the postintegral reality frame. Thus it is by acknowledging that the integral reality frame is a temporary yet highly useful construct that we actually incorporate the postmodern critique of all such frames while simultaneously moving beyond postmodernism's debilitating limitations.

So with these considerations in mind, we now turn to a presentation of the integral reality frame as I understand it.

The Integral Map of Reality

As we explored in the previous chapter, the canon of integral philosophy has evolved over the last two hundred years as a result of the efforts of many geniuses. Wilber's philosophy is thus just the latest development in a larger overall effort by some of humanity's most gifted thinkers to come to terms with the full significance of the revelation of evolution. So as integral theory carries forward the mantle of the great evolutionary philosophers, it recognizes that not only is matter and life evolving in the exterior realm, but evolution is also fully active in the internal realms as well. When we begin to see and better understand these internal aspects of the universe, we begin to recognize that just as the external universe has habits and laws, so too does the internal universe. When we look at the external, objective universe from the perspective of science, we can see its principle components. We can see that the external universe finds its extension in the coordinates of time and space and its content in the form of matter, energy, and life. Likewise, as we now observe the subjective and intersubjective universe from the perspective of integral philosophy, we find a similar set of essential components. We can now begin to see that the internal universe finds its extension in the coordinates of consciousness and culture and its content in the form of meaning, value, and love. These parallels are not merely poetic; they are the starting place for the "physics of the internal universe," a broadly empirical yet metaphysical understanding of interiority that opens up new dimensions of human understanding and corresponding new powers of improvement. And here it bears repeating that the emergence of the integral worldview, with its new abilities to access the internal universe, is in almost every way the evolutionary equivalent of the emergence of the modernist worldview, which demonstrated similar abilities in the way that it provided new access to the external universe through science. The rise of the integral worldview thus marks the beginning of history's Second Enlightenment.

But in order for us to achieve the developmental promise of this Second Enlightenment, our grasp of the internal universe has to be firm. We need to see how the internal structures and patterns revealed by integral philosophy are not just metaphors, but real systems shaped by real forces. And our initial grasp of these internal structures is actually made possible by the integral reality frame's minimalist metaphysics. Looking at the relevant history of the first Enlightenment, we have seen how the power of the modernist reality frame was initially enacted by the way Descartes' metaphysics isolated and identified the entities of the objective universe. Integralism is similarly empowered in the way that its metaphysics isolate and identify the entities of the internal universe. That is, the integral worldview's reality frame creates a "new location" within the internal universe, a new vantage point from which the structures of consciousness and culture become more visible. Integral consciousness' world-changing power thus comes from its new ability to contact, work with, manage, and improve these internal structures. But this power cannot accrue to integralism unless it leaves behind postmodern philosophy's ontological prejudice, its insistence that philosophy is not qualified to offer descriptions of a larger reality.

Just as nineteenth-century scientists used early microscopes to see the previously invisible germs that were causing so much suffering in the world, integralists can use their philosophy's new understanding of the internal universe to see and actually make contact with the previously invisible structures of consciousness and culture. But just as scientists eventually abandoned optical microscopes in favor of more powerful electron microscopes, so too will we eventually transcend integral metaphysics in favor of an even more powerful understanding of reality. Nevertheless, when we recognize that most of the problems in the world today are really problems of consciousness (opportunities for cultural evolution), we can see how necessary this new understanding of consciousness is to our ability to make things better.

In the previous chapter we traced the development of the canon of integral philosophy all the way back to Hegel. So as we now consider the integral reality frame, we can see that from Hegel and the Idealists we received our understanding of the dialectical structure of evolution's progress; from Bergson we learned that reality is best understood as a creative process; with Whitehead we saw how, at every level, the internal and external dimensions of the universe are woven together in the experience of every actual entity; from Teilhard we learned that complexity and consciousness emerge simultaneously as the external and internal aspects of evolution; with Graves we came to see the systemic structure of the spiral of development;

and from Habermas we learned of the significance of intersubjectivity. And now with Wilber we have a map of the evolving universe that brings all of these insights (as well as many others) together in a way that constitutes an entirely new worldview. As we discussed above, Wilber's philosophy succeeds in creating a new worldview where Habermas's philosophy does not because it is, in practice, robustly ontological—because it describes real structures evolving within real domains.

Wilber based his new map of the universe on a concept from systems theory known as *holons*. The idea of a holon was first proposed by Hungarian thinker Arthur Koestler as a way to describe the basic units of organization in biological and social systems. Koestler observed that in both living organisms and in social organizations, entirely self-supporting, noninteracting entities did not exist. In every domain of evolution there could be found neither simple wholes nor simple parts because every entity subject to evolution was simultaneously a whole and a part. Koestler recognized how these whole-parts—these systems embedded in systems—were organized in natural hierarchies or "holarchies" (hierarchies of holons), with every holarchical line of evolutionary development itself behaving as a self-organizing dynamic system. Koestler also saw how these naturally occurring holarchic systems emerged through the process of transcendence and inclusion—molecules transcend and include atoms, cells transcend and include molecules, organs transcend and include cells. This concept of holons and holarchy thus arose as a way of modeling these complex systems, and it also works well as a method of analysis that reconciles the seeming contradictions of atomism and holism.

As Wilber contemplated these evolutionary lines of development, he saw how every externally observable, natural evolutionary structure has a corresponding "interior"; after Whitehead, he recognized how every holon has some form of consciousness, observing how even the most primitive cells exhibit a certain type of proto-consciousness or "irritability." Wilber also recognized that as the complexity of a biological organism's exterior form increases, there is a corresponding increase in the complexity of that organism's consciousness. Thus, after Teilhard, Wilber saw how the development of the "without" coevolves with the development of the "within." Wilber accordingly began to construct his model by tracing the inextricable connections between the exterior and interior holarchies of evolutionary development.

But in addition to evolution's symmetrical expression of corresponding interior and exterior domains, Wilber also observed that evolutionary structures have both an individual and collective dimension. Building on the work of systems scientist Erich Jantsch, Wilber traced the coevolution of individual evolutionary entities and their corresponding collective environments. For example, where there is individual consciousness, there is a collective culture to which that individual belongs. And as the consciousness of the individuals within a culture evolves, so does the culture as a whole. Wilber thus postulated a model containing four different strands of hierarchical development, "each of which is intimately related and indeed dependent upon all the others, but none of which can be reduced to the others. The four strands are the interior and the exterior of the individual and the social, or the inside and the outside of the micro and the macro."[12] As reproduced in Figure 8-1 below, Wilber's four-quadrant model represents his attempt to account for what he sees as the four types of related evolutionary development unfolding within what he calls the "four corners of the known universe."

Overall, the quadrant model is an important foundation of the integral reality frame. Its exposition has certainly marked the beginning of integral philosophy's twenty-first-century synthesis. And there are obviously many important details and nuances to this model that are beyond the scope of this chapter to describe. However, as Wilber admits, when he originally formulated the quadrant model, he did not take into account the existence of *human artifacts*. The difference between a holon and an artifact is that a holon is a naturally occurring, self-organizing evolutionary system, but an artifact is not a natural system; it's an artificial human creation and thus it does not have an interior. For example, a human being is a holonic evolutionary system with an external biological body and an internal subjective consciousness, but a computer is an artifact that consists only of its exterior matter. A computer may have software, and it may perform internal operations, but it does not have a true interior—its reality does not extend into the internal universe. Thus when we attempt to draw a comprehensive map of the evolving universe, it is critical that we include not only holons, but also the reality of human artifacts, because in our increasingly "technicized lifeworld," the influence of artifacts cannot be ignored. Now, we must admit that Wilber's model does include artifacts in a way, it just mislabels them as holons. However, this seemingly technical distinction does reveal some of the limitations of the quadrant model.

The problem is found in Wilber's lower-right "interobjective quadrant," which is said to contain the holonic systems that comprise the exteriors of culture. But when we look at the exteriors of human culture, when we look for the objective aspects of human society, we can see that these are almost all man-made constructions such as (quoting Wilber): "architectural structures, transportation systems, physical infrastructure, even written (material) forms of books, legal codes, linguistic structures, verbal signifiers."[13] These artifacts clothe the internal systems of human culture with the external manifestations of art, technology, and human organizations, but these man-made constructions cannot be accurately described as "self-organizing systems of dynamic ITs." The physical structures of our complex society have not arisen autopoietically, they have been carefully designed and created through human intention, ingenuity, and effort. A problem thus arises because the quadrant model suggests symmetries that overstate the interdomain relationships. The symmetrical connections between the inside and the outside of an individual person may be perfectly correlated, but the connections between the holarchy of intersubjective human relationships and the external artifacts with which those relationships are associated are not always so perfectly correlated or symmetrical. As integral philosophy evolves and more and more weight is placed on the quadrant model, these weaknesses become increasingly problematic. However, in order for me to fully explain why the distinction between holons and artifacts in the lower-right quadrant matters, it requires a level of argument that is best reserved for Appendix B entitled "Consid-

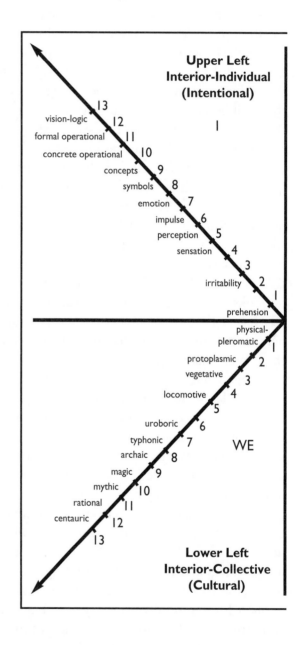

Figure 7-1. Wilber's four-quadrant model of evolution.

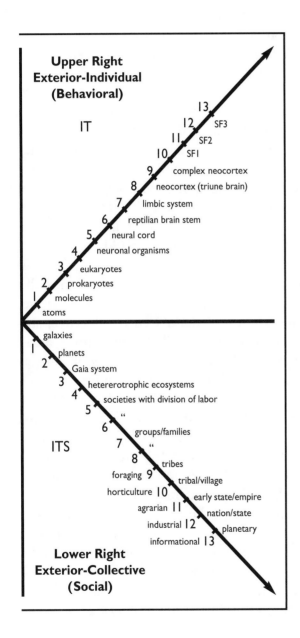

**Upper Right
Exterior-Individual
(Behavioral)**

IT

13
12   SF3
11   SF2
10   SF1
9   complex neocortex
8   neocortex (triune brain)
7   limbic system
6   reptilian brain stem
5   neural cord
4   neuronal organisms
3   eukaryotes
2   prokaryotes
1   molecules
atoms

1   galaxies
2   planets
3   Gaia system
4   hetererotrophic ecosystems
5   societies with division of labor
    "
6   groups/families
7   "
8   tribes
foraging 9   tribal/village
horticulture 10   early state/empire
agrarian 11   nation/state
industrial 12   planetary
informational 13

ITS

**Lower Right
Exterior-Collective
(Social)**

eration of Wilber's Four-Quadrant Model of Evolution." So I invite those who are interested in the finer points of integral philosophy to continue with this discussion in Appendix B, where we delve deeper into the nuances of integral metaphysics.

But for purposes of our present discussion, we can acknowledge that the four-quadrant model represents one of the best maps we have of the internal universe and its relation to the external realm. Despite its limitations, I think we can continue to use the quadrant model as long as we do not take it too literally. And this, of course, is the best way to use any kind of metaphysics. Yet the metaphysics of integral philosophy is still evolving, and as Wilber himself has said, a good theory is merely "one that lasts long enough to get you to a better one."[14] So in my opinion, the quadrant map has provided an excellent beginning for the emerging reality frame of integral consciousness; but this map is not the final word on the integral worldview.

As described in chapter 2, I do think that integral philosophy is on much firmer footing when it comes to its identification of the *three* basic and observable domains of evolution found in nature, self, and culture. This recognition of the objective, subjective, and intersubjective dimensions of evolving reality forms the foundation of integral metaphysics and frames the worldview of integral consciousness. Wilber has acknowledged this through his emphasis on the importance of what he calls the "Big Three." In fact, Wilber often reduces the four quadrants to simply the "Three Big" domains: objective, subjective, and intersubjective. Throughout his writing he frequently collapses the individual and collective aspects of the "right hand," external side of his model into a single domain. The individual objective and the collective interobjective—"It and Its"— become simply "It." Thus by reducing these two exterior quadrants to one single domain, thereby condensing the four quadrants to three essential realms, Wilber is able to connect his model of reality to the heritage of many of the world's greatest thinkers who have consistently recognized, in one form or another, these three basic domains of reality. For example, in his 1998 book *The Marriage of Sense and Soul*, Wilber writes:

I refer to these three value spheres as the "Big Three" because they are three of the most significant of modernity's differentiations, destined to play a crucial role in so many areas of life. This is not simply my own idea. The Big Three are recognized by an influential number of scholars. They are Sir Karl Popper's three worlds: subjective (I), cultural (We), and objective (It). They are Habermas's three validity claims: subjective sincerity (I), intersubjective justness (We), and objective truth (It). They are Plato's Beautiful, Good and True. They even show up in Buddhism as Buddha, Dharma, and Sangha....

And of enormous historical importance, the Big Three showed up in Kant's immensely influential trilogy: *Critique of Pure Reason* (objective science), *Critique of Practical Reason* (morals), and *Critique of Judgment* (aesthetic judgment and art). Dozens of examples could be given, but that is the general picture of the Big Three, which are just a shorthand version of the four quadrants.

The fact that the four quadrants (or simply the Big Three) are the results of an extensive data search across hundreds of holarchies; the fact that they show up cross-culturally nearly universally; the fact that they strenuously resist being reduced or erased from consideration—ought to tell us something, ought to tell us that they are etched deeply into the being of the Kosmos, that they are the warp and the woof of the fabric of the Real, announcing abiding truths about our world, about the insides and outsides, about its individual and communal forms.... [15]

As this passage makes clear, the metaphysics of integral philosophy, which frame the evolving universe with the interrelated categories of nature, self, and culture, are solidly grounded in observable reality. Although what is "observable" is not always visible, it is nonetheless very tangible and very valuable. Integral metaphysics are thus not "occult" or antiscientific in any way. When we ask ourselves what matters most, we can perhaps all agree that nature, self, and culture describe what's important in life. And if we wish to engage life to the fullest, it helps if we have a philosophy that adequately accounts for these dimensions of existence and clearly shows us what they are and how they relate to each other. However, there is more to integral metaphysics than the objective, subjective, and intersubjective dimensions of evolution. Another central feature of integral philosophy is the way it connects with spirituality.

Integral Philosophy and Human Spirituality

Integral philosophy has always been a spiritual philosophy. That is, every one of the founders of integral philosophy we've discussed (save the de facto founder, Habermas) have recognized, in one way or another, the centrality of spirit in the universe. So as integral philosophy works out the metaphysics that will frame its worldview in the twenty-first-century, it must decide how and where spirit fits in. In this endeavor, integral philosophy has essentially three options: under what I'll call *Option 1* it can incline toward science and declare that the realities of spirit are empirically discoverable and that integral philosophy can serve as a kind of spiritual science; Under *Option 2* it can incline toward religion by associating itself with a particular religion and by declaring the teachings of that religion to be essentially right; or under *Option 3* it can carefully situate itself in between science and religion by recognizing that spirit is real, but that science is too objectivistic and religion is too subjectivistic for either of these institutions to be given the final word on spiritual reality.

Under Option 3, integral philosophy expands the empirical methods of science so as to open up the internal universe to exploration and discovery. And as it does so, it takes notice of the ubiquitous presence of spirit's unmistakable influence; it recognizes how values are directly connected to spiritual experience. Yet it also recognizes that the approach to spirit is a deeply personal quest that leads through the heart of every subject. Under Option 3, integral philosophy limits its inquiries about reality to the noosphere, leaving the larger, theological explanations of the "theosphere" to the realm of spirituality. Option 3 thus supports the time-honored idea that science, philosophy, and religion are the three essential fields of human endeavor that are needed to support the development of higher levels of civilization—that all three of these disciplines are necessary for us to approach the truth in its fullness, that none can be reduced to any other or erased from consideration, and that the task of philosophy should be to harmonize science and spirituality while leaving each of these disciplines secure in its own domain. Thus, as explained in this section, I advocate Option 3.

However, by arguing that integral philosophy should impose limits on itself and thereby preserve the province of spirituality as a distinct category apart from philosophy, I occupy a different position than Wilber on this issue, and so it is worth discussing this in some detail. Even if you don't care what Wilber thinks, the evolving spirituality of integral consciousness can be fully understood only by appreciating the debate out of which it is being formed. It thus behooves us to examine Wilber's position and then to examine my suggested alternative, so as to bring out the significance of these formative issues. But let me say first, that with regard to our spiritual differences, Wilber and I are in complete agreement about the reality and centrality of spirit in the universe. And we firmly agree that no philosophy can be truly "integral" unless it acknowledges the significance of humanity's experience of spirit and attempts to account for and integrate this ultimate human concern. The fact that Wilber's philosophy is a spiritual philosophy gives it an essential credibility that much of philosophy since the Enlightenment has lacked. Overall, I agree with and applaud many of Wilber's insights on the movement of spirit in the world. My differences with Wilber in this area are not really with his religion—his notions of spirit are rich and beautiful and I have no need to argue with them or otherwise try to invalidate them. Everyone who has deeply felt the unifying embrace of spiritual experience knows that any perceived differences in these matters are ultimately of little importance, and that "behind the veil," the intense light of our essential oneness blasts away the shadows of our separation. So I disagree with Wilber not so much about matters of spirit but rather about how integral philosophy relates to spirituality. I've followed a variety of spiritual paths and experienced the light of a number of traditions, including Wilber's

Vedanta/Vajrayana path. At this point, I don't profess belief in any specific religious tradition, but in general I'm most deeply moved by Jesus of Nazareth's teachings about the love of God and the universal family. There are obviously many excellent paths to spirit, and I think the integral worldview is roomy enough to embrace all forms of authentic spirituality.

Wilber has demonstrated a strong commitment to spiritual pluralism through his recent inauguration of the *Integral Spiritual Center*, which seeks to bring together spiritual teachers from different traditions to "explore a trans-path path to the future." But even as Wilber celebrates spiritual diversity and advocates the inclusion of all authentic approaches to spirit, he is simultaneously attempting to develop a spiritual science (a version of Option 1) that claims to provide a perspective on the empirical nature of spiritual reality.

From the beginning, Wilber's writing has included descriptions of the higher states and stages of consciousness experienced by mystics. Wilber has argued that the consistency with which many saints and sages have described their mystical experiences points to an empirical domain of spirituality that can be explored and mapped through neoscientific methods that acknowledge the broadly empirical validity of mental and spiritual experience. As I explained above, I think broad empiricism is a good idea; however, I have always felt that Wilber goes too far by claiming that his "levels of mysticism" represent the future of humanity's evolution, and that these higher states and stages can be investigated and established with similar degrees of certainty as the stages of human history revealed by the spiral of development. Nevertheless, until recently I've been willing to overlook these claims and to recognize this part of Wilber's philosophy as simply his laudable attempt to integrate spirit according to his own lights. But as Wilber's writing has evolved his claims for an empirical spirituality have become more pronounced. In his latest book, *Integral Spirituality*, Wilber writes: "The metaphysics of the spiritual traditions have been thoroughly critiqued—'trashed' is probably the better word—by both modernist and postmodernist epistemologies, and there has as yet arisen nothing compelling to take their place."[16] Accordingly, Wilber attempts to bring forward a spiritual system of his own that is said to be based exclusively on broad empiricism and thus free from all "metaphysical baggage." But unsurprisingly, Wilber's postmetaphysical spirituality continues to appear very similar to the spiritual teachings of Vedanta Hinduism.

Wilber has been previously criticized for trying to reduce spirituality to a science, and in answer to these criticisms he writes:

> But science—broad or narrow—is not, as I said, the whole story of deep spirituality. The broad science of the interior domains only gives us the immediate data or immediate experiences of those interior domains. Those experiences are the ingredients for further elaboration in aesthetic/expressive and ethical/normative judgments. Thus, even with broad science, we are not reducing the interiors to merely science (broad or narrow). Science, in both its broad and narrow forms, is always merely one of the Big Three and simply helps us investigate the immediate data or experiences that are the raw material of aesthetic and normative experiences. Charges that my approach is positivistic missed this simple point.
>
> Thus, in *Sense and Soul*, I do indeed try to show that there is a *science* of the body realm (gross), the subtle realm (subtle), and the causal realm (spirit). But I point out that there is also the *art* of the body realm, the subtle realm, and spirit; and there are the *morals* of the body realm, the mind, and spirit. Thus, *all* of the manifest waves of the Great Nest have an I, We, and It dimension—that is, all of the levels actually have art, morals, and science. Hence, even if we expand science into the higher realms, as I suggest, science and its methods are still only "one third" of the total story, because the higher levels also have art and morals, *which follow their own quite different methodologies* (following their different validity claims, namely, truthfulness and justness, respectively).... A few critics proclaimed that in expanding science to include the higher realms, I was somehow reducing the higher realms to science.[17]

So, acknowledging his position in the quote above, I am not accusing Wilber of trying to reduce spirituality to a science. But despite his suggestion that an integral science of spirituality can be supplemented and expanded by spiritual art and morality, Wilber is nonetheless claiming that integral philosophy can provide a kind of scientific insight into the "causal realm" whereby questions such as the true path of spiritual growth and the Ultimate nature of reality can be answered definitively and authoritatively.

As we discussed in chapter 6 on "Integral Spirituality," the trouble with this approach can be seen when we realize that by claiming to be broadly empirical, Wilber's purportedly postmetaphysical spiritual system leaves room for only one "empirical" perspective on spiritual truth. According to Wilber, "This 'post-Kantian post-metaphysics'—or something like it—is the only avenue open to a spiritual philosophy in the modern and postmodern world."[18] Thus, even though he acknowledges that there is more to spirituality than its objective investigation, Wilber nevertheless claims that integral philosophy can definitively describe the "It" or objective truth of "deep spirituality." And I think this would be a good thing if it were possible. But as we explored in chapter 6, because different spiritual traditions and practices can produce significantly different experiences of spirit, it is not possible to create a reliable science of human spirituality that can bring forth objective and empirical descriptions of the spiritual universe. To claim to do so is to engage in a form of belief system imperialism that asserts an objective status for a particular theology.

Wilber acknowledges that spiritual realities are not simply empirical in a pregiven sense—he explains that such realities can be accessed only by those whose internal development has reached a level that corresponds to these spiritual realities. Yet he also claims that the spiritual features of the universe and the general ascension scheme of spiritual growth described by his own religion is in fact an empirical account of what's actually out there in the spiritual worldspace. So unless we are willing to simply accept his belief system on its face, we have to explain why such empirical claims are suspect. And this serves as a test of the integral reality frame's attempt to steer between the Myth of the Given and the Myth of the Framework, which we discussed above. In other words, it seems to me that the Mystery of spiritual reality, as it can be approached by humans in this age, lies somewhere in between a relativistic pluralism (leading to the Myth of the Framework) and a facile universalism (leading to the Myth of the Given).

Ultimately, I think there is "a unity of truth" about the real nature of spiritual reality; and as we ascend I trust we will all come to know this truth in its fullness. But the human mind is so small and the spiritual universe is so large that at this point no human mind can credibly claim to describe its features in objective terms. While integral philosophy can describe certain empirical features of the internal universe of consciousness and culture (the noosphere), as we venture into the spiritual worldspace (the theosphere), our perspectives become increasingly subject to our own spiritual expectations. Mystical experience can indeed illuminate spiritual truth, but there are many scholars of mysticism who reject the notion that these experiences can disclose empirical realities. On this point, Ian Barbour, who is considered the "dean" of the field of science and religion, describes the position of religious scholar Steven Katz:

> A report of religious experience is determinatively *shaped* by the *concepts* a person brings to it. [Katz] examines mystical writings in various traditions and is impressed by their diversity. For example, Jewish mysticism does not involve loss of identity in the experience of unity but preserves a sense of God's otherness. Belief in a personal God and the importance of ritual and ethical action is simply assumed. "The mystic brings to his experience a world of concepts, images, symbols and values which shape as well as color the experience he eventually and actually has." Prior expectations impose both form and content on experience; we cannot say there is a universal experience that is then interpreted by diverse cultural concepts. The symbols of religious communities are at work before, during, and after the experience.[19]

Thus, even if you subscribe to Wilber's religion, even if you believe that the "psychic, subtle, causal, and nondual" levels are exactly what the spiritual universe looks like, you must allow that other integralists can have differing ideas about spiritual growth. Surely you must see that integral philosophy cannot become substantially identical to a particular form of spirituality if it is ever going to achieve its important work of helping to form the next historically significant worldview in humanity's cultural evolution. The mission of integral philosophy is too important to allow itself to be burdened by any specific or official version of spirituality. If integral philosophy is to flourish, it must acknowledge the validity of spirituality as a category of human experience without asserting a supposedly empirical description of spiritual reality. It is only by doing this that integralism can achieve its full potential and remain a progressive, evolving philosophy that is open to all forms of genuine spiritual experience.

Again, I do not wish to discourage Wilber's spiritual teaching or otherwise argue with his position that there is "nothing higher." But I do want to separate these essentially theological assertions from the main body of integral philosophy because it is critical to integral philosophy's success that it impose limits on its own explanations of spiritual reality. In other words, as a philosophy, as a form of reason-based (and vision logic–based) public agreement about nature, self, and culture, integral philosophy can effectively enact the next historically significant worldview only by limiting itself to the realm of philosophy—to the realm of the noosphere—effectively reserving the realm of the theosphere for religion and thereby acknowledging the reality of spirit, but not the final authority of any particular explanation thereof. As we discussed in chapter 6, religion serves humanity best when it provides an orienting and comprehensive explanation of the meaning of life, the purpose of the self, life after death, and the nature of the Ultimate. Teachings about these realities are not all outmoded myths and premodern relics; they are the essential elements of every form of vital spirituality, and they need to be preserved and protected (even as these teachings differ among traditions) if religion is going to continue to fulfill its crucial role in human society.

Wilber is admirably attempting to harmonize science and spirituality by seeking a broadly empirical "trans-path path" that can unite the various approaches of the great wisdom traditions. But because, as William James discovered early on, spirit consistently shows itself to be elusive to empirical investigation, Wilber's quest for a trans-path path cannot produce a credible empirical spirituality; it can only pretend to do so by effectively exalting and privileging one of the previously existing paths. Thus by seeking to connect integral philosophy to spirituality through Option 1, Wilber ends up with an approach that looks very much like Option 2.

That humans have spiritual experiences is undeniable; and having directly experienced spirit myself, I can say that not only is the *experience* of spirit real, but *spirit itself* is the most real thing in the universe. But as we have discussed, the methods of broad empiricism break down in the realm of spiritual experience. Some spiritual experiences confirm the personal nature of Deity, and others point to the impersonal nature of the Ultimate. If integral theory preserves religion as a category distinct from philosophy, it can allow for the full truth of both of these kinds of spiritual experience. But if integral philosophy maintains that it can only recognize "empirical spirituality," then to be consistent it must recognize either the personal or the impersonal nature of the Ultimate as the most empirically valid—it must choose between a loving God and Nondual Emptiness. However, this is not a choice that integral philosophy can or should make. It seems unlikely that a clear consensus can be reached about which type of religion is right, even within the integral stage of cultural development. Nor does it seem likely that integral culture will produce an entirely new understanding of spiritual reality that effectively unifies the differences between the impersonal and the personal approaches to Divinity without effectively totalizing one of these paths. In fact, at this point in cultural evolution it seems that these theological differences provide a kind of valuable diversity that enriches our spiritual culture, even as we attempt to move beyond the relativistic limitations of postmodernism's polite spiritual pluralism. Thus in order for integralists to be free to choose among the different kinds of authentic spirituality, the philosophy that enacts their worldview must not be tied to a spiritual system that claims to be empirical. Is spirit real? Yes; but is spirit subject to being systemized by a broadly empirical philosophy? My answer is no, or at least not in this century.

So where does this leave us? Well, there is one approach to spirituality left open to integral philosophy that is broadly empirical but which does not end up privileging one particular spiritual path over others. This philosophical approach to spirituality, which remains consistent with the position I describe as "Option 3," is found in the examination of the directions of evolution itself. And this is the subject of the final chapter, entitled "The Directions of Evolution." However, before we end our discussion of the metaphysics of integral philosophy, as promised, we'll now consider some possible critiques of the integral reality frame.

Some Critiques of the Integral Reality Frame

As we observed at the beginning of this chapter, whenever we attempt to explain the universe in terms that humans can understand, wherever we find a metaphysics that frames reality in a useful way, we naturally find critiques of that metaphysics. Our examination of these critiques begins by remembering that as long as our consciousness is situated within a material body and brain, we generally require a worldview to frame our experience and organize our perspectives. In other words, all understanding occurs within a worldview, and thus all critiques are ultimately situated within one worldview or another. So let's consider some potential critiques that arise from each of the major worldviews we've discussed.

1) From the perspective of traditional consciousness, the metaphysics that frames the integral worldview is weak because it lacks a robust theology. Even though it generally recognizes spirit, because it does not acknowledge the final authority of ... [and here we could insert a number of different spiritual traditions], it does not really transcend postmodern relativism. Thus from a traditional perspective, the integral worldview is just another New Age belief system lost in a sea of relativism and unconnected to the essential justifying authority of scripture.

2) From the perspective of late-modernist consciousness, integral metaphysics fails because it is not subject to falsifiability. In other words, it is not meaningful because it cannot be proved or disproved as a matter of sensory-empirical fact. Integral philosophy maintains that spiritual experience is the experience of something real, but because such experiences are always thoroughly subjective, there is no way to distinguish a spiritual experience from any other kind of fantasy. Thus if integral philosophy is going to honor science, as it says it does, then it must dispense with all claims that have to be taken on faith. From a scientific perspective, ideas such as an "internal universe," downward causation, and vague notions of "spirit" are clearly religious and thus hopelessly premodern.

3) From the perspective of postmodern philosophy, the integral worldview is a Eurocentric reification of white male thinking that is nothing but a transparent attempt at domination through the use of a false metanarrative. Integral philosophy's attempt to assert universal truth claims is a pretentious (and potentially dangerous) fiction designed to justify Western capitalism's neocolonial globalization. Integral philosophy is essentially attempting to resurrect the now discredited Enlightenment worldview, and by doing so it becomes complicit in the ongoing sins of modernist oppression. Despite paying lip service to postmodern insights, integralism ignores the fact that modernism's reality frame has been effectively deconstructed and unmasked. Thus, because it fails to acknowledge the inherent illegitimacy of the modernist worldview, but rather claims this worldview as part of its foundation, integral philosophy fails at even understanding postmodernism, let alone transcending postmodernism, as it naively claims to do.

4) In connection with the postmodern critique above, we should also consider a related set of criticisms that arise from postmodern culture rather than postmodern philosophy per se. These critiques are that integral philosophy is too masculine, too cerebral, and too concerned with THE truth, rather than the many truths. Integral philosophy privileges progress over sustainability, and its ideas on cultural evolution are disturbingly neoconservative.

5) Now in addition to these critiques, we can also speculate

about the postintegral critiques that will inevitably begin to appear once the integral worldview becomes more successfully established. Postintegral critiques might point out that the attempted separation of science and religion into two categories that require the "bridging and separating" function of a third category, identified as philosophy, is an unnecessary and artificial construct. From a postintegral perspective, the essential unity of all human knowledge and experience calls for a reality frame that does not rely on separate categories, but rather seeks a category-free perspective that can make contact with being as it is in itself. This unmediated apprehension of reality is found by simply allowing oneself to be in the moment. However, because integral philosophy is overly concerned with distinguishing between worldviews, it allows the "concept of worldview" to get in the way of seeing things as they really are.

I think these criticisms all have some validity, but I don't think any of them completely overcomes the value of the integral worldview or its potential to improve human conditions in the twenty-first century. As we discussed earlier in this chapter, integral consciousness clearly recognizes that its worldview is, in a sense, designed to make progress only with respect to certain problematic life conditions. Thus, like all historically significant worldviews, the integral worldview is a creature of its time in history, not an end state of cultural evolution. But even as it recognizes that it is merely a temporary stage and only a relative step forward, integralism must have the confidence and the courage to carry on in the face of all the criticisms that will inevitably be leveled against it.

Thus, in answer to the specific criticisms listed above, I can briefly respond that: 1) Theological unity is a laudable goal, but at this point in history it could be achieved only through coercion, and such coercion would be contrary to any theology worthy of unifying under. 2) Scientific proof is certainly valuable and important, but a culture that believes that only science can deliver truth is one that is destined to be severely retarded in its evolution. In fact, one of integral philosophy's primary goals is to secure a place for the ongoing authority (but not the final authority) of science in the face of postmodernism's attempts to delegitimize the scientific worldview.

But given the ubiquitous nature of mental and spiritual experience, it seems that the burden of proof should be on scientific materialism to show why these experiences have no ontological referents. 3) The integral worldview acknowledges the historical crimes of modernity and it is sensitive to the suffering that arose in the wake of the Enlightenment. However, integral consciousness can also see where modernism has been a force for good in the world, and integralism thus seeks to carefully distinguish between those elements of the modern world that must be eliminated and those aspects that must be carried forward and further improved. 4) If the dialectic spiral is a real system of consciousness and culture, then it is the very structure of history that gives integralism its essentially "yang" character. Without its emphasis on progress and achievement, the integral worldview would fail at being what it claims to be: the next step in contemporary culture's evolutionary advance. However, unlike modernism, which generally ridicules postmodern culture, integralism celebrates postmodernism as the most advanced form of culture that has yet to appear. Integral philosophy thus does its best to honor and include the virtues of the postmodern worldview even as it attempts to transcend the limitations of these values. And finally, 5) as a result of spiritual growth, people often come to the place where worrying dissolves and life is seen as already perfect just as it is in the present moment. Thus, from the perspective of advanced states of consciousness, concepts and theories about the future can sometimes seem silly in comparison with the awesome truth of being as it simply is in the now. However, no matter how far we progress as individuals, as long as we are alive on this planet there will be millions of others who live in a world of trouble and suffering. And if we are going to care about these others by trying to improve their conditions, we may find the concepts of integral philosophy to be somewhat helpful.

Now, the fuller answers to these criticisms are found in the context of this book as a whole, as well as within the larger body of integral philosophy. But the foregoing lists the rejoinders to these criticisms in summary form. I'm sure there are many other valid criticisms of integral philosophy that I have not addressed here. However, this discussion has provided an overview of the main objections that might be raised against the integral worldview.

This concludes our discussion of the integral reality frame. But this has really been only a description of what the integral reality frame looks like from the outside. As we will discuss in the next chapter, to fully understand any internal structure, it is necessary to experience what it is like from the inside as well as from the outside. That is, in order to truly know what integral consciousness is, we have to actually adopt the values of this worldview and use it to define the location of our identity.

CHAPTER 9

Structures of the Human Mind

LET'S REVIEW OUR PURPOSES. WE'RE PROCEEDING FROM THE DIRECT observation that life conditions here at the beginning of the twenty-first century call for some kind of significant cultural evolution. And now, through integral philosophy's understanding of "internal history"—the history of the development of consciousness and culture—we can see that in response to these life conditions, a historically significant new worldview is beginning to emerge in our time. Those of us who can recognize this new perspective here at its beginning have a unique opportunity to participate in this worldview by being among the first to adopt its values and practice its methods. These methods, these practices that can improve the human condition in large and small ways, are found in the integral worldview's ability to better understand human values as they are manifested in the various stages of consciousness. As Gebser saw early on, the integral worldview arises in people as the stages of consciousness become transparent to them. And this recognition of the stages of human history within the minds of individuals yields a method of working with consciousness that can produce meaningful evolutionary progress.

However, the emerging worldview of integral consciousness is entered into not by merely knowing about the stages, but by personally identifying with the values of integral consciousness and by using the power of the integral perspective as a practice that raises consciousness in ourselves and in others. Knowledge of the spiral of development may raise the cognitive level of our consciousness, but in order to raise our consciousness permanently and overall, in order to move our "center of gravity" into integral consciousness, we have to raise not only our thinking, but also our values, and our loyalties. We have to embrace the expanded vertical perspective of integral consciousness with our feelings and our intentions as well as with our thoughts. And the most effective way to do this is to actually use this new perspective to improve conditions in our world.

But if we're going to use the spiral, sooner or later we're going to have to defend the spiral. We're going to have to explain not only the nature and behavior of the spiral itself, but also where this structure comes from and how it relates to a person's consciousness as a whole. Thus, in order to take the spiral structure seriously, in order for us to rely on it as an important foundation of our worldview, we have to have a clear idea of how the structure of the spiral fits within the structure of the mind.

While there is little agreement in academic psychology about the actual structure of the human mind, most integralists agree that our minds include subconscious, conscious, and superconscious aspects. And in addition to these *general domains* of psychic activity, integralists also recognize *states* of consciousness (such as waking, dreaming, sleeping, and nonordinary states) as well as *structures* of consciousness, which can be defined as stable patterns that consistently recur over time. Within this general understanding of the mind, the stages identified by the spiral of development can be classified as structures of consciousness. And, as we've seen, these same structures that organize the consciousness of individuals are writ large in the societies in which those individuals live. So the structures of consciousness can be loosely correlated with the structures of culture, making them very relevant to the overall state of the human condition.

Moreover, as Piaget recognized, "There is no structure that lacks a development." This insight suggests how every structure in consciousness is ultimately a part of a larger line of development—every identifiable level is part of a system of multiple, unfolding levels. However, when it comes to the evolving structure of the spiral, there is some disagreement among integralists about the place of this line of development within the larger scheme of things. On one side of the issue are those who recognize the worldview structures identified by the spiral as generally defining and encompassing the overall trajectory of the evolution of consciousness as a whole. And on the other side are those who recognize multiple, relatively independent lines of development that evolve at different rates within each person. These theorists see the spiral as simply "one among at least a dozen" developmental lines. But from my perspective, this deemphasis of the importance of a person's cultural worldview weakens the foundations of the integral worldview itself.

As I mentioned at the end of chapter 7, although the different structures or types of human intelligence, such as cognitive ability or emotional intelligence, can develop relatively independently, I'll argue in this chapter that these various lines of development are themselves organized within a larger holarchic structure wherein three primary lines of development encompass the rest. And it is from this perspective that we can begin to see how values-based worldviews come to have a significant influence on the overall "internal location" of our consciousness. However, a person's worldview serves to generally establish their cultural location not because it is part of a monolithic, singular line of absolute development, but because a person's worldview serves as the focus of their intention and their *will*. As we'll explore in this chapter, that which orients our attention and our intention has a powerful affect upon our consciousness as a whole.

In order to really understand the larger holarchic structure of the human mind and see where the spiral fits in, we will need to first discuss some current theories of consciousness. Fortunately, at this point in the development of humanity's knowledge, theories about the structure of the mind are not idle speculation. As we've noted, in the last hundred years, scientifically minded researchers working in the social sciences have uncovered considerable evidence of psychic structures and lines of development within consciousness. We are thus at a point in history where we're actually close to discovering the authentic structure of the mind through the straightforward process of pattern recognition. This is similar to how the structure of DNA was originally recognized: We can observe bits and pieces of the structure from the research of the social sciences; all we have to do now is envision an overall structure that fits the observable data and that makes sense within the larger scheme of evolution. And just like with the structure of DNA, once we have a good idea of what the internal organization of the mind looks like, we can then design specific tests to confirm or refute this postulated structure.

As we discussed in chapter 2 on "The Internal Universe," there is definitely something going on here: Through the advances of culture, the consciousness of individuals has shown its ability to evolve independently from the underlying evolution of the brain. While there is a neurological basis for all conscious activity, the mind's demonstration of its ability to evolve and grow, even while the structure of the brain remains relatively constant, makes clear that the mind takes form around structures that cannot all necessarily be found in the neurological physiology of the brain. And the evolving system of values-based worldviews we recognize as the spiral of development is a prime example of a psychic structure that interacts with the brain but which is not made out of gray matter. So if we can put the pieces together and see the overall structure of the mind as it actually exists, this will be hugely important because, like the pattern recognition that revealed the structure of the DNA molecule, correctly seeing the structures of consciousness will allow us to dramatically improve the human condition.

In the discussion that follows, we'll briefly survey what developmental psychologists have concluded regarding the structures of consciousness and the lines of development within the mind. Then we'll examine Ken Wilber's latest ideas on the subject. Wilber's theory of the lines of development has become a major focus of his most recent writing, and his conclusions in this area challenge the ideas of some of developmental psychology's most distinguished thinkers. So no theory of the structure of the mind can be adequate unless it takes notice of the problems Wilber identifies.

Then with this background in mind, we'll explore an alternative theory of the structure of consciousness that rests on the original insights advanced by James Mark Baldwin, and which has now been updated to account for the latest thinking and research. In my opinion, this alternative theory comes closer than any previous theory to explaining the overall internal organization of human consciousness in the way that it accounts for what can be felt from the inside as well as what can be observed from the outside, and in the way that it reveals an elegant structure that reflects the larger patterns of evolution as a whole. However, in order to appreciate why the theory I'm proposing works so well, it is necessary to first examine the theories of Wilber and the developmental psychologists. But this effort is certainly worthwhile because, as Einstein famously said, "Theory is very important because your theory ultimately determines what you can see."

Lines of Development Recognized by Psychologists

Researchers working within the field of developmental psychology have adopted a variety of conceptual approaches in their investigation of consciousness. Baldwin organized his research on the human mind around his understanding of the three essential categories of thought outlined by Kant and known as judgment (aesthetics), theoretical reason (science), and practical reason (morality). Baldwin's structural inquiries focused primarily on the latter two modes. According to prominent developmentalist and Baldwin scholar John Broughton: "First, there is the development of theoretical reason and scientific intelligence, primarily dealt with by Baldwin in his (1906) *Thought and Things*. Second, there is the development of practical reason and the active, rather than cognitive, life of the mind. This is dealt with in *Social and Ethical Interpretations* (1897), an earlier work which treats morality in combination with religious consciousness."[1] Later in the century, Piaget would carry on the cognitive side of Baldwin's research, and Kohlberg would focus on the moral side of human development. And both of these now world famous researchers rediscovered and confirmed that these two distinct lines of mental development naturally unfold through the specific stages originally found by Baldwin.

The developmental psychologists who would follow Piaget and Kohlberg designed research programs that essentially focused on variations of either the cognitive or the moral line of development originally outlined by Baldwin (after Kant). Although Maslow did not make any reference to Baldwin, Piaget, or Kohlberg in the original description of his stage theory outlined in his 1954 masterpiece *Motivation and Personality* (despite including the names of close to five hundred other academics in the book's index), Maslow's research on human motivation was explicitly centered on human needs and their corresponding values. So although we can perhaps draw fine distinctions between the investigation of values and the investigation of the kind of moral choices in which values are expressed, there is little doubt that the research of both Maslow and Kohlberg was generally concerned with "practical reason" and the moral line of development.

As we discussed in chapter 7, Graves originally designed his research program to confirm Maslow's stages. So it is clear that Maslow and Graves were also studying the same thing. Graves, however, relied on the research of Piaget[2] as well as Maslow, and thus concluded that the worldview stages he identified encompassed and included a wide variety of developmental lines. Graves specifically identified "feelings, motivations, ethics and values, biochemistry, degree of neurological activation, learning systems, belief systems, ... education, economics, and political theory and practice" as all being governed by a person's overall worldview.

Similarly, Robert Kegan, who we identified in chapter 3 as the most well-respected living developmental psychologist, attempts to integrate the work of both Piaget and Kohlberg by recognizing within the stages (which he identifies as "orders of consciousness") three primary lines of development. Kegan identifies these lines as "the cognitive, the interpersonal, and the intrapersonal."[3] Thus, according to Kegan, a person's overall worldview or order of consciousness encompasses the cognitive line, the moral line, and the emotional line of development. Hence, Kegan's conception of the structures of consciousness is very similar to the original thinking of Baldwin.

After Kegan, the second most influential living developmentalist is undoubtedly Howard Gardner (who teaches in the same academic department at Harvard as Kegan). Unlike Kegan, however, Gardner has focused exclusively on cognitive development, which he sees, like his intellectual mentor Piaget, as the only type of mental activity that can be reliably investigated by science. Through his research Gardner has sought to challenge "the widespread belief—one held by many psychologists and entrenched in many languages—that intelligence is a single faculty and that one is either 'smart' or 'stupid' across the board."[4] By defining intelligence as "the ability to solve problems or to create products that are valued within one or more cultural settings," Gardner developed eight criteria for what constitutes a specific type of human intelligence. And by using these criteria in his extensive research, Gardner has now identified eight "intelligences" which he claims "account for human cognition in its fullness."[5] As illustrated in Figure 9-1 below, these eight distinct intelligences are identified as: linguistic, logical-mathematical, musical, bodily-kinesthetic, spatial, interpersonal, intrapersonal, and naturalist. Gardner has also considered adding "spiritual or existential intelligence" to the list (which he admits is a structure of consciousness with which

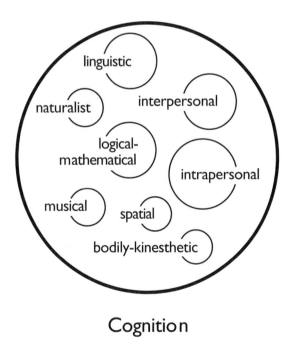

Cognition

Figure 9-1. Gardner's "eight intelligences" found within human cognition.

he is not personally acquainted), but he has ultimately declined to recognize this as a distinct form of intelligence. Writes Gardner: "Despite the attractiveness of a ninth intelligence, however, I am not adding existential intelligence to the list. I find the phenomenon perplexing enough and the distance from the other intelligences vast enough to dictate prudence—at least for now. At most, I am willing, Fellini-style, to joke about '8-1/2 intelligences.'"[6]

In anticipation of our discussion of Wilber's view of the lines of development, below, it is important to emphasize that Gardner has limited his inquiry strictly to the cognitive line(s) of development. In his elucidation of these various lines of development, which together constitute the overall cognitive line, Gardner has been careful to distinguish cognitive intelligence from emotional intelligence and moral intelligence. Although he recognizes that the idea of emotional intelligence "fits comfortably with my own sense of interpersonal and intrapersonal intelligences," he believes that most ideas about emotional intelligence cannot really be investigated scientifically, and he thus prefers to speak of "emotional sensitivity" rather than conceptualizing emotion as a formal type of intelligence. Gardner also distinguishes his idea of intelligence from a person's moral development, which he recognizes as resulting from "the exercise of one's will" rather than from a specific cognitive ability. According to Gardner, "'Morality' is then properly a statement about personality, individuality, will, character—and, in the happiest cases, about the highest realization of human nature."[7]

Mainstream professional academics such as Gardner define themselves as social scientists, so it is understandable that they want to "stick to science" and avoid any theoretical descriptions of consciousness as a whole. And Gardner is right when he says that the emotional and moral aspects of the mind are largely beyond the reach of science. But as we've seen, just because a subject is beyond the reach of science does not mean that it is beyond the reach of human knowledge in general. So as we now move beyond our brief discussion of developmental psychology's understanding of the lines of development within consciousness, we turn to a similarly brief examination of Wilber's ideas on the subject. Because Wilber transcends the limitations of the social sciences and approaches the structures of the mind from a broader philosophical perspective, it is worth examining his ideas in some detail.

Wilber's Theory of the Lines of Development

In some of his most recent writing, Wilber has gone to great lengths to justify the accuracy and legitimacy of his account of the structures of consciousness. Wilber maintains that his understanding of these structures has been informed by the investigations of the academic researchers he calls "adequate structuralists." According to Wilber, "adequate structuralists generally define a structure as a '*holistic, dynamic pattern of self-organizing processes* that maintain themselves as stable configurations through their ongoing reproduction.'"[8] A "structuralist" is defined as a theorist working within the social sciences who examines the internal structures of consciousness and/or culture from a third-person perspective. Wilber writes that one of the advantages of a structuralist approach to consciousness is that it discloses aspects of a person's interiors from an outside perspective, which reveals forms of consciousness that cannot really be seen from "the inside," from a first-person perspective. In other words, by observing the behaviors and beliefs of statistically significant numbers of people over time, structuralists have been able to recognize empirical patterns and universal processes of development that are occurring within the mind. However, according to Wilber, in order for an internal structure to be adequately (integrally) understood, it needs to be apprehended from both the outside and the inside. If we are going to really understand what an internal structure is, we have to be able to see it both objectively and subjectively—we have to know what it is like for ourselves in order to be able to really say what it is. Thus an "adequate structuralist" is one who knows the objects of her study by both external observation and personal acquaintance. And, according to Wilber, this method of seeing internal universe structures from both without and from within is one of the techniques that gives the integral approach its expanded grasp of interior realities.

After outlining the criteria for what he considers to be adequate structuralism, Wilber then goes on to take notice of the variety of research questions that have been asked by the various developmentalists (adequate structuralists) who have studied consciousness. From this he concludes that each line of questioning reveals a different "organ in the psyche."[9] This reasoning then leads to Wilber's psychograph model (reproduced in Figure 9-2 below), which charts the relative height of the independent developmental lines that have been revealed through the research of the various developmentalists. According to Wilber:

> Early developmental theorists tended to assume that there was one thing called development, and they were getting at it. Their stages were simply a map of "the" course of development. Piaget assumed that his cognitive line was the only fundamental line, and everything else hung off it like lights on his Christmas tree. Clare Graves assumed that his "values systems" were actually "levels of existence" into which everything could be plopped (despite the fact that his initial research was conducted on American, white, middle-class college students and consisted in their responses to only one simple question ...). Still, the early researchers could hardly have assumed otherwise, given the unknown and uncharted nature of the territory they were traversing.
>
> But after 4 decades of this pioneering research, we can put all their results on the table and have a look, and if we do so, an unmistakable pattern emerges. There is not one line of development that the dozens of models are giving different maps of; rather, there are at least *a dozen different developmental lines*—cognitive, moral, interpersonal, emotional, psychosexual, kinesthetic, self, values, needs, and so on. Each of the great developmentalists tended to stumble onto a particular developmental line or stream and explore it in great detail. They then often assumed that this was the only fundamental stream and all others could easily be reduced to something happening within their stream, an assumption that only history and further research could disclose as unwarranted (we call this *stream* or *line absolutism*).[10]

After introducing the psychograph model, Wilber then addresses the question of how the various lines relate to each other. Referring to the work of Gardner, Wilber concludes that the structures in the different lines are "apples and oranges," and that the stages exhibited in one line of development cannot be used to explain or categorize the stages in another line. As an example of line independence, Wilber cites the case of the "Nazi doctor" who is highly developed cognitively but poorly developed in the moral line. Yet with regard to the various lines, Wilber also recognizes how the research shows that each of the lines "nonetheless traverse the same general levels, waves, or orders of consciousness." In other words, no matter what line of development the structuralists have studied, they have consistently found that every line exhibits the same developmental progression from preconventional to conventional to postconventional and beyond. Wilber then comments that this evident similarity found within each line's development, when coupled with the apparent developmental independence of each line, "has been the great puzzle to developmentalists for the last several decades."[11] Then as a proposed solution to this puzzle, Wilber offers his theory of the "degrees of consciousness."

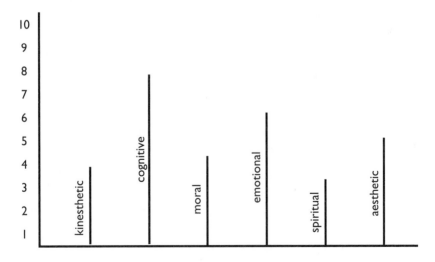

Figure 9-2. Wilber's psychograph model of the lines of development within consciousness.

Under this theory, the "y-axis" of the psychograph, the measure of the relative height of the various lines of development, is recognized as simply the degree of development in "consciousness per se." According to Wilber, "the levels of consciousness [measured by the y-axis] are not levels of a particular and separate stream, but *a measure of the degree of awareness in any particular stream*. In that sense, the levels of consciousness are indeed like degrees, inches, or kilograms: measures that do not exist in themselves, or by themselves, but are simply measures of concrete realities. As meters measure distance or degrees measure heat, levels of consciousness measure the amount of awareness or consciousness present in any specific stage/level/wave in any of the streams."[12] Wilber explains that his conception of consciousness as "empty" is in accord with the "Madhyamaka/Yogachara schools of Buddhism, which point out that, if consciousness is to be conceptualized at all, it is a pure Emptiness, devoid of specific characteristics, but allowing specific characteristics to arise in the manifest world; ... This is why nobody has ever been able to satisfactorily define consciousness—it doesn't exist, but is the space in which things exist. And a 'level of consciousness' is a measure of the spaciousness of the space in which in they exist."[13]

In his overall theory of the lines of development within consciousness, Wilber is adamant that the lines are independent. Yet later in his discussion of the lines of development in culture, Wilber addresses the fact that it often appears as though an individual or group is "behaving as if from one level" overall. Wilber explains this perception by acknowledging that most people have a general center of psychic gravity around which their lines of development tend to cluster. According to Wilber, "Individuals and groups have something like a center of gravity that expresses the sum total of their overall inclinations in all levels and lines. In individuals, the center of gravity is usually in the vicinity of the proximate self in the self-identity stream; and in groups, it usually 'resides' in the communal action systems (whether educational, governmental, medical, etc.). ... The center of gravity is simply the probability space in which you will most often find a particular holon, and it is a useful concept to just that degree."[14]

The inclusion of the idea of a center of developmental gravity in Wilber's recent writing connects back to his ideas about the self articulated in the 1999 book *Integral Psychology*. There, Wilber described the overall self as consisting of three parts: a proximate self (what we experience as "I"), a distal or distant self (what we experience as the objective self, or "me"), and the ultimate Witness (the transcendental self, or "I-I"). In his discussion of the self, Wilber writes: "As the locus of integration, the self is responsible *for balancing and integrating all of the levels, lines, and states in the individual*."[15] Overall, I think this is an excellent definition of the self with which I can generally agree. However, after describing the self and its elements and functions, Wilber then makes clear that he considers the proximate self to be just one of at least a dozen developmental lines. After discussing how the proximate self navigates through the mind's overall development, on the very next page he says: "Thus, there are the developmental lines in general (cognitive, affective, aesthetic, kinesthetic, mathematical, etc.), and, as a subset of those, there are the developmental lines that are especially and intimately associated with the self, its needs, its identity, and its development—and those are the self-related lines."[16] Thus, despite his suggestion that the self is responsible for integrating the various lines of development, his position in *Integral Psychology* ultimately comes back to the idea that the self and its sublines do not constitute a structure over and above the other lines of development in consciousness. And this stance is now more clearly explained and affirmed in his latest writing.

Wilber's theory of the development of consciousness obviously contains additional details and nuances not described here. But the foregoing provides a general summary of his thinking in this area. And this allows us to now consider some possible critiques of his theory.

A Critique of Wilber's Theory of Developmental Lines

Before I respectfully disagree with Wilber, I need to say that I'm grateful that he has chosen to explore these matters in the detail that he has, and I hope that the field of developmental psychology will take notice of integral philosophy's advances in this area. I've carefully read the developmental psychology literature, and, looking at the same research data as Wilber, I see a different pattern. But before I advance an alternative theory of the structure of consciousness, it will be helpful to briefly list my objections to the structure described by Wilber. I offer this critique because it shows why an alternative theory is needed and because it lays the groundwork for the discussion that follows. However, depending on how you feel about Wilber, it is possible to skip over these specific objections (or simply read the italicized headings) and move directly to the alternative theory of the structure of consciousness described in the section after this.

Although the six specific objections discussed below are related and overlap, describing them in a numbered list makes the argument easier to follow.

1) *The position that all the various lines of development have no higher-level organizing structure, short of the overall self, seems to violate the "twenty tenets" of holonic evolution articulated by Wilber in Sex, Ecology, Spirituality.* Wilber describes his "twenty tenets" as the "'patterns of existence' or 'tendencies of evolution' or 'laws of form' or 'propensities of manifestation.'" These are the "stable habits" uncovered by systems scientists, which "are operative in all three domains of evolution—the physiosphere, the biosphere, and the noosphere ..."[17] As we discussed in chapter 8, these tenets of evolution center around the recognition of the structures formed by hierarchies of holons known as holarchies; and within this understanding, each line of development in consciousness represents a distinct holarchy. However, as the twenty tenets make clear, as individual holarchical lines evolve, they are themselves organized and integrated within larger wholes. In his description of the twenty tenets, under the heading of the directionality of evolution, Wilber observes, "The differentiating processes are obviously necessary for the undeniable novelty and diversity created by evolution, but integration is just as crucial, converting manyness into oneness ... Thus Whitehead's view that 'the ultimate character pervading the universe is a drive toward the endless production of new syntheses [integration].' ... Thus Whitehead's all-important dictum: 'The many [differentiation] become one [inte-

gration] and are increased by one [the new holon]."[18] (bracketed additions in original). Now perhaps Wilber would say that the lines of development are simply integrated in the overall self, or in "consciousness per se." But as a matter of structure it seems unlikely that there would be more than a dozen relatively independent lines with no major or primary lines through which these various lines would find higher levels of organization.

2) *A model of relatively independent lines, with no higher-level organizing structure, does not represent what contemporary developmental psychologists in fact believe.* Wilber cites Gardner as an authority for the proposition that the developmental lines are relatively independent. And Gardner confirms this in his 1999 book *Intelligence Reframed*, where he writes: "[T]he human mind is better thought of as a series of relatively separate faculties, with only loose and nonpredictable relations with one another, than as a single, all-purpose machine ..."[19] However, as Gardner makes clear, the "mind" he is talking about is the cognitive mind exclusively. The "8-1/2 intelligences" described by Gardner are all subsets of "cognition in its fullness." And in *Intelligence Reframed*, Gardner spends a considerable number of pages distinguishing the mind's cognitive functions from the faculties of morality and emotion, which he recognizes as distinct organizing domains of the psyche. So while Gardner concludes that the lines of development he has studied are relatively separate, he also concludes that the lines he identifies all fall within the cognitive domain, with this cognitive organizing domain being merely a subset of the overall organization of the mind, which also includes a moral and emotional domain. In distinguishing morality and emotion from cognition, Gardner says that he insists "on a strict distinction between being emotionally sensitive and being a 'good' or 'moral' person."[20] This quote shows that Gardner understands the overall organization of the mind as consisting of three different aspects: cognition, emotion, and a moral sensibility, and that the independent lines of cognitive development that Gardner has researched are in fact encompassed by this larger threefold organizing structure. And in addition to Gardner, as we discussed above, Kegan also understands the levels

of consciousness revealed by his research to encompass and contain three primary lines of development, which he calls the "cognitive, interpersonal, and intrapersonal." According to Kegan, the subject-object relationship that makes up an overall "order of consciousness" "organizes cognitive and affective and interpersonal experiencing."[21] Kegan thus occupies a position close to Graves in that he recognizes a given stage of consciousness to be an overall organizing structure that encompasses multiple lines of development. In fact, there are no developmental psychologists who conceive of the mind as being simply a collection of relatively independent lines, as does Wilber.

3) *The conclusion that every research question posed by developmentalists corresponds to a separate and distinct line of development seems unlikely.* After surveying and summarizing the various questions posed by developmentalists to their research subjects, Wilber concludes that each of these questions reveal different "organs in the psyche that specialize in responding to them—multiple intelligences, if you will, devoted to being 'smart' about how to answer life's questions." However, the questions cited by Wilber, such as "What is significant to me?; What do I need?; and What should I do?"[22] could easily be understood as questions about the same thing. Wilber's conclusion that these clearly similar questions in fact reveal relatively independent lines of development seems unwarranted. I do not think that there is a separate line of development for every research methodology, and I think it is possible to recognize a plethora of lines without concluding that these lines are all relatively equal and independent. Further, knowing what we do about the structures of evolution, we would expect to find certain primary lines that each envelope a series of sublines. Thus, in an otherwise legitimate effort to move away from "line absolutism," Wilber seems to be embracing the other extreme in a kind of "line relativism."

4) *The "center of gravity" phenomenon points to a larger enveloping structure that encompasses the multiple lines.* Wilber's comments about a center of psychic gravity, quoted in the previous section, are hard to reconcile with his comments about the separate lines being "apples

and oranges." That is, in Wilber's psychograph model the "proximate self" line is said to be just one among at least a dozen different developmental lines. Yet in his discussion of the center of gravity concept, Wilber says that a person's self-identity line "expresses the sum total of their overall inclinations in all levels and lines." And this suggests that the self line exercises some kind of agency or control over the other lines. However, the psychograph model clearly indicates otherwise.

5) *The idea that consciousness is empty is inconsistent with the idea of the actual structures of consciousness exhibited in the lines of development.* Wilber's assertion "If consciousness is to be conceptualized at all, it is a pure Emptiness" is an expression of his spiritual belief system. And as we discussed in the previous chapter, I have no need to argue with this. I will only point out that if, as Wilber says, "Consciousness is not anything itself, just the degree of openness or emptiness, the clearing in which the phenomena of the various lines appear,"[23] then what do the lines consist of, if not consciousness? In fact, in a footnote to the sentence quoted directly above, Wilber writes, "Cognition is simply a qualified type of consciousness appearing as an actual developmental line ... with its own structure and content." Perhaps Wilber has a way of reconciling these inconsistencies, but this is not made clear in his writing.

6) *A psychograph model that shows only multiple independent lines does not account for the phenomenology of, nor the widely held understanding of, the two basic systems of knowing: thinking and feeling.* In 1995, psychologist and *New York Times* reporter Daniel Goleman published one of the most influential books of the decade called *Emotional Intelligence: Why It Can Matter More Than IQ*. In this book, Goleman marshals considerable scientific evidence that shows how "the folk distinction between 'heart' and 'head'" actually approximates real neurological and psychological structures. According to Goleman:

> In a very real sense we have two minds, one that thinks and one that feels. These two fundamentally different ways of knowing interact to construct our mental life. One, the

rational mind, is the mode of comprehension we are typically conscious of: more prominent in awareness, thoughtful,
able to ponder and reflect. But alongside that there is another system of knowing: impulsive and powerful, if sometimes
illogical—the emotional mind. ... These two minds, the
emotional and the rational, operate in tight harmony for the
most part, intertwining their very different ways of knowing to guide us through the world. Ordinarily there is balance between emotional and rational minds, with emotion
feeding into and informing the operations of the rational
mind, and the rational mind refining and sometimes vetoing
the inputs of the emotions. Still the emotional and rational
minds are semi-independent faculties, each, as we shall see,
reflecting the operation of distinct but interconnected cir-
cuitry in the brain.[24]

As this quote makes clear, there is significant evidence that the
rational mind and the emotional mind are "metastructures" that
organize distinct areas of the psyche. Thus it seems clear from both
Gardner's work and Goleman's work (which Gardner approvingly
discusses in *Intelligence Reframed*) that the overall rational mind and
the overall emotional mind each encompass and contain a variety of
developmental sublines. However, a psychograph model that shows
a dozen different lines, some more rational and some more emotional, but that does not group these lines within, or otherwise take
notice of, the organization revealed by Goleman's "two minds," does
not adequately account for these evident structures.

We will return to our consideration of Goleman's work in the
next section. But this concludes my critique of Wilber's model of
the structures of consciousness. I'm sure Wilber could advance some
interesting counterarguments, but these objections are certainly
worth further consideration.

An Alternative Theory of the Structures of Consciousness

The beauty of Goleman's description of the "two minds" is that it
brings together psychology, neuroscience, and direct personal expe-

rience to provide an explanation of the structure of consciousness that satisfies both scientific sense and common sense. So by combing the work of both Goleman and Gardner, as illustrated in the abstract diagram in Figure 9-3 below, we have a reasonable starting place in our conception of the structure of the mind. Within the spheres of emotion and cognition (and within their overlapping intersection), we can locate a number of important developmental lines or types of mental activity.

As we recognize the spheres of feeling and thinking as meta-structures of the human mind, we must also take notice of how these modes of consciousness are supported by immediate sensory experience on the outside and memory on the inside. But when it comes to the activity of the mind, the general categories of emotion and cognition explain much of what is actually going on. However, as we look at this diagram of the various developmental lines represented as spheres of mental capacity within the larger overall structures of feeling and thinking, we can detect that there is still something miss-

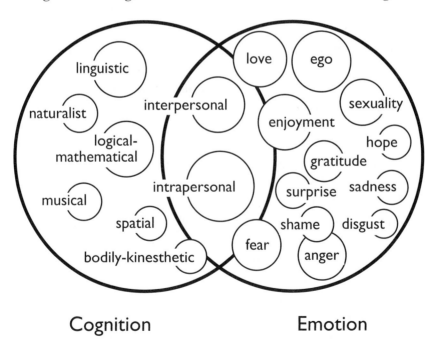

Figure 9-3. Spheres of emotion and cognition, after Gardner and Goleman.

ing. And what's missing are the developmental lines associated with values and morality. As we've seen, research on moral development has been the focus of developmental psychology's most gifted theorists: Baldwin, Kohlberg, Gilligan, Maslow, Graves, and Kegan have all done important work within what we can generally recognize as the sphere of values and morals. Although the work of these theorists covers a wide range of mental activity, all of them have studied values and morals in one way or another.[25] As Gardner makes clear, while there is certainly some overlap between the spheres of emotion, cognition, and morality, the sphere of morality is clearly distinct from feeling and thinking.

So what is the best way to understand and conceptualize the sphere of values and morals? If we are going to recognize a third sphere of development that is similar in structure and function to the spheres of emotion and cognition, then we would expect to find a third "system of knowing." That is, Goleman's most significant contribution is his recognition that "emotional intelligence" is a "way of knowing" that "can matter more than IQ," as his book's subtitle proclaims. But is there a third "way of knowing" that can be compared to feeling and thinking in terms of its overall significance in the organization of the mind? I think the answer is yes. And the structure/function of the human mind that fulfills these considerations is *free will*, the faculty of choice and evaluation—the consciousness of intention. So in this section I'll argue that the primary spheres of the mind—the major lines of development within consciousness—are emotion, cognition, and volition, or simply feeling, thought, and will.

It is only through the exercise of free will that humans can be considered moral agents. And it's only by our choices and by our evaluations that we really come to know morals and values. That is, we can certainly think and feel about values, but we do not really come to know them until we actually choose them. To choose a value is to know what it is like from the inside, to make it our own by our intentional selection. The human will can thus be recognized as a distinct way of knowing—as an *organ of perception for values*. In fact, every choice, no matter how trivial, always involves an inherent determination of relative goodness. If one makes a real choice, even if this choice is between the "lesser of two evils," such a choice evidences the assessment that one alternative is "better" than another. Even though the choice of "better" can be made according to a wide variety of value criteria, an exercise of will inevitably involves an evaluation—if there is nothing to value, then there is nothing to choose. Thus even a bad choice or a wrong choice constitutes an act of valuation, although a faulty one.

Yet unlike emotion or cognition, volition—free will—is a highly metaphysical concept. Unlike the structures of feeling or thinking, will has not yet been located as a definite structure in the brain. Thus Gardner correctly recognizes that while free will is real, it constitutes a subject that is beyond the reach of the sciences. In fact, materialist philosophers have gone to great lengths to try to show how the idea of freedom of choice is merely an illusion. The scientific worldview is embarrassed by its inability to explain the mysterious notion of uncaused causation that underlies the apparent phenomenon of free will, so as with all metaphysical subjects, materialistic philosophers simply deny that it exists. These thinkers maintain that preexisting physical, biological, and cultural forces ultimately predetermine all human choices. However, while every choice is certainly influenced (and while some "choices" are actually coerced) by outside factors, whether we believe in free will or not, we all *inevitably presuppose in practice* that we have freedom of choice, we really can't act otherwise. And this is a marker of the essential truth that humans indeed have relatively free will.

If we consider free will from the perspectives of the developmental psychologists, we find additional support for the idea that volition can be understood as a sphere of mental activity that is comparable to the spheres of emotion and cognition. For example, Gardner clearly recognizes that free will is the primary determiner of moral development, writing that "the central component in the moral realm or domain is a sense of personal agency." Gardner believes that morality is properly a statement about "the exercise of one's will."[26] And like Gardner, in his discussion of emotional intelligence and morality, Goleman recognizes the significance of what he calls "character," which he says was "in a former day called will." According to

Goleman, it is the will or character that supplies the "psychological muscle that moral conduct requires." He quotes Thomas Lickona for the proposition that: "It takes will to keep emotion under the control of reason."[27] And it is in this crucial sentence where we see that, with Gardner, Goleman likewise recognizes the three essential spheres of mental development to be feeling, thought, and will.

But does the will also develop? Maslow clearly thought so. In *Motivation and Personality*, he writes:

> Finally I must make a statement even though it will certainly be disturbing to many theologians, philosophers, and scientists: self-actualizing individuals have more "free will" and are less "determined" than average people are, However the words "free will" and "determinism" may come to be operationally defined, in this investigation they are empirical realities. Furthermore, they are degree concepts, varying in amount; they are not all-or-none packages.[28]

Indeed, like emotion and cognition, most of us have had the experience of the development of volition as a faculty of our minds.[29]

Many (if not most) philosophers have also recognized will or intentionality as a central factor in the life of the mind. According to the influential German philosopher and psychologist Franz Brentano (1838–1917), all genuinely mental states are intentional, and all genuinely intentional states are mental. Brentano's ideas are underscored by integral theorist Allan Combs, who writes: "Consciousness is always *about* something. ...In other words, consciousness always has a point. In formal terms it is said to be *intentional*. Something is *intended* by it. ...Intentionality is dynamic. Like a polarizing magnetic field that draws iron filings into formations of multiple ellipses, consciousness aligns the processes of the mind into patterns with direction and purpose."[30]

In addition to the thinking of philosophers and psychologists, we can also find support for the idea that feeling, thought, and will are the primary organizing structures of the mind in some religious traditions. According to Wilber biographer and integral theorist Frank Visser:

Inspired by Hindu sources, the theosophical literature describes consciousness as having three aspects: will, thought, and feeling (or, in Eastern terminology, *sat, chit, ananda*). Western psychology seems to be exclusively interested in the intellect, is reluctantly beginning to pay attention to emotion, and shows absolutely no interest in the will; a true integral psychology will need to honor all three aspects. This view of consciousness maintains that spirituality can be attained via the line of the will (*karma yoga*), the line of the intellect (*jnana yoga*), and the line of feeling (*bhakti yoga*). Theosophy even goes as far as to suggest that these are the three fundamental lines of development by means of which consciousness evolves.[31]

Now, my spiritual path has followed neither Hinduism nor Theosophy, so I was unaware of what these traditions had to say on the subject when it first became evident to me that consciousness was organized around the lines of feeling, thought, and will. So I was obviously pleased to learn that the significance of these structures had been previously recognized by these traditions.

But from the perspective of integral philosophy, as we try to discern the basic organizing structures of the mind, we are ultimately led back to Baldwin, who saw it all clearly in the beginning. Baldwin was explicit in his recognition that "the three great modes of mental function" are "intellect, will, and feeling."[32] Thus, with Baldwin (together with the other numerous thinkers in different cultures throughout the centuries who have also seen this truth), we are on solid ground in our recognition of this threefold overall organizing structure. We can use other words to label these general overlapping functions of the mind, but there is good evidence, both structurally and phenomenologically, for the recognition of feeling, thought, and will as the primary lines or spheres of development within consciousness. Each of these primary spheres or lines of development contain sublines, but like all holonic structures, these subsystems are transcended and included by larger enveloping structures (i.e., each sphere as a whole), which also exhibit a developmental progression in themselves. That is, all the various sublines of consciousness exhibit a self-similar pattern of stage-wise progression that mirrors the stage-wise progression of the larger lines of which they are a part. And this self-similar mirroring of the part and the whole is, of course, a common pattern found in many evolutionary structures from fern leaves to blood vessels.

Once we recognize that the metastructures of emotion, cognition, and volition are the primary lines or spheres of evolving consciousness, we can begin to see how these subjective spheres are shaped and influenced by both objective and intersubjective structures. That is, our consciousness is formed not only by our body and our brain, but also by the culture in which we live. And as we have discussed throughout this book, like our body and brain, our evolving culture also has a systemic structure—the structure of the spiral of development. This intersubjective structure serves to guide, orient, and direct the subjective structure of our will through its influence on our value choices and agreements. By serving as a major influence on our volitional sphere of consciousness, by providing the values that our will desires and pursues, the spiral becomes a significant structure within our consciousness as a whole. Although this dialectical structure of history is not made out of gray matter, it nevertheless has a profound effect on the mind.

Within the sphere of human volition, the values that serve as the locus of our attention and the focus of our intention find their origin primarily within the worldview systems in which we participate. For example, if your consciousness is influenced primarily by the postmodern worldview, if postmodernism is your center of gravity, then it is almost certain that your heart will desire things like a sense of like-minded community, personal growth and development, natural foods and products, and a world at peace. Conversely, if your center of gravity is rooted in the modernist worldview, your determination may be focused on things like class mobility and wealth, physical fitness, and the academic success of your children.

We have seen how most people in the developed world participate in more than one value system, so it is not uncommon to find people who aspire to both modernist and postmodern values. But regardless of the actual values a person may hold, those values almost always find their origin within one or more of these worldview systems.

In chapter 3 we saw how these successive stages of consciousness and culture evince a tendency to alternate dialectically between individualistic and communitarian orientations as the spiral of development is ascended. And we can perhaps observe that those centered within the communally oriented stages are somewhat more subject to being externally influenced by the values of their community. But even people who are centered within more individualistically oriented worldviews, as well as those who are motivated more by intrinsic or internal sources rather than by external rewards, nevertheless find that their desires and aspirations are in fact mightily influenced by the goodness, the truth, and the beauty they see around them in the world (including all of the subtle shades and combinations that are subsumed within these primary values). As we explored in chapter 6, the values of beauty, truth, and goodness do serve as the "eternal images" that influence the evolution of consciousness at every level. And we have also seen how these general values are made relevant and applicable in the way that they are contained, conditioned, and adjusted to local life conditions by each of the systemic structures of consciousness and culture that make up the spiral of development. That is, the universal "value directions" of beauty, truth, and goodness actually *gain traction* upon the human will as they are adapted and translated by the historically significant worldview systems that have evolved in relation to the specific circumstances of a given time in human history. And it is in this way that the evolutionary attractors we recognize as values "gently persuade" the human will to make the choices that cause it to evolve.

However, as illustrated in Figure 9-4 below,[33] the worldview stages of the spiral serve as more than just the source of our values—our cultural worldview also strongly influences a number of different lines of development that can be found within the sphere of volition, including our sense of morality, personal identity, and group belonging (to name only a few). For instance, if your psychic center of gravity is postmodern, you will probably dress like a postmodernist (personal identity) and relate best to your own "tribe" of other postmodernists (group belonging). Moreover, your estimates of right and wrong will be strongly colored by postmodern sensibilities (morals). For most people, the worldview that guides and directs their will can be clearly observed to have a significant and pervasive influence on almost every aspect of their lives. And this is perhaps why the "worldview or values line" appears to measure our overall state of existence, as Graves and Kegan conclude.

Once we understand how the primary structure of the mind arises from the three distinct but overlapping domains of feeling, thought, and will, we can reconcile the appearance of an "overall

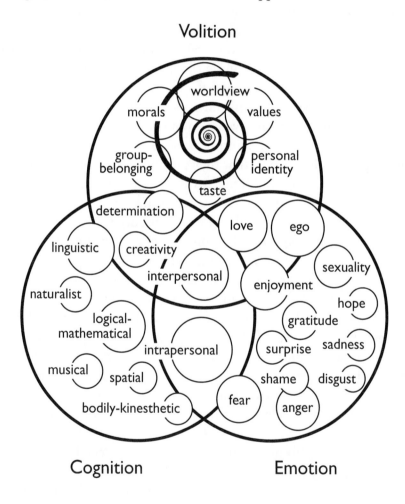

Figure 9-4. The spiral's influence on consciousness through its effect on the lines of development within human will.

state of existence" or "center of gravity" with the simultaneous observation of uneven development among the different lines. Once we understand that the spiral structure is not merely one among a dozen factors, but a primary influence on our will, which is at least a third of our overal consciousness, we can begin to solve the puzzle of line independence identified by Wilber without resorting to the rather disjointed conception of mental structure represented by his psychograph model.[34]

Even though emotion and volition cannot be smoothly conceptualized as formal types of intelligence similar to the varieties of cognition identified by Gardner, we can nevertheless recognize the degree of a person's relative development in emotional sensitivity, and we can also recognize the relative development of their worldview along the spiral of development. And this leads to the idea, introduced in chapter 3, that the "quotient" or degree of development among the three primary lines can be loosely understood as *EQ, IQ,* and *VQ.* The idea of VQ provides a way to conceptualize the development of our ability to evaluate; it serves as a measure of our moral center of gravity, as well as the stage of culture with which we identify ourselves. EQ is the measure of our emotional sensitivity and the strength of our empathy and intuition. And IQ, after Gardner, can be understood as a profile of the various lines of our cognitive development considered together.

But to this you might say, how can IQ (or the others for that matter) be a measure of evolution? Isn't IQ a genetic predisposition fixed at birth? And my answer is that although there are some aspects of IQ that are inherited, there are others that can clearly be developed. As an example from my own life, after three years of law school, there was no question that my cognitive abilities had been strengthened and that my IQ had increased in some very real ways. It has also been demonstrated that "emotional intelligence" can likewise be learned and developed. Goleman cites a variety of research and education programs that have achieved significant success in raising the emotional intelligence and emotional literacy of both children and adults.[35] And when it comes to the will, we can see how self-discipline, self-determination, and the quality of our decisions all develop as our will grapples with life's dilemmas. Like EQ and IQ, "willpower" has a partially predetermined genetic basis, but also as with EQ and IQ, no matter where we start out biologically, we can clearly evolve our values and strengthen our will. VQ can thus be recognized as both a measure of the strength of a person's convictions and values (no matter where they are developmentally) and as a gauge of their "time in history" relative to the developmental stages of consciousness.

Although most people do not experience significant vertical movement along the spiral once they reach adulthood, as we've seen, there have been times in history when large demographic segments of a population have adopted new value systems and produced new levels of cultural evolution. And it is just this sort of evolutionary growth—just this advance in VQ—that integral philosophy seeks to produce in our time.

As I have argued in this chapter, like all naturally evolving structures, the structure of the mind is holarchic. It consists of a whole-part hierarchy wherein its subsystems (its multiple lines of development) are transcended and included within larger enveloping structures, which I have identified as the spheres or modes of feeling, thought, and will. However, the holarchy does not end there. Just as the many lines of development are transcended and included by the primary modes of consciousness, these modes are themselves unified within the larger holon of the self as a whole. In fact, no model of consciousness can be complete without a clear recognition of the overall self. We thus conclude our discussion of the structures of the human mind with a brief examination of the structure of the self.

The Self as a Whole

Although the subject of the self has been investigated and described by many psychologists and philosophers, there is little general agreement among them as to what the self really is. This is because it is not really possible to understand the nature or the structure of the self without bringing in spiritual explanations. This is why every discussion of the self either quickly becomes spiritual or quickly comes to an end due to its unwillingness to acknowledge the self's essential spirituality. Complicating the matter further is the fact that different forms of spirituality understand the self differently. Integral philosophy thus does well to approach this subject modestly, leaving the primary description of the self to the realm of religion. Nevertheless, once we recognize that consciousness takes form around a multiplicity of developmental lines, and once we see how these lines are contained within a larger encompassing system organized by the three essential categories of feelings, thoughts, and intentions, we can anticipate that these three types of knowing will themselves be unified within a larger overall system identified as the self. Accordingly, I believe integral philosophy can describe certain aspects of this self-system, even as it allows for a plurality of definitions of the spiritual aspects of selfhood.

As we consider the structure and function of the self relative to human consciousness as a whole, we need to keep in mind Wilber's definition of "adequate structuralism," which requires that we take account of both the third-person and the first-person perspectives of any internal structures we may be examining. From a first-person perspective, there seems to be little question that we all generally experience our own consciousness as a unified whole. Although this unity can become divided, as when our feelings and thoughts conflict, all mentally healthy people generally have a sense of themselves as a whole self. The unity that we all experience from a first-person perspective thus provides evidence that there is an overall self that unifies the various developmental lines and modes of consciousness. And we can also expect that this self-structure can be seen and understood from a third-person perspective as well. That there is a unifying holon of the overall self is also suggested by our understanding of the systemic nature of consciousness—as with all evolutionary systems, it is inevitable that as consciousness evolves, the many (the primary lines and their constituent sublines) will become one and will be increased by one (the self).

So in order to complete our model of the major spheres of developing consciousness, we can locate the self (or at least one aspect of it) in this model within the overlapping intersection of these three

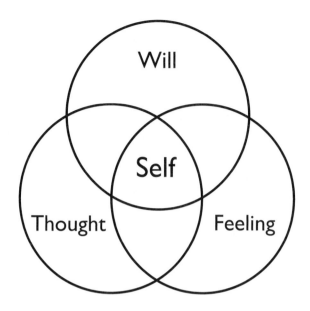

Figure 9-5. The holonic structure of the self and its primary spheres of development.

spheres, as illustrated in Figure 9-5.

As Wilber has observed, although each of the primary lines of mental development show the distinct pattern of growth by stages, the overall self as a whole does not generally exhibit such stage-wise growth. So it would be a mistake to try to locate the "whole self" along any monolithic or absolute line of development. But I think we can observe that, as a *holon*, the self has an *agency* that is centered around the will, and a *communion* that finds its connection to other people largely through the emotions. Moreover, while the self does not develop by stages, the self does have a definite "location" in culture that can be understood as the profile of the lines of development considered together. And this internal location of the self can be recognized as a person's overall "center of gravity." The center of gravity concept helps us recognize that although the lines of development can exhibit degrees of developmental independence, they are also clearly influenced by the "gravity" of the self's general intersubjective location. In fact, when a person's lines of development become unevenly developed, this inevitably creates the kind of internal psychic dissonance that leads either to further development, or to a crisis or breakdown, as we might anticipate in the case of some "Nazi doctors." Thus, not only can a person's center of gravity be determined by reference to the overall profile of their development lines, but a person's lines of development are themselves influenced by that person's overall center of gravity. And as we can see throughout history, as new worldviews emerge, they not only produce evolutionary development in people's feelings, thoughts, and intentions, they also move the center of gravity of entire cultures.

However, the idea of "the self" in its fullness includes not only the overall encompassing self illustrated in the diagram above, but also lesser and greater kinds of self. Here we can recall Wilber's definition of the self which recognizes three essential aspects of selfhood: a proximate or personal self (the "I"), a distal or separate self (the "me"), and a higher self (the indwelling spirit). If we consider these three aspects of self from the theoretical perspective just described, we find the "proximate self" in the position of the overall holon of the self. As we have noted, this holon of the overall self serves to unify and integrate experience. It does not develop by stages, but its internal intersubjective location can change as the lines it contains evolve and their developmental profile changes. Conversely, the distal self or "me" is the aspect of the self that identifies with, and is connected to, the various developmental lines (primarily, but not exclusively, with the will). It is through our distal self that we invest our identity in the worldview stages and in our cognitive or emotional life. This is thus the aspect of self that becomes objectified and transcended as one stage is left behind and another stage of development is achieved; it is the process described by Kegan through which *"the 'I' of one stage becomes the 'me' of the next."*[36] Therefore, although the proximate self does not develop by stages, the distal self (that is embedded within the lines) clearly does.

But in addition to the overall self, and the separate or temporary self, we can also recognize the "higher self," which is known in Buddhism as the *Buddha Nature*, in Hinduism as the *Atman*, and in the Bible it is often referred to as the *Still Small Voice*. According to my understanding, the higher self is the fragment of infinite spirit that lives within us. This seed of spirit in our personality does not change or grow, because it is not "a thing of this world." But here I'm describing my personal beliefs, and I recognize that this goes beyond the bounds of integral philosophy as I'd like to define it. Nevertheless, many forms of spirituality practiced by integralists do recognize that the mind has a connection to spirit and that the higher self is real. However, I think it's best to leave it to these various forms of spirituality to define respectively exactly what the higher self is and how it works within the mind.

There is obviously more to the structure of the human mind than what I've described here. But as we've seen, there is a significant amount of evidence which suggests that this threefold pattern of feeling, thought, and will does in fact exist as an actual organizing structure of the mind. And this internal mental structure can be recognized as an expression of an even larger organizing pattern that influences evolution in every domain of its unfolding. So in the next and final chapter we'll look more closely at this larger organizing pattern to see how it reflects the overall direction and process of evolution as a whole.

10

The Directions of Evolution

ACCORDING TO THE FAMOUS RENAISSANCE SCIENTIST SIR FRANCIS Bacon, "A little science estranges a man from God; a lot of science brings him back." And I think Bacon's insight applies as much to the subject of evolution as it does to science itself. As we discussed in chapter 6, as our worldview grows wider and deeper, it becomes increasingly evident that the story of evolution in nature, self, and culture has unmistakable spiritual implications. Indeed, it is hard to deny that evolution's advance from the isolated atoms of hydrogen gas to the blue jewel of planet earth, then from single-celled prokaryotes to the first self-conscious humans, and then finally from the first humans to the twenty-first century's global civilization, is an astonishing odyssey of development, a magnificent production of form and diversity, and an unfathomable outpouring of creativity. The spiritual message of evolution was not lost on Alfred Russel Wallace, the English naturalist who discovered the process of natural selection independently and contemporaneously with Darwin. Writes Wallace:

> These three distinct stages of progress from the inorganic world of matter in motion up to man, point clearly to an unseen universe—to a world of spirit, to which the world of matter is altogether subordinate. ... We, who accept the existence of a spiritual world, can look upon the universe as a grand consistent whole adapted in all its parts to the development of spiritual beings capable of indefinite life and perfectibility.[1]

Among the many astonishing features of evolution, that which makes its essential spirituality most evident is its inexhaustible creativity. The significance of evolution's boundless display of creativity was well appreciated by Alfred North Whitehead, who wrote:

> "Creativity" is the universal of universals characterizing ultimate matter of fact. It is that ultimate principle by which the many, which are the universe disjunctively, become the one actual occasion, which is the universe conjunctively. It lies in the nature of things that the many enter into complex unity.[2]

And as evolution "enters into complex unity," we can see its spiritual quality not only in the creative *products* or forms of evolution, but also in the creative *process* of evolution as a whole. So in this chapter we'll examine evolution's overall process, and we'll consider the essential direction or directions of evolution's advance. Understanding where evolution is headed is a central inquiry for a philosophy that defines itself in evolutionary terms. But questions about of the directions of evolution's unfolding are not just relevant to integral philosophers; properly understood, these questions relate to every situation in which the need for improvement can be recognized. And as it now becomes increasingly necessary for humanity to participate in guiding cultural evolution toward a more positive future, knowledge of evolution's essential methods, techniques, and directions is of critical importance.

We begin our discussion with an examination of what science has revealed about the unfolding of evolution. Our intent is to honor science by making sure that nothing we conclude about evolution as a whole contradicts or negates science. But as we make sure that our inquiry rests on scientific foundations, we will also need to distinguish the facts of evolutionary science from certain materialistic philosophies that have become closely associated with these facts. As we will discuss, in the last few decades a variety of scientists have claimed that science has now proven that evolution is completely random and meaningless, that it does not progress, and that the products of evolution are essentially accidental. Integral philosophy, however, can clearly see how this is not the case through its broader, more inclusive understanding that comes from its ability to see evolution at work in both the internal and the external universe. In other words, when we begin to see the common habits and methods of evolution in all of its domains at once, we can then begin to discern the larger organizing pattern that is the shape of the process of evolution as a whole. And it is through this effort to discern the overall movement of evolution as a whole that we begin to behold the glimmers of spirit that underlie every instance of evolutionary progress. Indeed, if there really is spirit in this universe, then the all-encompassing, ever-present activity of evolutionary development can be accordingly recognized as the universe's essential form of spiritual practice.

Evolution and the Idea of Progress

Evolution is a scientific fact. There is no doubt that life has evolved over the last three and a half billion years from single-celled prokaryotes to the wide diversity of species that populate the earth today. There is also no doubt that the process of natural selection—the mechanism through which random genetic mutations that are favorably adapted to environmental pressures are perpetuated, thereby producing change in an organism's form over generations—has been a central factor in the origin of species. Integral philosophy's account of evolution rests on these facts. However, we have seen how these facts of evolution have been used not only for scientific purposes, but also for the cultural purposes of undermining the authority of premodern worldviews by showing how the reality-framing creation stories of these worldviews are false. And from an integral perspective this has been evolutionarily appropriate. In fact, modernism's struggle to break the all-encompassing grip of religion and to overcome the myths and superstitions of traditionalism is clearly not over, as the continuing battle between creationism and evolutionism attests. But even as science fights the good fight of evolving beyond traditional religious explanations of our world, many scientists have unwittingly made the theory of evolution into a belief system of their own. In the course of its battle with traditionalism, neo-Darwinism has been expanded by a variety of popular science writers in ways that make it seem like the same kind of dogmatism it seeks to combat. Darwin's spectacular presentation of the scientific facts of evolution has spawned the development of a materialistic philosophy of evolution that has sought to extend the theory of evolution beyond its objective facts so as to serve as a complete explanation of the universe. In the course of their cultural mission of undermining the authority of traditional religion, neo-Darwinists have claimed that their philosophy of evolution—their metaphysical interpretation of evolution—is itself a simple and straightforward presentation of scientific facts which prove that evolution has no direction, no purpose, and no meaning.

Thus, because the line between science and philosophy has been blurred, it becomes necessary to emphatically state that science by itself cannot prove that evolution has no meaning or that it is simply random and without purpose. The process of natural selection may make use of chance and random mutation, but this fact is not a scientific proof of evolution's meaninglessness. In fact, science as such is not qualified to determine whether something has a larger meaning (or no meaning); this is the job of philosophy. Scientific materialists are certainly entitled to argue for a philosophy which claims that the universe is a random accident. But they are not entitled to claim that this pessimistic philosophy of the universe is the only one supported by science. As we will see in this chapter, the scientific facts of evolution can also be shown to be consistent with a philosophy that recognizes meaning, direction, and purpose in the evolutionary process.

One of the most fundamental questions raised by science's investigation of evolution is whether it progresses. Neo-Darwinians have generally eschewed the idea of "higher" or "lower" forms of evolution, claiming that such ranking involves a value judgment that has no part in the scientific discourse. The very idea of progress in evolution has been attacked by a number of prominent scientists, including biologist Stephen Jay Gould, who argues that the only legitimate criterion for progress is the effectiveness of an organism's adaptation to its local environment, and by this criterion, the most progressive organisms are bacteria because they have shown themselves to be the most successful at adaptation. Following this reasoning, many in the scientific community claim that a major triumph of the modern evolutionary synthesis has been the removal of outdated ideas about direction, progress, or increasing value in natural evolution. Advocates of scientism argue that the science of evolution has shown how undirected forces, blind and unintelligent, are the *sole* causes that have produced the order we observe in biological systems, and that this proves that evolution is not progressive. Thus while they maintain that science cannot make value judgments about higher and lower, neo-Darwinians are perfectly willing to claim the status of "science" for their value judgment that there is no value in evolution.

However, despite the attempt to eliminate any notions of progress from the scientific understanding of evolution, many biologists do continue to recognize *advancing complexity* as an unmistakable form of material progress. The well-known scientific materialist E. O. Wilson states this case as follows:

> It is, I must acknowledge, unfashionable in academic circles nowadays to speak of evolutionary progress. *All the more reason to do so.* In fact, the dilemma that has consumed so much ink can be evaporated with a simple semantic distinction. If we mean by progress the advance toward a preset goal, such as that composed by intention in the human mind, then evolution by natural selection, which has no preset goals, is not progress. But if we mean the production through time of increasingly complex and controlling organisms and societies, in at least some lines of descent, with regression always a possibility, then evolutionary progress is an obvious reality.[3]

Thus after we have weeded out the assertions of atheistic philosophies, we find that science does recognize at least one direction of evolution's progress, and this is the direction of expanding systemic complexity, or an increase over time in the number of functional parts in any given system. Humans are more complex systems than bacteria, and this evident increase in complexity is a direction of evolution that many scientists are willing to acknowledge. The progressive nature of increasing complexity is well articulated by Erich

Jantsch, who writes: "The evolution of the universe is the history of an unfolding of differentiated order or complexity. ... Evolution acts in the sense of simultaneous and interdependent structurization of the macro- and the micro-world. Complexity thus emerges from the interpenetration of processes of differentiation and integration."[4] Systems scientists like Jantsch have generally been more willing than neo-Darwinian biologists to recognize evolutionary progress; in fact, some prominent systems scientists have actually celebrated it. For example, Ervin Laszlo writes:

> Among the foreseeable characteristics of development are increasing coordination of formerly relatively isolated entities, the emergence of more general patterns of order, the consolidation of individuals in superordinate organizations, and the progressive refinement of certain types of functions and responses.
>
> In evolution there is a progression from multiplicity and chaos to oneness and order. There is also progressive development of complex multiple-component individuals, fewer in number but more accomplished in behavior than the previous entities. Evolution does go one way rather than another, and keeps on going that way as long as it does not come into conflict with basic physical laws. ... We cannot see how evolution could fail to push toward organization and integration, complexity and individuation, whatever forms it may choose for realization.[5]

Laszlo is one well-respected scientist who has been willing to look beyond the prejudice against the idea of evolutionary progress that infects many in the scientific community. And his statements in the quote above are based on three decades of research in general evolution theory. In his conclusions about the "characteristics of development," Laszlo identifies the progressive unfolding of not only "complexity," but also the progression of "integration." And from this we can begin to see that material evolution advances in more than one direction only. Laszlo's quote brings out a characteristic of evolutionary development that is not adequately described as "increasing complexity," and this is the countervailing force of increasing *unification*.

Unity, Complexity, and Consciousness

As evolution advances and organisms become more complex, this accumulating complexity results in an increasing interdependence among the system's components. In other words, the more complex a system becomes, the more it needs to hold together its complex parts in ways that require a significant degree of integration. For a system or structure to maintain integrity in the face of greater complexity, it must become more unified—each part of the system must work together with a large number of other parts, and together with the system as a whole. For example, a squirrel is a more unified system than a starfish. We can cut off the leg of a starfish, and not only will the starfish grow a new leg, but the old leg will grow a new starfish. However, if a squirrel is deprived of one of its legs, it will almost certainly die from starvation (in its natural environment), if not from the wound itself. This is because mammals, being more complex systems than echinoderms, require greater degrees of systemic unity for their existence. The parts of the system are more interdependent—each part is absolutely necessary for the proper functioning of the system.

Part of the confusion that has caused many scientists to privilege complexity as the primary descriptor of evolution's progress may have come from the fact that *within* the overall process of complexification we can observe the two forces of differentiation and integration. Complexity appears to subsume these two forces within itself, which is brought out in the quote above from Jantsch, who sees complexity emerging "from the interpenetration of processes of differentiation and integration." On the other hand, the quote by Laszlo describes how increasing complexity itself is actually balanced by the complementary force of increasing integration. This apparent contradiction can be reconciled when we see how the pattern of the two basic forces of differentiation and integration is a self-similar pattern that occurs both within the levels and across the levels. In other words, as will become more clear as our discussion unfolds, the master patterns of evolution are manifested across the scale of the universe from the micro to the macro. And like many other features of evolutionary development, the interpenetrating forces of differentiation and integration can be seen functioning in both the part and the whole.

However, it is perhaps predictable that in their estimates of the significance of the two identifiable evolutionary forces of complexification and integration scientists would privilege complexity because their primary tool is analysis. Science goes about understanding the complex world by breaking it down into its parts, by analyzing a system through its components. Science is good at recognizing and analyzing complexity, so it naturally sees complexity as "the fundamental principle of the development of pattern." But science is not as good at recognizing unity as it is at recognizing complexity. And this is because (as we will see below) recognizing unity is primarily the job of art, and not the job of science.

As another example of increasing unity in evolution, consider the artful unity of the higher mammals. What makes the higher mammals more evolved is not just their greater complexity, but also the way they exhibit greater unification. Cats, for instance, are not just more complex than frogs, they are also more graceful, more refined, more elegant, and more beautiful. And these expressions of feline beauty arise more from the singularity or unity of what it is to be a cat than from any attributes of a cat's evolutionary complexity—the grace is not in the parts, it is in the coordinated functioning of the whole. So we can perhaps see that as evolution advances, its forms exhibit not only greater complexity but also greater unity—not just more "partness" but also more wholeness.

Thus, as the systemic forms of chemical and biological evolution develop over time, a clear trend can be observed in the general increase in both the overall complexity and the overall unity of these systems. In fact, the ubiquitous presence of these two basic forces was recognized early on by Herbert Spencer, who, as we noted in chapter 7, provided a definition of evolution that still holds today: "Evolution is a change from an indefinite, incoherent homogeneity, to a definite, coherent heterogeneity; through continuous differentiations and integrations."

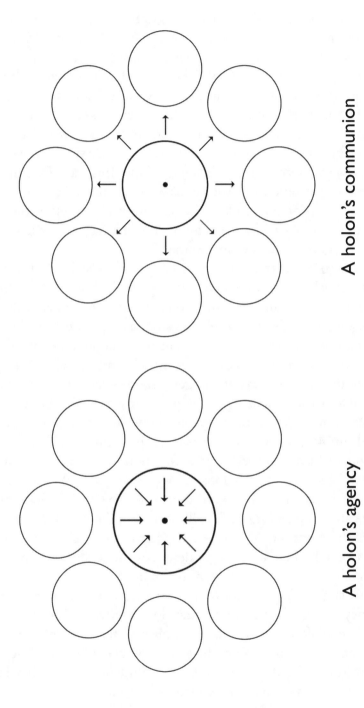

A holon's communion

A holon's agency

Figure 10–1. Holonic agency and communion.

The way evolution functions through the interpenetrating forces of unity and complexity becomes particularly evident within the understanding of evolutionary development provided by the theory of holons. In chapter 8 we briefly discussed systems science's recognition of the ubiquitous pattern of organization seen in physical, biological, and cultural evolution wherein every system, every evolutionary form, functions within a hierarchy of *systems embedded in systems.* The theory of holons recognizes how every system is a *whole* that is always already a *part* of a larger whole. This way of seeing the systemic organization of evolutionary development has become a cornerstone of integral philosophy because it ties together the different domains of evolution at a foundational level by revealing what all forms of evolution have in common.

But how is it that every evolutionary system is able to function simultaneously as both a whole and a part? As Wilber and others have explained, the answer is that every evolutionary system exhibits both *agency* and *communion.* As illustrated in Figure 10-1 on the previous page, each whole-part holon is an autonomous whole in itself—this is its *agency,* its drive toward self-unity or wholeness; yet every system is also a part of a larger system—this is its *communion,* its drive to participate in a greater complexity beyond itself.

According to these theorists, not only can we see these drives toward unification and complexification within each individual holon, we can also see the manifestation of these forces within multilevel hierarchies of holons known as *holarchies.* Within every holarchical system can be found the twin drives that Wilber (after Plato) calls "*Eros* and *Agape.*" As illustrated in Figure 10-2 opposite, Eros is the tendency of every systemic level to "reach up from the lower to the higher," and Agape describes the tendency of higher-level holons to "reach down from the higher to the lower."

This simple diagram shows the force of unity as the universal tendency of higher levels to embrace lower levels, and it shows the force of complexity in the equally universal tendency of the entities of each level to combine to form new encompassing levels of organization—the drive identified by Whitehead through which "the many become one, and are increased by one."[6]

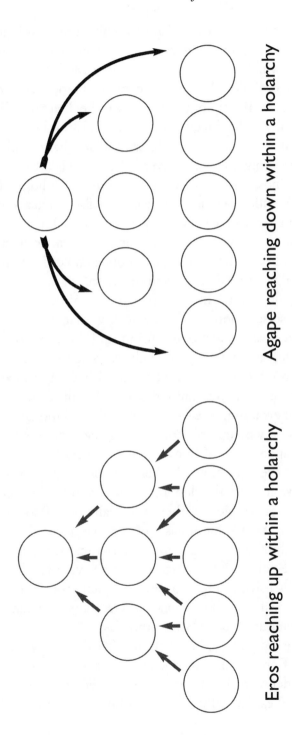

Agape reaching down within a holarchy

Eros reaching up within a holarchy

Figure 10–2. Holarchic eros and agape.

This illustration of the forces of Eros (reaching up toward greater complexity) and Agape (reaching down toward greater unification) shows how these twin drives are simply another way of describing the overall advance of evolution through the combined processes of *transcendence and inclusion*. Put simply, complexity is the direction of transcendence, and unity is the direction of inclusion. Even though these processes can be intermittent and nonlinear, and are always subject to pathology or regression, they have nevertheless managed to produce our bodies, our minds, and this marvelous world we call home. Thus, through this examination of what scientists have discovered about the process of evolution, we can see how development unfolds through the combined outworking of two basic forces, forces that can be described alternatively as differentiation and integration, complexification and unification, or simply transcendence and inclusion.

However, in addition to the "interpenetration of these two processes," we can also see another "obvious reality" that is rarely mentioned as a progressive product of evolution, and this is *consciousness itself*. Consciousness is generally ignored by the scientists who study evolution for two reasons: because of science's inability to explain subjective phenomenon, and because the inclusion of consciousness in any estimate of evolution reveals unmistakable evolutionary progress. In fact, it is only by ignoring or denying the evolutionary significance of the appearance of human consciousness that scientists have been able to even question whether evolution is progressive or not. But when we include the development of mind or consciousness in the evolutionary picture, there can really be no doubt that evolution has progressed—that it has produced a sequential series of organisms that exhibit increasing degrees of awareness, and that this in itself constitutes an objective increase in value over time. In other words, it is only by leaving consciousness completely out of the picture that neo-Darwinist philosophers can credibly avoid acknowledging that humans are "higher" than amoebas.

However, integral philosophers have not failed to recognize that the production of organisms with increasing degrees of consciousness is clear evidence of evolution's progress. For example, we've noted how Whitehead actually defined evolution as "an increase in the capacity to experience what is intrinsically valuable." Teilhard similarly recognized the inseparability of the growth of complexity and the growth of consciousness in his famous "law of complexity-consciousness," which maintains that these two terms are simply the inside and the outside of the same essential pattern of growth. Yet Teilhard also understood the way increasing complexity works in partnership with increasing unity to produce organisms with increasing degrees of awareness.[7]

Thus, when we include the growth of mind within our assessment of evolutionary development, we can actually see *three* major trends or products of evolution's advance—increasing unity, complexity, and consciousness. As illustrated in Figure 10-3 below, without violating any scientific principles, and without resorting to any kind of metaphysics, we can see that material evolution (in at least some lines of development) has produced systems that exhibit increasing integration, differentiation, and sentient subjectivity.

Although scientists centered in modernist consciousness often fail to recognize these three essential elements of evolution, these organizing principles are more clearly visible to scientists who have

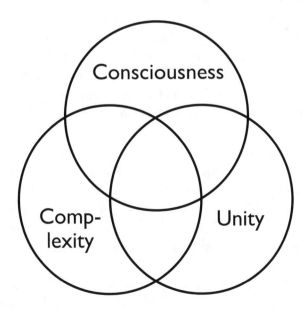

Figure 10-3. Products of material evolution.

attained a postmodern perspective, and who are thus better able to discern these larger cosmological patterns. An example of such "postmodern science" can be found in the influential 1992 book *The Universe Story*, in which cosmologist Brian Swimme and historian Thomas Berry weave together the latest science into a coherent narrative of the long sequence of transformations, beginning with the Big Bang, that have led to the development of the universe, planet earth, and human consciousness. By carefully observing and evaluating the scientific evidence, Swimme and Berry identify the essential dynamics of evolution that are embodied in what they call the *Cosmogenetic Principle:*

> The Cosmogenetic Principle states that the evolution of the universe will be characterized by differentiation, autopoiesis and communion throughout time and space and at every level of reality. These three terms— differentiation, autopoiesis and communion—refer to the governing themes and the basal intentionality of all existence, and thus are beyond any simple one-line univocal definition. … Some synonyms for differentiation are diversity, complexity, variation, disparity, multiform, nature, heterogeneity, articulation. Different words that point to the second feature are autopoiesis, subjectivity, self-manifestation, sentience, self-organization, dynamic centers of experience, presence, identity, inner principle of being, voice, interiority. And for the third feature, communion, interrelatedness, interdependence, kinship, mutuality, internal relatedness, reciprocity, complementarity, interconnectivity, and affiliation all point to the same dynamic of cosmic evolution.
>
> These three features are not "logical" or "axiomatic" in that they are not deductions within some larger theoretical framework. They come from a post hoc evaluation of cosmic evolution; these three will undoubtedly be deepened and altered in the next era as future experience expands our present understanding.
>
> The sequence of events in the universe becomes a story precisely because these events are themselves shaped by these central ordering tendencies—complexity, autopoiesis

and communion. These are the cosmological orderings of the creative display of energy everywhere and at any time throughout the history of the universe.[8]

Let's pause and reflect on the significance of this quote. As Swimme and Berry recognize, these "governing themes" of evolution, which I am calling unity, complexity, and consciousness, and which they call communion, differentiation, and autopoiesis (together with other synonyms), represent a very important teaching about the nature of the universe. Although these authors' understanding of what they call the "central ordering tendencies" of evolution is not informed by the clarifying perspective of integral consciousness, they have nevertheless come very close to describing the threefold character of evolution's overall master pattern.[9]

Although *The Universe Story* may not be a definitive scientific text, it is certainly more than mere New Age speculation—the authors attest that the threefold nature of evolution's "basal intentionality" has been discovered through a "post hoc evaluation" of the facts of science. However, we don't have to take their word for it; I trust our discussion so far has also shown how evolution develops through increasing differentiation and integration, how the results of the outworking of these two forces is increasing consciousness, and how this is perfectly evident to anyone willing to consider the patterns of evolutionary development.

Swimme and Berry's discernment of a "Cosmogenetic Principle" is thus an idea I want to adopt, modify, and explore further, because we can see this principle at work not only in the external universe of chemistry and biology, but also in the internal universe of consciousness and culture. So throughout the rest of this chapter we will expand and develop the idea of this Cosmogenetic Principle to see how its "governing themes" apply to the larger understanding of evolution advanced by integral philosophy. Because at this point we have really only begun our exploration of evolution's directions (both in this chapter and in integral philosophy in general). And as these authors presciently state: "These three will undoubtedly be deepened and altered in the next era as future experience expands our present understanding."

Accordingly, now that we have a basic grasp of what integral philosophy can discern within science's disclosure of the patterns of evolution in the external universe, we can begin to explore the outworking of this threefold Cosmogenetic Principle within the evolving internal universe. And this brings us back to an examination of the structures of evolving consciousness which we discussed in chapter 9.

Directions of Evolution in the Internal Universe

It is worth repeating here that in this investigation of the directions of evolution, my goal is to present a philosophy that carefully builds upon science, but which includes the internal universe of consciousness and culture within the purview of its investigation. So now that we've seen how the products of material evolution, when considered together as a whole, suggest principles which, according to Swimme and Berry, are "the cosmological orderings of the creative display of energy everywhere and at any time throughout the history of the universe," we are ready to see whether this Cosmogenetic Principle holds true in the internal universe as well as the external. Recall that in chapter 9 on the "Structures of the Human Mind" we examined the scientific evidence presented by Daniel Goleman that there are "two minds, one that thinks and one that feels" and that these two minds operate by "intertwining their very different ways of knowing to guide us through the world." Additionally in chapter 9, we saw how cognition and emotion are not the whole story of the human mind; volition or free will is also a central feature. In fact, the operation of free will is a major function of consciousness that has been widely recognized by thinkers throughout the centuries who have considered the subject.

So with this in mind, perhaps we can now begin to see the parallels between the development of nature and the development of self. In the external universe we can see how two material forces—differentiation and integration—intertwine to produce structures that generally exhibit increasing degrees of awareness or consciousness. Similarly, within the evolving domain of consciousness itself, two types of neurological activity can be seen interacting within subjective awareness, and out of this interaction (or somehow closely related to it) there arises the third and distinct aspect of intentional volition, through which the human mind is directed. And as we further consider the similarities between the objective evolution of biology and the subjective evolution of human consciousness, we can also see that the third element in both cases is of a different order than the other two elements. That is, increasing complexification and unification are clearly observable physical trends, but consciousness, although observable, is not physical. Although science does not generally account for consciousness in its estimates of evolutionary progress, few scientists deny that it exists or that it is indeed a product of material evolution. But as we've also noted, biologists generally ignore consciousness because it is *in* the body, but it is not entirely *of* the body—consciousness transcends the objective systems of biology through its extension into the subjective domain of evolution. Likewise, within the evolution of subjective consciousness itself, we can identify the scientifically observable features of emotion and cognition, together with a third feature that is not directly accessible to science. Now, this third feature, this *uncaused causation* of free will, is, as we have discussed, a thoroughly metaphysical reality. Yet like consciousness, free will is undeniable to all but the most ardent materialist fundamentalists. And as I argued in the last chapter, this is because free will is *in* the mind but not entirely *of* the mind—the value choices of free will are shaped not only by the subjective structures of consciousness but also by the intersubjective structures of evolving human culture.

In light of these arguments it becomes possible to see how there is something very similar behind the basic characteristics of both internal and external evolution. As illustrated in Figure 10-4 below, unity and complexity interact in the course of advancing objective evolution to produce biological forms containing minds that are increasingly aware. Then, with the appearance of self-reflective human mind, this threefold pattern of evolution continues within the subjective realm wherein emotion and cognition interact to produce forms of consciousness that contain volitional will that is increasingly free.

These nested diagrams are not intended to suggest that the Cosmogenetic Principle is some kind of deterministic mold, only that

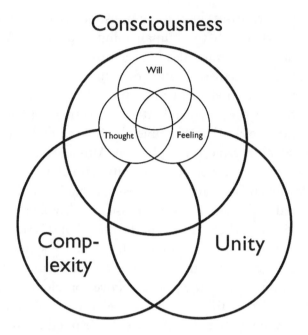

Figure 10-4. External and internal expressions of the Cosmogenetic Principle.

these observable patterns do reveal faint traces of the larger currents of a progressive universe.

But as you know by now, this is not the whole story. The evolution of individual organisms or individual minds always proceeds in relationship with a community. As Wilber has shown, not only is the inside connected to the outside, but the individual is also connected to the social and cultural. However, when we extend our investigation of the directions of evolution beyond the realm of objective biology and subjective consciousness to look for these larger patterns of growth within the intersubjective domain of human culture, we must acknowledge that we are leaving science behind and relying exclusively on the arguments of philosophy. And this is because the structures of cultural evolution are not the products of *natural selection*, but rather the products of *actual selection*—they are the results of the outworking of the human will. Nevertheless, although the trends of cultural evolution are not as well evidenced as the trends of mental and biological evolution, it is possible to detect the influence of the Cosmogenetic Principle even within the evolution of human culture.

Toward this end, in this section of the chapter we will explore the conclusions of a variety of thinkers regarding the direction or directions of cultural evolution. In this analysis, we will find that some of the most widely respected scholars who have considered this subject have indeed detected a threefold influence that appears to be shaping the development of human societies. And this threefold influence within culture becomes easier to see when we examine both the inside and the outside of collective human development together as a whole. Moreover, when we then compare the inside and the outside of collective human cultural development with the inside and outside of individual human development (as we have already explored), the influence of the Cosmogenetic Principle becomes even more evident.

We begin our inquiry by briefly considering two recent books, both written by scientifically minded authors, and both coming to similar conclusions about the direction of cultural evolution. The first is the 2000 publication, written by the American journalist Robert Wright, entitled *Non-Zero: The Logic of Human Destiny*. In this book, Wright employs game theory to show how human cultures continually devise ways to cooperate, and how in the long run this cooperation inevitably produces a non-zero-sum gain in the form of progress and cultural evolution. According to Wright: "When you look beneath the roiled surface of human events, beyond the comings and goings of particular regimes, beyond the lives of the 'great men' who have strutted on the stage of history, you see an arrow beginning tens of thousands of years ago and continuing to the present. And, looking ahead, you see where it is pointing."[10] Similarly, in the 1999 book *Evolution's Arrow: The Direction of Evolution and the Future of Humanity*, Australian economist John Stewart argues that the direction of cultural evolution is toward increasing human cooperation. According to Stewart: "Evolution progresses by discovering ways to build cooperative organisations out of self-interested individuals."[11] While I agree with the conclusions of both these authors that increasing cooperation is an observable direction of cultural evolution, this is not the only direction or even the main direction. It seems clear that as culture progresses, *cooperation interacts with competition*, and that both of these forms of relation are necessary for a healthy society. Can there be any doubt that competition as well as cooperation has produced advances in culture? The "space race" between the United States and the Soviet Union comes to mind as a recent example from history. And from a personal perspective, many of us have experienced how competition has helped us achieve greater academic or athletic excellence. As we will explore further below, understanding how dualities such as competition and cooperation work together as a system is one of the central insights of the Cosmogenetic Principle properly understood. In the process of evolution, when either side of a duality becomes privileged or over-extended, pathology results. This does not mean, using our example, that competition and cooperation must be equally balanced, but rather that they need to be understood together through the lens of the third synthetic element that unifies the system and causes it to transcend the apparent duality. Thus, while increasing cooperation is clearly a direction our culture needs to grow toward, characterizing cultural progress as the unidirectional advance of cooperation is an overly simplistic understanding of the dynamics of evolution.

However, we find a clearer recognition of the process of cultural evolution in the writing of famous German sociologist Max Weber. Weber dedicated his scholarly life to understanding how the astounding evolution of the culture of modernity was achieved. Writing in the early twentieth century, Weber recognized that during the Enlightenment, in the process of rationalization and secularization, different aspects of the once-monolithic religious culture of Europe became separated and differentiated into three distinct "value spheres," which he identified as *art, science,* and *morality.* As a result of their societal differentiation into three distinct spheres of endeavor, science, art, and political organizations were liberated from the constraints of the Church and were able to achieve new progress by following their own inner logic. The differentiation of these cultural value spheres allowed science, morality, and art to be judged not according to "religious correctness," but according to the now better understood categories of "truth," "justice," and "beauty," respectively. Weber thus built upon Kant's critical analysis of human thinking in terms of pure reason, practical reason, and aesthetic judgment by showing how the spectacular achievements of modernism were actually brought about by the emergence of separate realms of cultural development, which allowed for the fuller expression of these three essential aspects of human thought.

Weber's philosophy of cultural evolution has influenced a wide variety of writers, and most notably Jürgen Habermas, whose recognition of these three "differentiations of modernity" has featured prominently in his work. Following Weber and Habermas, Wilber has also made use of the concept of these three value spheres in his depiction of the historical evolution of modernist consciousness. Wilber, however, has extended the concept by showing how this initial differentiation became distorted in the twentieth century as science came to dominate and colonize the other spheres, rendering a healthy differentiation into a pathological dissociation.

Now, unlike the rather evident unfolding of material evolution in the directions of unity, complexity, and consciousness, or the similarly evident differentiation of the structures of consciousness into feeling, thought, and will, this characterization of the structures of cultural evolution as science, art (or more properly, aesthetics), and morality is not as well evidenced. We can employ physics and biology in our recognition of the directions of objective evolution, and neurology and psychology in the recognition of subjective evolution, but as we have noted, our understanding of the directions of intersubjective evolution can be confirmed only through philosophical insight. However, we can certainly use the apparent correspondence between the objective, subjective, and intersubjective domains to strengthen our argument. And this correspondence between the threefold character of the objective and subjective development of individuals and the threefold character of the collective evolution of culture becomes easier to see when we recognize that, like the development of individuals, cultures also have an inside and an outside. That is, once we understand the significance of the internal value spheres of aesthetics, science, and morality, this suggests an elegant correspondence with the development of the external artifacts of *art, technology,* and the *human organizations* that make up our society. As we discussed in chapter 8 (and as we explore further in Appendix B), although these external artifacts are not natural, self-organizing systems of evolution like the entities of the other domains we're discussing, the development of these objective artifacts does reveal the character of the underlying natural systems from which they arise.

So let's briefly consider the evolution of each of these spheres of collective development—*aesthetics-science-morality* on the inside, and *art-technology-organizations* on the outside—to see whether these lines of advance do indeed reflect the outworking of the Cosmogenetic Principle. There is certainly no doubt that science and technology constitute a significant direction of cultural and societal evolution; and whether this has been good or not is something we discussed in chapter 3. It also seems clear that human organizations—political, economic, religious, and social—have demonstrated undeniable progressive development in human history. Whether the development of these external societal institutions corresponds to the internal development of a culture's morality is obviously a complex subject, which I won't address here. However, the external evolution of political organizations (at least in developed countries) has definitely resulted in both greater freedom and an increased recognition of human rights. Few would argue that the emergence of democracy throughout the globe does not constitute moral evolution. However, when it comes to aesthetics and art, unlike the evolution of science and technology, or the evolution of morality and human organizations, the evolution of aesthetics and art (with the idea of "art" being defined as generally as possible to include fine art, music, architecture, entertainment, styles, etc.) is not always as easy to recognize. But when we remember that the most dramatic examples of cultural evolution are produced through the emergence of historically significant new worldviews, aesthetic progress becomes easier to see. For example, when the traditional worldview reestablished itself across Europe during the eleventh and twelfth centuries, it was accompanied by the aesthetically significant emergence of Gothic art and architecture. Similarly, modernism's European beginnings were marked by the fresh art of the Renaissance, and later by the classical music of the Enlightenment. And music also played a crucial role in the emergence of postmodernism in the 1960s, as we have discussed. Newly emerging, historically significant worldviews always arise in connection with new aesthetic sensibilities and new forms of art.

Thus when we consider all the domains of evolution together, when we look for the directions of evolution within each dimension of its advance using Wilber's quadrant model (illustrated in Figure 10-5), we can begin to discern the faint traces of a pattern emerging. As the diagram below shows, the three-term Cosmogenetic Principle can now be recognized in the inside and the outside of both the individual and the collective dimensions of evolution. And this four-quadrant description of the Cosmogenetic Principle brings our understanding of the outworking of evolution full circle from objective biology, through subjective consciousness, then through

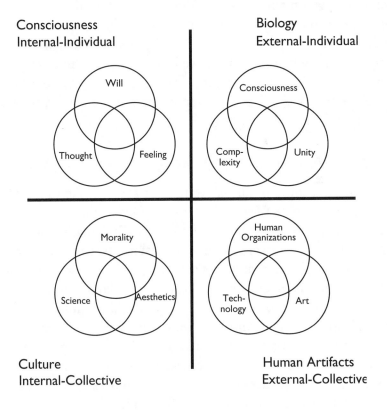

Figure 10-5. Directions of evolution in each quadrant.

intersubjective culture, and then finally back to the objective manifestations of material civilization.

Obviously, examples of regression and pathology can be found in all of these trends. Moreover, we can identify other institutions of society that do not fall squarely within these categories. Religion, for example, cannot be completely subsumed within the category of morality. But as we look for the primordial influences at the heart of all evolution, traces of these shaping forces can definitely be found within the collective development of culture and society. As Whitehead recognized, "Science, art, religion, and morality, take their rise from this sense of values within the structure of being."[12]

So although there is no conclusive proof that this threefold pattern is actually serving to organize or otherwise influence evolution in every domain of its unfolding, it seems to me that this is an intriguing proposition, which if true, could usher in a new era in our understanding of how the universe progresses. When we consider evolution as a whole, and when we begin to discern ubiquitous patterns such as the Cosmogenetic Principle, this inevitably has the positive effect of guiding us in our efforts to produce further evolution in our lives and in our world.

The Dialectical Quality of the Master Patterns of Evolution

So if we are willing to allow, even if just for the sake of argument, that there is a master systemic pattern of evolution that is shaping the contours and character of evolution in each domain of its unfolding, what can we discern about this pattern as a whole? Swimme and Berry employ a variety of synonyms in their description of the Cosmogenetic Principle, but their analysis is largely limited to the external universe. However, when we now add the insights of integral philosophy, which disclose evolution in the internal universe, the recognition of these internal manifestations of the pattern allows us to see its overall form more accurately and more completely. And as we begin to consider both the internal and external expressions of the Cosmogenetic Principle, the first thing that becomes apparent is the pattern's dialectical character. Integration and differentiation, feelings and thoughts, art and science—these categories clearly exhibit contrasting or opposing tendencies. We can also discern a certain sequence in their priority. In the dialectical movement, before something can be a part, it must first be a whole—although they work together as a system and unfold simultaneously, we can perhaps sense how integration precedes differentiation in a subtle way. Similarly, evolving consciousness exhibits feelings before it develops thoughts, and in culture the arts generally appear before the sciences. And, of course, these contrasting poles of development are always in relationship with a third element, which we have identified as consciousness in the body, free will in the mind, and morality in the organization of culture. Just as the first two elements suggest the dialectical relationship of thesis and antithesis, each of these third elements reveals a synthetic or transcendental quality. As we've discussed, consciousness is *in* the body but not entirely *of* the body, free will is *in* the mind but not entirely *of* the mind, and morality is generally recognized as being more important than either aesthetics or science.

The characterization of evolution's dialectical movement through the use of the three terms "thesis, antithesis, and synthesis" has been criticized as a "vulgarization" of the dialectic's subtlety. It has been pointed out that the reduction of the dialectic into three separate terms suggests a mechanical process, or that the explication of this triad somehow implies that these contradictions come from outside of things. However, we can make effective use of the idea of thesis, antithesis, and synthesis if we keep in mind Hegel's explanation of how the dialectical tension between thesis and antithesis is internal and inherent in the very nature of things and beings. That is, in a universe populated by imperfect, partial entities, we can almost always find an existential conflict resident in the separation between the real and the ideal. And it is out of the intrinsic energy of the inherent tension of this conflict that systems of development arise.

One of the most important things to keep in mind about this apparent dialectical pattern of universal development is that it is a *system*. That is, just as every naturally occurring form of evolution is a system, the process of evolution as a whole can, through this broad philosophical understanding, be recognized as a kind of master dialectical system. And in order to make this claim more apparent, I'd like to examine the outworking of this master system of evolution across a spectrum of analysis in the following concluding arguments. On one end of the spectrum we'll consider this systemic pattern in its most abstract form through an examination of the geometry of the relationships exhibited in the interaction of its three basic terms. Then on the other end of the spectrum, we'll consider the implications of this pattern in its fullness by discerning how the Cosmogenetic Principle points to evolution's overall purpose and goal.

Every relationship suggests a geometry. Whenever two or more entities interact or communicate, their exchange casts a shadow that falls in the abstract realm of mathematics. However, as we examine the relationship geometry of the Cosmogenetic Principle's three terms, we need to keep in mind that the following mathematical description of evolution's dynamics creates a distortion. Modeling the Cosmogenetic Principle with a three-dimensional map is like trying to describe a sphere with a circle. Nevertheless, the oversimplification of this geometrical abstraction does provide some insight into how the system works.

In our discussion of holons and holarchies above, we noted how every evolutionary system exhibits both agency and communion. And we saw how these twin holonic drives exhibit a correspondence with the larger overall tendencies of integration and differentiation. Thus, considered geometrically, these two forces of holonic cohesion suggest an *inward pull* toward wholeness emanating from the center of every holonic system, which is balanced by an *outward pull* that compels every holon to become part of something larger, to participate in a level of organization more complex that its own. As illustrated in Figure 10-6 opposite, if we think of these influences in terms of unity and complexity, we can see how unity can be expressed abstractly as the pull from the center, and complexity as the pull on the circumference or boundary of every evolutionary system. The direction of complexity is continually reaching out to encompass more, to produce organisms and organizations with more and more complex parts, whereas the direction of unity keeps making each individual part as complete as possible.

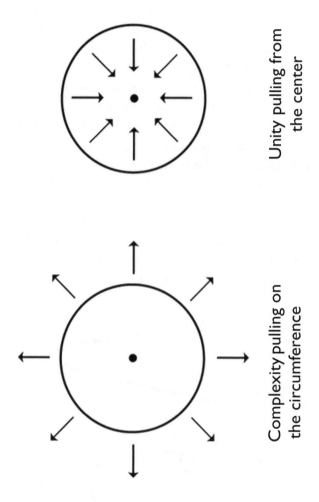

Unity pulling from
the center

Complexity pulling on
the circumference

Figure 10–6. The opposing forces of holonic organization.

But how do we overcome this duality? How do we reconcile the inherent conflict found in these opposing evolutionary forces? Well, we move in a direction not contained in the conflict, we transcend to a new level, or in this illustration, we move to a new dimension. The only way to transcend the opposing forces of part and whole is to move beyond them in a way that includes them both on their own terms. Thus as illustrated in Figure 10-7, this two-dimensional opposition is transcended through a third-dimensional movement whose form continues to be shaped by the influences of both opposing forces. In the diagram below, as the curve of the spiral grows outward, its extension responds to the influences of increasing complexity. Yet as it expands, the spiral also continually curves in on itself, yielding its outward extension to the inward gravity of its center and thereby exhibiting the influence of the abiding unity that gives it form. This diagram suggests the technique whereby evolution achieves the transcendental movement that originates *in* a given domain but which is not actually *of* that domain. Evolution as a whole thus exhibits the continuous ability to transcend the duality of conflict and the limitations of any given container by moving in the direction of an entirely new domain.

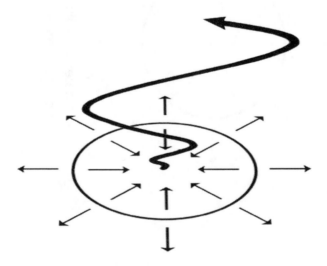

Figure 10-7. The geometry of inclusive transcendence.

And this logarithmic spiral pattern is, of course, a simplified geometric model of the dialectical relationship of thesis, antithesis, and synthesis. The opposing forces of unity and complexity are synthesized through a transcendental movement that resolves the conflicting duality inherent in every "incomplete" situation by moving in the direction of a new level. As we are beginning to see, evolution's advance is never unilinear; progress emerges at every level through the interplay of two opposing forces that produce (and are produced by) the continuous improvement achieved through their synthetic transcendence.

However, before we go too far in these universal conclusions, let's consider the other end of the spectrum of possible interpretations of the Cosmogenetic Principle. As we've just discussed, when the directions of evolution are understood in their most minimal, mathematical expression, they appear to unfold through a simultaneous pull from both the center and from the circumference of every form of universe organization. And as we've also discussed, evolution harmonizes these opposing forces through its continuous transcendence to new levels. But in contrast, when the directions of evolution are considered in their most maximal, spiritually robust expression, they can be recognized as the different ways that the forces of the universe are striving for improvement, striving to make things better, striving for what can, in the fullness of its natural extension, be recognized as a striving for *perfection*.

As we will now explore, viewed with the eye of spiritual discernment, the primordial influences at the heart of the evolutionary impulse begin to appear as the *directions of perfection*. As Whitehead recognized, within the deepest dynamics of evolution we can perceive "the urge towards the realization of ideal perfection." And as we explored in chapter 6, this overall urge toward increasing perfection is itself differentiated into the three "eternal forms" of the beautiful, the true, and the good. Beauty, truth, and goodness are the lures of perfection, the subtle spiritual *attractors* behind all forms of evolutionary development.

The existential connection between the beautiful, the true, and the good and the dialectical directions of evolution's advance is evidenced by the kinship that these values share with the differentiated expressions of evolution found in each of the domains of development we've discussed. In other words, within each of the distinct domains of objective, subjective, and intersubjective evolution, we can discern a different aspect or phase of the expression of the primary values. *Unity-complexity-consciousness, feeling-thought-will,* and *aesthetics-science-morality*—each kind of evolution reveals this threefold striving for perfection in different ways. And it is by seeing how beauty, truth, and goodness are manifest in each domain through this process that we are led to a deeper understanding of these values, and of perfection itself.

So let's briefly consider how each of the primary values finds expression in the distinct domains of evolution, starting with the value of beauty. Although beauty cannot be reduced to the material patterns of unity, although beauty is not simply integration, beauty's kinship with "the pull from the center" can definitely be recognized. Beauty often arises from the different kinds of unity that find expression in the material world such as *symmetry, harmony, proportion,* and *self-similarity.* Even *originality* can be understood as a form of unique wholeness or individuality—a form of unity—that is often recognized as beautiful. These different forms of unity all exhibit beauty in their own way, but beauty's essentially spiritual quality renders it elusive to any fixed pattern. Beauty's primordial influence upon evolution can also be seen as an organizing principle in the realm of feelings and aesthetics. While beauty is certainly not the only value for these realms, it is clearly a central element. As we consider the role of the primary values as "attractors of evolutionary development," it is important to remember that in every vital expression of beauty, truth, or goodness, each value contains and discloses the others. As the early integralist Pitirim Sorokin observed:

> Though each member of this supreme [value] Trinity has a distinct individuality, all three are inseparable from one another. ... The genuine Truth is always good and beautiful. ... Goodness is always true and beautiful; and the pure Beauty is invariably true and good. These greatest values are not only inseparable from one another, but they are trans-

formable into one another, like one form of physical energy, say, heat, is transformable into other kinds of energy, electricity or light or mechanical motion.[13]

As we consider the spiritual implications of evolution's dialectical striving for perfection, we can see how the primordial influence of beauty occupies the position of the *thesis* (or the tentatively completed beginning of the dialectical movement) in the way that beauty gives us a fleeting glimpse of relative actual perfection. As we discussed in chapter 6, the extent to which something is beautiful is the extent to which it is relatively complete; its evolution can proceed no further. Although it is often possible to make something more beautiful, our perception of the beauty itself arises from our intuition of the way that something exhibits the faint traces of perfection. It is worth repeating here that the feelings of pleasure that accompany the experience of beauty come from the temporary relief of the relentless background pressure caused by the subtle compulsion of the incomplete—the pleasure of psychic rest arises from a beauty experience as the need to improve things is briefly satisfied.

And just as beauty reveals the thesis of relative *actual* perfection, the value of truth occupies the position of the dialectical *antithesis* in the way that it represents the *potential* for relatively *more* perfection. That is, truth can be expansively understood as the direction of progress by which subjective consciousness can increase its understanding of the realities of the objective and intersubjective realms that are external to it. According to Hegel, "the true ... is merely the dialectical movement."[14] This insight of Hegel's helps us see that just as beauty serves to define the present good, truth helps to define the future good, which we all strive for. That truth is a *direction* can best be appreciated by remembering that truth is always relative, that it is always tied to the understanding of a subject who is himself growing and developing. Subjective consciousness thus grows in truth as it increases the relative perfection with which it knows that which is outside itself—even as it increasingly recognizes the relative and contingent nature of its expanding perspectives. However, knowledge of the truth includes not only an understanding of "what's out there," but also the knowledge of "how to get there." The goodness of truth—the usefulness of truth—is seen in the way that its possession provides the power to improve things (and the power to avoid mistakes). The quest for truth (defined in this way) can thus be recognized as the drive to achieve greater relative potential perfection. Just as beauty (working within the realms of feelings, aesthetics, and material unity) can be understood as the appearance of what is relatively actually perfect, truth can be contrastingly understood as the recognition of what can be potentially more perfect. The "direction of truth"—as it is pursued in our thinking, in our science, and in the unfolding of increasing complexity—can thus be envisioned as *the way forward*, the direction of evolution's potential for increasing perfection.

So now we come to the value of goodness. And as we consider this value in the context of the other primary values, and in the context of evolution's overall progress, it is important to keep in mind that we are here engaged in a philosophical attempt to discern the movement of spirit in the world. In our efforts to glimpse the realities of spirit with the use of simple terms such as beauty, truth, and goodness, these words quickly overflow with more meaning than they are capable of holding. Even the use of numerous synonyms pointing to different aspects of these dialectical directions of evolutionary progress provide but an inkling of insight into how the universe is moved by the perfect nature of spirit. And when it comes to the idea of evolving goodness, these linguistic limitations are compounded. Nevertheless, most will agree that objective evolution's production of organisms that are increasingly aware, subjective evolution's production of human will that is increasingly free, and intersubjective evolution's production of cultures that are increasingly moral all provide clear evidence of a trend toward the good. Obviously, countervailing regressions or stagnations in the development of all these domains can be cited, but this does not negate the fact that increasing consciousness, free will, and morality are evident products of the evolutionary process.

Goodness occupies the position of the *synthesis* in the way that it defines the useful limits of beauty and truth, in the way that it mediates between the maximum extension of inclusion and transcendence relative to each other. That is, as we've seen, evolution precedes though the interplay of opposing forces, and when either of these opposing forces is privileged or extended too far, the result is pathology. The avoidance of such pathology in any developmental situation is achieved by finding the dynamic equilibrium, the right relation, that brings these dialectical forces together in progressive, synthetic harmony. Goodness is thus revealed as it contrasts with the pathology it seeks to avoid.

The way that the countervailing forces of beauty and truth provide content for the synthetic advance of goodness is well articulated by Whitehead:

> The factor in human life provocative of a noble discontent is the gradual emergence into prominence of a sense of criticism, founded upon appreciations of beauty, and of intellectual distinction, and of duty. The moral element is derivative from the other factors in experience. For otherwise there is no content for duty to operate upon. There can be no morality in a vacuum.[15]

From this perspective, the synthetic character of the good, which finds its expression through the harmonization of whole and part, self and other, thesis and antithesis, inclusion and transcendence, and beauty and truth, can be more fully appreciated. And as we've seen, this dialectical relationship can be illustrated as the systemic motion of a logarithmic spiral, as shown in Figure 10-8 below.

In light of these arguments, if we can recognize how the beautiful, the true, and the good do act as subtle compass headings of universal improvement, we may then ask: What are the causal mechanisms through which these value attractors actually influence evolutionary progress? How do these ideals exert a gravitational pull on evolutionary systems? The most obvious answer is that these ideals influence the *choices* of subjective consciousness. In chapter 6 we discussed how the primary values, as specifically translated into goals and mores by each historically significant worldview, serve to generally define the overall directions of improvement, regardless of the assessor's psychic location. The way that evolution influences our choices, stimulating our *perfection hunger*, our appetite for intrinsic value, is well understood by David Ray Griffin, who writes: "We are attracted to Beauty, Truth, and Goodness because these values are entertained appetitively by the Eros of the universe, whose appetites we feel."[16] And through this understanding we can begin to see how evolutionary progress in the internal universe comes about as a result of "gentle persuasion through love."

But what about the rest of life, how is it influenced by these value attractors? According to prominent evolutionary biologist Lynn Margolis, "Life is matter that chooses."[17] And the outworking of the choices of biological systems can be seen in two significant areas that point to the "gravity" of the primary values in the realm of life. The first is simply the choice to survive. Survival value can be recognized as a primitive form of goodness for which all life evidently strives. But beauty is also a value that is apparently accessible to a wide variety of life forms through their evident power of sexual selection. The aesthetic sense required for the selection of the "most beautiful" mate does not depend upon intellectual development, as evidenced by the way that even the most primitive life forms discriminate for markers of biological fitness in the selection of their reproductive partners. Darwin himself recognized the functioning of this aesthetic sense in animals, writing: "I fully admit that it is an astonishing fact that the females of many birds and some mammals would be endowed with sufficient taste for what has apparently been effected through sexual

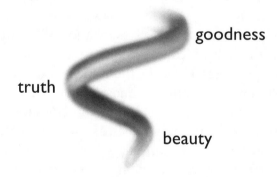

Figure 10-8. The dialectical relationship of the beautiful, the true, and the good.

selection; and this is even more astonishing in the case of reptiles, fish, and insects."[18]

Now, as I mentioned above, integral philosophy is just beginning its exploration of the directions of evolution. Just as it required three hundred years for Enlightenment science to master the mysteries of the external universe (and there is obviously still much that remains unexplained), it will likewise require further development for integral consciousness to understand the "physics of the internal universe" in greater fullness. But at this point we can begin to detect the outlines of this Cosmogenetic Principle as it is seen functioning in each of the domains of evolution we've discussed. And we can also detect the self-similar quality of this master evolutionary system in the way that it shapes evolution not only in each domain, but also in the *containing structure* of these domains. That is, the threefold pattern of the Cosmogenetic Principle can be recognized in the integral worldview's reality-framing conception of nature, self, and culture as a whole. Thus, in light of our discussion it becomes possible to see how the objective, subjective, and intersubjective character of the developing universe is itself a reflection of evolution's dialectical advance toward increasing perfection. As illustrated in Figure 10-9 below, the directions of development that can be seen unfolding in each *part* of evolution's manifestation, can also be seen in the character of evolution as a *whole*.

As we consider the recurring patterns of this threefold Cosmogenetic Principle, it must be emphasized that the description of evolution in terms of these various three-part systems provides only a snapshot of a moving, developing process. In every case, the nature of these elements is more like a *whole together* than it is like three separate parts. But although these elements always share a systemic unity, it is in their differentiation that we see the system in action. The beautiful, the true, and the good; the objective, the subjective, and the intersubjective; and even the thesis, the antithesis, and the synthesis are like musical tones within an octave. They form each other, containing each other in harmonic relation. These differentiated elements are thus merely like the notes of the score; the actual music is found in the play of spirit in the world as it strives to achieve perfection in time. Integral philosophy's dialectical understanding of evolutionary development merely tunes our ears so as to better hear the melodies inherent in the universe's creative process.

It is important to state again that in our attempts to discern the larger cosmological currents of our developing universe, as humans we can only glimpse faint traces of spirit's role in evolution. The primordial influences at the heart of the evolutionary impulse are not subject to being understood as mechanical or physical forces. And it is unlikely that those who ignore or deny the realities of spirit will be able to detect the way that spiritual gravity pulls us toward greater states of completion. But for those who can experience spirit, this spiritual philosophy

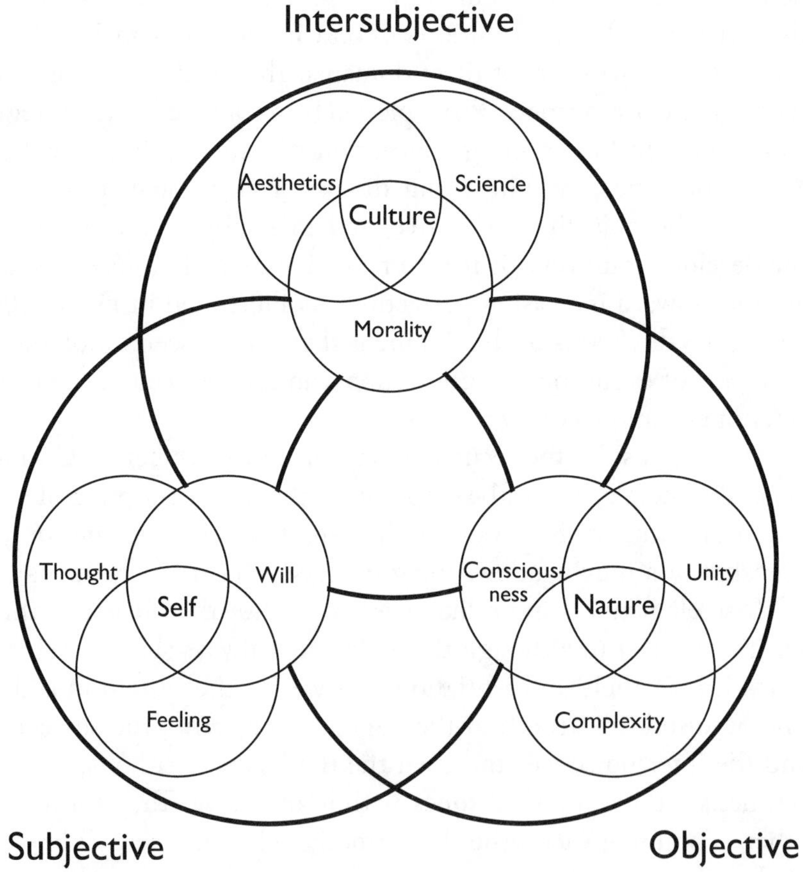

Figure 10-9. The self-similar patterning of evolution's Cosmogenetic Principle in nature, self, and culture.

of evolution can serve as a "natural supplement" to a wide variety of spiritual cosmologies. That which is behind the apparent threefold nature of evolution's systemic character can be explained differently by various spiritual traditions. But if those who follow different spiritual paths can find philosophical agreement about the spiritual nature of evolution, this can help us partially overcome the limitations of polite spiritual pluralism, and it can even help us make progress in our efforts to harmonize science and spirituality.

Are the parallels between advancing *unity-complexity-conscious-ness, feeling-thought-will,* and *aesthetics-science-morality* too fanciful or abstract? Does the description of these patterns overgeneralize the way that evolution actually unfolds? Am I trying to force-fit the staggering diversity and originality of evolution into simplistic conceptual molds that suggest a pattern that is not really there? These are always good questions to ask when one is trying to describe a universal pattern or system that is said to characterize "the creative display of energy everywhere and at any time throughout the history of the universe." And I have certainly asked myself these questions many times in the course of my investigation of these larger cosmological currents of evolution. However, the more I use this philosophical recognition of the Cosmogenetic Principle as a lens of understanding, the more the pattern becomes apparent through the useful results produced by its application.

Potential Applications of a Dialectical Understanding of Evolution

After considering Figure 10-9's diagram of the tripartite nature of evolution's structure and function, in the spirit of pragmatism you may ask: If this is true, what's it good for? What are the potential applications of this aspect of integral philosophy? How can an understanding of the dialectical directions of evolution be used to actually make things better?

The most obvious application of dialectical philosophy is something we all do instinctively in the process of being in relationship. For example, in a marriage, a healthy relationship is achieved when the couple's mutual best interest is found through the balance of the needs of the self and the needs of the other. In an intimate relationship pathology can occur through either selfishness (too much thesis) or codependence (too much antithesis). Thus in any human relationship, the correct relation between self and other is found by reference to the *transcendent purpose* of the overall health of the relationship as a whole (the synthesis), which is ultimately in the best interest of both parties. While this approach to a healthy relationship may at first seem mundane and already evident without the use of any fancy philosophy, seeing how such a common situation partakes of a larger universe process helps us remember that it is not just a middling compromise we're after, but rather an improved condition in which both original positions are exalted and transformed in the process of being transcended.

However, the most exciting and rewarding application of integral philosophy's new understanding of the dynamics of evolution is found through the use of the spiral of development as a method of raising consciousness. As we've discussed throughout this book, knowledge of the systemic and dialectic behavior of the spiral actually opens our eyes to the realities of the internal universe. It allows us to clearly see each historically significant type of consciousness (together with the perceived life conditions that animate each of these worldviews) both in the minds of our fellows and in the institutions of our society. And with this new vision accrues the power to act and communicate in ways that provide creative solutions. In chapter 4, in the section entitled "Practicing the Integral Lifestyle— Value Metabolism," and also in chapter 6 in the section entitled "The Practice of Beauty, Truth, and Goodness," we discussed a variety of specific examples.

Those with the ability to make meaning at the level of integral consciousness will, for the foreseeable future, be among a small minority. Thus in almost every situation in which we may find ourselves in the world at large, we will be with others whose centers of gravity are resident in older worldviews. And in every one of these situations we will have the opportunity to raise consciousness in both subtle and dramatic ways. When we begin to metabolize the values of the spiral as a whole, when we begin to make meaning from the level of integral consciousness, we become endowed with the skill that motivates us to help uplift the values held by others. This skill comes from the enhanced solidarity, empathy, and compassion for the worldviews of others that is a defining characteristic of integral consciousness. However, while integral consciousness helps us be more empathetic, it also helps us to be more discriminating; with integral consciousness we can see stagnation and pathology more accurately, and we can thus "tell the truth" about the real problem—the internal problem that is behind almost every conflict. Put simply, integral consciousness gives us the power to evaluate more effectively. And integral philosophy's understanding of the primordial values found at the heart of all evolution naturally fortifies this enhanced ability to see and work with values in general.

When we learn the details of what we already knew intuitively, when we recognize the dialectical dance of evolutionary progression more clearly through the use of this system of understanding, this inevitably reveals new opportunities for us to directly participate in cultural evolution. These opportunities for improvement have been there all along, but we can now begin to see them better as we are awakened to this new conception of evolution. That is, what all forms of consciousness really need, what feeds people spiritually and causes them to grow, are services of kindness, teachings of truth, and expressions of beauty. The skillful application of beauty, truth, or goodness makes any situation more evolved. And the values of beauty, truth, and goodness can be applied most skillfully when we recognize how they work together in a dialectical system. Thus, when we use integral philosophy to see how every conflict contains a transcendent synthesis that is waiting to be achieved, we are practicing the method of integral consciousness.

However, there is one more application of this understanding of the directions of evolution that serves not so much as a method or a means, but rather as an end in itself. Through the use of this evolutionary philosophy of beauty, truth, and goodness, we can glimpse the deep spirituality that is at the heart of the process of universe development. And when we see for ourselves how the master patterns of evolution are shaped by spirit's appetite for perfection, this results in a kind of spiritual experience that is indeed an end in itself. But this spiritual experience of the sacred nature of evolution is not merely a fleeting epiphany. As we increasingly align ourselves with these evolutionary currents of development by practicing beauty, truth, and goodness in our lives, our spiritual experience of evolution's perfecting purpose is continually deepened.

Appendix A
A Proposal for Integral Global Governance

THIS APPENDIX SUPPLEMENTS THE DISCUSSION OF "INTEGRAL Politics" in chapter 5 by providing a brief but specific example of the kind of structure that a world federal constitution might take if it was informed by the insights of integral philosophy. Just as the wisdom of Enlightenment philosophy was used in the original design of the constitutional structures of the United States and other democracies, so too can integral philosophy be used for the important task of designing proposed structures for a world federal constitution. However, despite the fact that integral thinking can shed significant light on this topic, I approach the subject with some hesitation because a proper and thorough treatment of "integral constitutional theory" would require a large and difficult book of its own. Nevertheless, I've decided to describe the outlines of this specific proposal because doing so helps bring out some of the difficult issues that a world federation will confront; and the sooner we come to grips with these issues, the closer we will be to achieving this next crucial step in the evolution of human society. There are certainly other integrally informed potential constitutional structures that could be used for a world federation, and I would be open to any of these as long as they resulted in peace, justice, freedom, environmental protection, and opportunities for cultural evolution.

In chapter 5 we touched on the basic outlines and goals of an integral world federation, which would be instituted to provide democratic oversight of the global economy, protect the world's environment, establish a universal bill of human rights, preserve cultural diversity, and bring an eventual end to war, disease, and poverty. After briefly describing how a world federation might be gradually implemented, I spent the rest of the chapter arguing that, with the rise of the integral worldview in the developed world, this new form of global political organization becomes achievable, safe, and desirable. However, for purposes of our discussion in this appendix, I will not argue further for the merits of such a system, but rather make a specific recommendation for how the structure of such a government might be organized. (For those interested in more extensive arguments in favor of world federal government, I offer some references in an endnote.)[1]

The idea of a world government was first proposed by the great Italian poet Dante Alighieri in the thirteenth century. Since then it has been championed by historical figures from Immanuel Kant to Albert Einstein.[2] The idea reached the height of its popularity shortly after World War II when world federalist organizations had hundreds of thousands of members, including scores of college campus chapters, and the desirability of a world federal government was even a national debate topic for all high schools in the United States. However, with the onset of the Cold War in the 1950s, the movement for world federation lost momentum. Nevertheless, since the late 1940s, scholars and activists centered in modernist consciousness have continued to advance specific proposals for a global constitution. Many of these proposals have focused on ways to reform and expand the United Nations Charter so as to convert the presently *confederal* United Nations into a *federal* United Nations with genuine sovereignty of its own. Other modernist proposals for world federation have advocated the creation of an entirely new global legal entity that would supersede the United Nations. In addition to the variety of academic proposals aimed at persuading foreign-policy establishment elites, there have also appeared several grass-roots proposals for a global constitution that have been conceived from a distinctly postmodern perspective. Many of these constitutional proposals have merit, but none of them have adequately addressed the central issue of effectively and fairly integrating the diversity of levels of consciousness that currently populate the world.

Others who have considered the future evolution of global governance believe that such global systems will not arise in a formal way through the ratification of a constitution, but rather through the gradual accumulation of treaties, nongovernmental organizations, trade agreements, and global economic institutions. However, while the incremental accumulation of issue-specific global systems is generally positive, I do not believe that we can achieve the full benefits of a world federation (as listed above) without the effective implementation of democratically enacted global law with jurisdiction over individual persons. Even if such jurisdiction over individuals is limited by the mandates of restricted federal authority (wherein national legal systems would be left largely in place with the world federation's authority being strictly limited to global-level concerns), for global law to be effective, nation-states will be required to relinquish some degree of their presently unrestricted sovereignty. And the only way that nation-states will likely be persuaded to give up some of their sovereignty is under a scenario wherein their relinquished sovereignty becomes reinvested in a higher authority. That is, to bring about the bright promise of a world without war, oppression, environmental degradation, or human suffering, a world federation will have to be adequately *empowered*—empowered by the master lawmaking authority of a democratically enacted global constitution.

One of the major benefits of "pushing power up" through the advent of a global constitution is that this would allow for more power to be "pushed down." We know this because it is exactly what has happened within the European Union. As the nation-states of Europe have transferred some of their sovereignty to the E.U., this has facilitated the reemergence of smaller political entities such as Scotland and Catalonia. Age-old power struggles that were once necessary for the maintenance of national borders become increasingly irrelevant when such individual states are protected within a larger democratic entity such as the E.U. In a similar fashion, the inauguration of a world federal constitution will make it possible for nation-states to safely push power up, making it then more feasible for a world federation to safely push power down, closer to the level of the people. And if such a program of local empowerment was implemented under the guidance of integral thinking, it could serve to strengthen traditional cultures and help them to better develop their own native forms of modernist culture—the kind of homegrown modernism that would complement and preserve the uniqueness and evolutionary genius of their own particular versions of traditionalism.

An important safeguard prerequisite for the greater empowerment of traditional cultures would be the inauguration of the global government's universal bill of human rights, which would ensure that any newly empowered governmental entities did not trample on the rights of their citizens. Just as the U.S. Constitution's Bill of Rights keeps the subordinate governments its constituent states from discriminating against their citizens, so too would a universal bill of human rights act as a safeguard that would allow more control to be invested in smaller, regional political entities. Ultimately, the opportunity to safely "push power down" that would be afforded by a world federal constitution may make such a proposal more acceptable to populations centered in traditional consciousness, because it would allow them to secure a degree of ethnic political identity currently denied many of them under the present international system of competing nation-states.

While the European Union provides a good contemporary example of how a supranational organization can be successfully implemented, a world federation will be confronted with problems that the E.U. has not yet had to tackle. But these problems come into clear focus only when we recognize how consciousness is distributed across the spiral of development. That is, the E.U. is a federal union that has been formed from nations that were for the most part already democratic; European populations are all relatively highly developed, and thus their amalgamation has not created a large disruption in the social fabric of the Continent. But when we contemplate forming a union that encompasses the large populations of the Third World, from an integral perspective we can see that a simple one-person, one-vote system would likely create major problems. If global laws were to be made by a world legislature elected exclusively by population size, this would effectively hand over power to the large populations of the Third World. And because these populations are still largely centered in traditional consciousness, the ethnocentric morality that generally characterizes this level of development would make for some predictably one-sided laws. Thus, a significant challenge for any would-be global democratic entity is to provide a certain degree of protection and insulation for modernist economies and modernist and postmodern cultures from the now significantly larger populations centered in traditional consciousness and below.

As is evident in the declining populations of Europe and Japan, and the stable population of the U.S. (excluding immigration), people who live in modernist cultures generally have fewer children than those who live in traditional cultures. While we can anticipate that as traditional cultures evolve, they too will have fewer children, it may take centuries before the majority of the world has evolved to the modernist level or above. However, we are confronted with a host of urgent global-level threats in this century. We must therefore find a way to provide for a system of global law that is thoroughly democratic but which also accounts for the disparity of cultural development in the state of the world today.

The integral worldview's *prime directive*—the principle which recognizes that every stage of the spiral of development needs to be nurtured and respected—requires that each stage of cultural development be afforded a certain degree of protection. And different developmental segments require different kinds of protection. Tribal cultures need to have their fragile ways of life protected and preserved (while also protecting individual human rights) lest they be dissolved and completely lost within the onslaught of globalization. Warrior cultures need to be protected from themselves, especially as these cultures increasingly acquire modern weapons. Traditional cultures also need to be protected from complete delegitimization by modernism and postmodernism. That is, the integrity of these ancient worldviews requires that their laws, customs, cosmologies, and general way of life be respected by the larger emerging global culture. When such societies feel respected, when their inherent legitimacy is acknowledged by more developed societies, this helps these societies remain *open to evolution*; it encourages them to create the conditions that allow for the gradual emergence of native forms of modernism within their midst. As we can see, it is extremely important to provide this kind of protection for traditional cultures because when these cultures are threatened with extinction, they cease to function as incubators of modernism and begin to instill fear and foment hostility toward all things modern, as has become the case in many Islamic countries.

An integral world federation could effectively protect these earlier stages of development while also protecting modernism and postmodernism from regression, by implementing a tiered approach to membership in the world federation. For a nation-state to be a full member, and for its citizens to be maximally enfranchised (politically and economically), there would need to be a requisite degree of modernist consciousness within that nation's population. It would be folly to try to create a world federation of equal democratic states that equally included states that have not yet become democratic. This is not to say that predemocratic populations would be denied membership in a world federation, but only that these traditional cultures would be protected as probationary members, receiving the basic protections and privileges while at the same time being insulated so that they can develop native forms of modernism (when and if they are ready).

So how would such safeguards be fairly implemented? Well, the key would be to expand on the essential genius of modernist democracy—the separation of powers. The proposed structure for a world federal constitution described below accordingly provides for a separation of powers into executive, legislative, and judicial branches. However, this proposed constitutional structure also provides for another kind of power separation, one that recognizes the three essential constituencies of populations, nation-states, and economies.

As illustrated in Figure A-1, this proposed constitution for an integral world federation recognizes that each of these constituencies—populations, nation-states, and economies—needs to be adequately represented for the world government to work. As in the bicameral structure of the U.S. Constitution, populations and state governments are each represented in the legislature; but in this proposal, a "tricameral house" (together with a tricameral judiciary and a tricameral executive branch) is recommended so that this third critical constituency of economic interests can find adequate protection and representation. This tricameral structure is thus intended: 1) to provide for democratic representation of all people within the federation while preventing the more populous countries from completely controlling the government and redistributing the world's wealth; 2) to give economic interests a segregated but legitimate voice in the government, reducing the incentive for these interests to try to corrupt the other branches as has happened to a certain degree in the U.S.; and 3) to achieve a twofold "separation of powers"—one form of separation that will provide for checks and balances between the branches of the government itself, and another form of separation that will provide checks and balances among the competing power

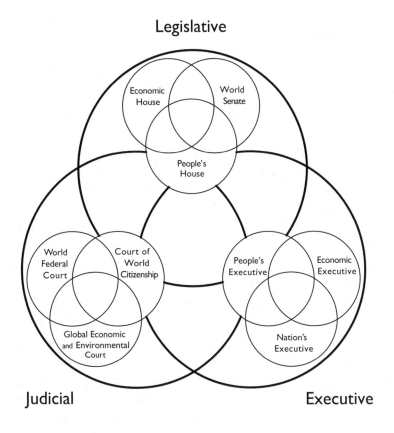

Figure A-1. A proposed structure for an integral world federal constitution modeled after the "Cosmogenetic Principle" described in chapter 10.

constituencies of populations, nation-states, and economic interests.

A government that provides democratic representation for economic interests may at first seem unfair, but any realistic assessment of the world will recognize that the evolution of civilization is at least partially based on economic development. Here at the beginning of the twenty-first century, power in the world is derived from economic and military might. And while a world government should rightly eliminate military might as the basis of power within the federation (requiring all member states to gradually disarm), if it denies representation to economic interests within a democratic world government, it would not be long before this policy did significant damage to the world's economy. And the disruption of modernist economies would inevitably lead to the collapse of much of modernist and postmodern culture.

As long as consciousness in the world is distributed across the spiral of development, communal schemes of wealth redistribution will not be sustainable. Wealth might be temporarily redistributed, but it would not be long before rich countries were rich again and poor countries were poor again. This is because economic development roughly traces the development of consciousness. Modernist consciousness, operating within the legal environment of free markets, is what creates most of the wealth of modern societies. Without a requisite degree of modernist consciousness, a First World economy is not sustainable. So before the Third World can be made as wealthy as the First World, the consciousness and culture of these peoples must be nurtured and cultivated, and these populations must also be protected from the ongoing legacy of colonialism and economic exploitation by wealthier countries. Until the Third World's cultural structures of traditional consciousness are healthy enough to produce their own native forms of modernism, free market economies alone will not produce the kind of evolution in these societies that leads to greater rights and freedoms. So if the world (or at least a good portion of it) is going to come together in a federal union, the evolutionary disparities in consciousness as well as the disparities in wealth must be given sufficient insulation to prevent the disruption of the natural course of evolution and the accompanying regression that would follow if a global democracy was established without such protections.

In this proposal each constituency would have its own bill of rights: There would be an international bill of human rights that would protect each citizen of the federation; a bill of state's rights that would limit the jurisdiction of the world federation and preserve the power of nation-states over much of their domestic affairs; and a bill of economic rights that would protect private property and secure a relative degree of freedom for economic entities. But in addition to a bill of rights for each constituency, this proposed constitution would also provide for a "bill of responsibilities" that would describe the affirmative obligations of each group to each other and to the world federation as a whole.

As illustrated in Figure A-1, the legislative branch of this proposed constitution would consist of three houses. The populist house of representatives would be elected directly by the enfranchised people of the federation in a one-person, one-vote structure that was not entirely constrained by national boundaries. The chamber of the legislature dedicated to nation-states, the world senate, would have its members appointed by the national governments in the federation, just as nations now appoint their representatives to the General Assembly of the United Nations. And the economic house could be elected through the device of enfranchising economic "stakeholders" such as investors, labor, management, small business, consumers, and environmental interests.

The laws enacted by these three legislative houses would be approved and interpreted by a tricameral judiciary consisting of a court that would rule on global economic and environmental issues; a court concerned with international human rights; and a court empowered to settle disputes between nation-states and to maintain the jurisdictional limits of world law. An integrally informed judiciary will play an especially crucial role in helping to create and preserve the conditions necessary for sustainable economic development while simultaneously protecting the world's environment. These integral jurists would understand the fragile ecology of markets and the needs of both local and global economies; but on the other hand these judges would, of course, also balance these concerns with the more fundamental concern over the fragile environment of our planet. Indeed, it is becoming increasingly apparent that environmental protection is a global-level issue that can be adequately addressed only by global laws enacted to preserve the global commons from economic exploitation and degradation.

Like the legislative and judicial branches of this proposed integral world federation, the executive branch would also consist of a committee of three world executives: a people's executive, a nation's executive, and an economic executive. Each legislative house would elect its respective executive for a four-year term—the economic executive would be elected by the economic house, the nation's executive by the world senate, and the people's executive by the populist house of representatives. However, unlike the legislative and judicial branches, which would focus primarily on their own spheres of influence, the committee of three world executives would be charged with the promotion of the prime directive. That is, the function of the world executive committee would be to work for the overall evolution of world civilization as such a course is illuminated by the insights of the integral worldview.

In practice, this would mean that the executive branch would work to harmonize communal and individual interests—sometimes they would champion transcendence and sometimes they would champion inclusion. For example, if a supermajority of people in a specific culture agreed to create (or more likely preserve) a traditional consciousness-based religious state governed by the rules of their scripture, the prime directive would prescribe that this group be given the autonomy to have such a state. But what if the bill of international human rights came into conflict with such religious laws? These two interests might be harmonized by ensuring that individuals within such a religious state had the right to leave the state and relocate to a more evolved culture. Certainly some of these conflicts would need to be resolved by the world courts, and some of the compromises might be codified by the world legislature. But again, the job of the executive branch would be to actively cultivate the overall health of the dynamic system we recognize as the spiral of development in consciousness and culture.

Toward this end, each of the three executives might have their own "cabinet of consciousness"—a committee of advisers with each member representing a different stage in the spiral of development. These cabinet members could be responsible for championing not only the causes of specific peoples and cultures in the world who evinced a given level of development, they could also serve as advocates for the ongoing contributions of early developmental stages as they continue to exist in transcended form within more developed societies. For example, a tribal-level adviser could serve not only as the advocate of the interests of the remaining tribal cultures in the world, he or she could also act as the advocate of family life and the ongoing necessity of the healthy forms of tribal consciousness that contribute to family loyalty and kinship bonds within modernist and postmodern cultures. Similarly, a warrior-level adviser could advocate not only respect for the warrior cultures in the world, he or she could also advocate the acceptance of healthy forms of warrior consciousness among the youth of developed nations.

The proposed structure shown in Figure A-1 is informed by integral philosophy in the way that it attempts to fulfill the prime directive by maintaining the health of the spiral of development and preserving evolutionary opportunities for everyone, regardless of their level of development. This structure seeks to harmonize the needs of the modern and postmodern developed world with the needs of the traditional Third World. And not only are these power relationships designed from the vantage point of integral consciousness, the very shape of the structure of this proposed global government is also designed to reflect integral philosophy's understanding of the master patterns of evolution itself. Recall that in chapter 10's discussion of "The Directions of Evolution," I showed how the "Big Three" domains of objective, subjective, and intersubjective evolution each express the threefold "Cosmogenetic Principle" in their own way. The objective evolution of biological organisms is characterized by increasing unity, complexity, and consciousness; the subjective evolution of human consciousness advances through the development of feeling, thought, and will; and within the intersubjective evolution of human culture we can recognize the three essential value spheres of aesthetics, science, and morality. This proposed constitutional structure thus attempts to mirror the "three within three" structure that is the self-similar pattern exhibited by the Cosmogenetic Principle's ordering of all evolutionary development. I have thus attempted to use the insights of integral philosophy to inform both the *function* and the *structure* of this proposed world federal constitution by utilizing the "natural structure of evolution" as a model for its basic form.

As mentioned at the beginning of this discussion, proposing specific constitutional structures for an integral world federation may at this point seem premature or even ill-advised. There are obviously many details and important mechanisms that have not been discussed. But ultimately, despite the limitations and shortcomings of such a cursory proposal, it is important to begin defining and debating these issues now, even though most of us may not live to see such structures actually implemented. And even if you disagree with this specific proposal, perhaps your consideration of these issues will lead you to conceive of an even better constitutional structure.

However, in addition to this proposal for the future, I've also brought forward a modest program for the present—an online petition for integral global governance. This petition, launched in 2004 and formally entitled "A Declaration of the Value of Global Governance," is found online at www.integralworldgovernment.org. The text of this declaration, reproduced in Figure A-2 below and modeled on Thomas Jefferson's Declaration of Independence, names the enduring values of each stage of the spiral of development. This list of "enduring values" starts with the "kinship bonds" originating in the tribal stage of consciousness (with these values writ large to include the family of humanity), and moves through the sequence of development until it reaches the value of the prime directive that is perhaps the most "enduring value" of the integral worldview as a whole. This petition thus provides one way for people to get involved by signifying their agreement and by participating online in the growing community of those who recognize the urgent need for world federation guided by the values of integral consciousness and the prime directive of evolution.

A Declaration of the
Value of Governance

WE hold these truths to be self-evident.

—that the world can be made a better place through the evolution of consciousness and culture.

—that we each have a responsibility of care and compassion for others and for the natural and cultural environments in which we live.

—that in order to fulfill these responsibilities and to secure the blessings of world peace, justice, and prosperity, it is necessary to institute a new form of global governance deriving its just powers from the consent of the governed.

—WE, the free citizens of planet earth, thus affirm the need for a system of global governance founded on the values of integral consciousness, which include:

The value of the universal family of humanity;

The value of individual freedom and personal autonomy;

The values of decency, honesty, and respect for traditions;

The values of progress, prosperity, and economic development;

The values of multiculturalism, environmentalism, and egalitarianism;

The value of the channel of evolution as a whole—the system through which individuals and societies develop.

WE, the undersigned, therefore solemnly publish and declare our intent to work toward the establishment of a limited, democratic, federal, integral world government; so that through this organization, we can begin to solve the global problems of war, hunger, poverty, disease, injustice, terrorism, environmental degradation, unfettered corporate globalization, ignorance, and despair.

Figure A-2. The text of the online petition entitled "A Declaration of the Value of Global Governance."

Appendix B
Consideration of Wilber's Four-Quadrant Model of Evolution

THIS APPENDIX PICKS UP WHERE WE LEFT OFF IN CHAPTER 8 IN THE section entitled "The Integral Map of Reality." This extended discussion is necessary because Ken Wilber, contemporary culture's leading integral theorist, has made the quadrant model of evolving holons the centerpiece of his philosophy, and this has tended to define the integral worldview for many as essentially and necessarily requiring a four-quadrant understanding of reality.

As we explored in chapters 2 and 8, integral philosophy actually achieves its evolutionary advance by offering an expanded frame of reality that makes the internal universe of consciousness and culture easier to recognize and understand. And Wilber's quadrant model has served as an important first step in the framing of this new understanding of the internal universe. That is, the quadrant model is definitely valid in certain respects, and it is unquestionably important to recognize the inside and outside of both the individual and collective dimensions of evolution (as we did in chapter 10). However, as I explained in chapter 8, the quadrant model contains certain distortions and weaknesses that render it ill suited to serve as a central foundation for the integral worldview's reality frame.

As will be shown through the arguments in this appendix, by insisting on a distinct "interobjective" external domain of naturally arising holonic systems of human social evolution, Wilber's model effectively raises human-made artifacts to the status of natural holons. And it is in this attempt to locate interobjective systems (like those found in biological evolution) within the realm of human society that the quadrant model becomes burdened with a category error. As we will see, by trying to honor and include the work of the social systems theorists, in his depiction of human social evolution Wilber has inadvertently committed the opposite of "subtle reductionism"; he has created a kind of "subtle expansionism" by postulating a distinct interobjective realm of "social action systems" that were themselves the mistaken results of subtle reductionism in the first place. This serious mistake renders the quadrant model vulnerable to attacks that may undermine the credibility of the integral reality frame as a whole. So it is therefore prudent for us to recognize this category error now, before this mistake is pointed out by those who will eventually try to invalidate the integral worldview as it inevitably gains social power.

If you are not previously familiar with Wilber's work and the importance of holons as a foundation of his system, I do recommend that you review chapter 8's discussion of "The Integral Map of Reality" prior to reading what follows, as this discussion necessarily assumes that the reader already has a basic understanding of Wilber's four-quadrant model of evolution.

Problems with the Continuity of Wilber's Evolutionary Timelines

As illustrated in Figure B-1, the quadrant model works beautifully until we get to the beginning of human cultural evolution—what Teilhard de Chardin called the "point of reflection"—the point in evolution when consciousness becomes conscious of itself. In general, the problem is as follows: Once human culture begins to develop, and once we move beyond the biologically based objective organization of the family (or perhaps even the tribe), the externally visible structures that are the product of social evolution become less and less holonic and increasingly subject to human design.

Prior to the emergence of human culture, Wilber's fourfold timeline of development, which traces the evolution of both cosmological and biological structures, does reveal systems that are indeed *interobjective holons*. These prehuman evolutionary structures are natural, self-organizing systems that are collective in nature and also externally visible. These external structures are unquestionably authentic holons—products of the natural process of evolution. Ready examples of these external, interobjective structures can be

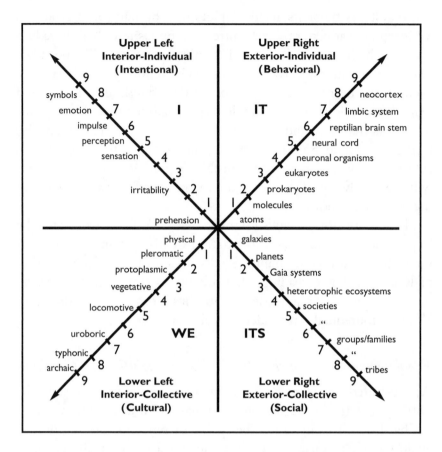

Figure B-1. A valid four-quadrant diagram of evolution prior to the appearance of humans. Note that the lower-right quadrant ends with "tribes" and the upper-right quadrant ends with "neocortex."

found in organizations such as flocks of geese or families of apes.

However, something changes at the "point of reflection" (a phrase we will borrow from Teilhard), and we can see this in both the upper-right and lower-right quadrants. As shown in Figure B-2 below, the evolution of new biological structures in the human brain effectively stops at "complex neocortex" (at the point Wilber labels fulcrum 10). Nevertheless, Wilber's model shows evolution continuing through "SF1, SF2, and SF3" (with "SF" standing for structure-functions in the human brain). By including these "post-complex neocortex" brain developments in the timeline of evolution, Wilber is trying to show how the emergence of new cultural worldviews result in measurable increases in electrical brain activity. As we discussed in chapter 4, the evolution of consciousness by stages does indeed result in increased neurological activation in the brain, and Wilber's model correctly accounts for this through his "structure-function" designations. But there is a difference between increased electrical activity in the brain and the emergence of new biological structures of evolution. Science is clear that the biology of the human brain has not evolved any new structures in at least the last 10,000 years; so whatever these structure-functions are, they do not constitute the evolutionary emergence of new biological structures (such as those shown along the upper-right quadrant's timeline prior to "complex neocortex"). Thus we find a kind of discontinuity once the timeline passes the point of reflection—the biology of the brain shows little or no structural change, yet a new kind of development, identified as increased neurological brain activation, is seamlessly grafted onto the timeline of development. However, while this conflation of two kinds of development into one continuous timeline does oversimplify evolution, I do not think it is particularly problematic for the validity of the four-quadrant model. But this minor discontinuity in the upper-right quadrant points to a more significant problem in the lower-right quadrant.

Continuing our consideration of Figure B-2, when we turn our attention from the upper-right quadrant (the exterior-individual) to the lower-right quadrant (the exterior-collective), we find a similar but more profound kind of discontinuity in the timeline beginning at the point of reflection (or soon thereafter). Although we could argue about the exact point in history when humans began to consciously design their social organizations, by the time we get to the point of recorded human history, we can see that the externally visible physical forms of social organization are unmistakably man-made.

As an example of the difference between a man-made artifact and a natural holon, consider the external structure of a nation-state (shown in the lower-right quadrant at fulcrum 12) like the United States. The exterior organization of the United States is an artifact with a consciously imposed design—it is a structure of law

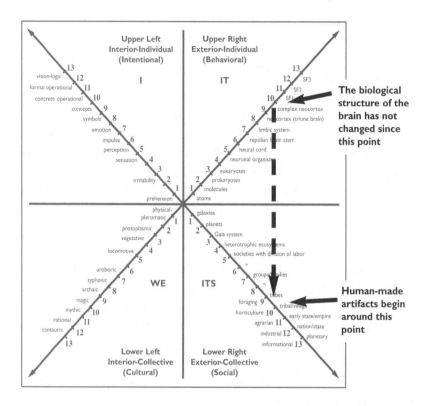

Figure B-2. The character of development changes with the emergence of the noosphere.

enacted by a constitution. But while the external legal structure of the United States is a nonholonic artifact, the U.S. also consists of an intersubjective cultural reality that is indeed an internal, holonic system (found in the lower-left quadrant) that coexists with its exterior national structure. And because the social reality of nation-states such as the United States have a combined holonic and artifactual structure, it is easy to confuse the two.

Another example of such a combined internally holonic and externally artifactual structure is found in a business corporation. The external, objective structure of a corporation does not arise auto-poietically like an ecosystem; its structure is designed and created by lawyers acting under the provisions of corporate law. And once the corporation becomes operational, the elements of its structure (as evidenced by the organization chart) are the result of conscious planning by the company's management. Although the external design of a corporation's structure is most definitely artifactual (including both its organizational design structure and its physical buildings and information systems), the company's internal culture and the way it is perceived by the market are holonic. The designs of management can influence corporate culture, but the opinions and morale of the corporation's employees arise from their actual experience and from the quality of the relationships they have with each other and with the company's leaders. The esprit de corps of an organization is a holonic self-organizing cultural system that can be influenced, but not directly designed and created in the same way that an external organizational structure can be.

Wilber has acknowledged that when he first formulated the quadrant model in the early 1990s, he was unaware of the important difference between holons and artifacts. In his original description of the quadrants, first published in 1995 in *Sex, Ecology, Spirituality*, Wilber correctly (if inadvertently) identified the postreflection contents of the lower-right quadrant as human-made artifacts. This can be seen in the following quote from *Sex, Ecology, Spirituality* (in which I have underlined the obvious artifacts):

> [I]n the Lower-Right quadrant, where evolution enters the human domain, I have only indicated the most concrete forms of <u>geopolitical structures</u>. But this quadrant includes the exterior of any of the social aspects of human interaction, including forces of production and techno-economic modes (<u>bow and arrow, horticultural tools, agrarian implements, industrial machinery, computers</u>, and so on), <u>architectural structures, transportation systems, physical infrastructure, even written (material) forms of books, legal codes, linguistic structures, verbal signifiers</u>, and so forth.[1] [Underlining added]

This description, which identified the contents of the lower-right quadrant as essentially artifacts rather than holons, went unnoticed until integral theorist Fred Kofman pointed out the important difference between holons and artifacts in a 2001 article entitled

"Holons, Heaps, and Artifacts."[2] But soon after the publication of Kofman's article, Wilber did admit that his failure to distinguish between holons and artifacts in *Sex, Ecology, Spirituality* had been an oversight. This admission appeared in an interview Wilber posted on his publisher's website, which echoed Kofman's analysis and thoroughly explained the difference between holons and artifacts. However, in this interview Wilber did not really explain whether or how this correction impacted his four-quadrant model.

Revisions to the Contents of the Interobjective Quadrant

Two years later, however, Wilber's writing did begin to address the place of artifacts within his evolutionary model, thus modifying his position on the contents of the lower-right quadrant. Toward the end of "Excerpt D" to his forthcoming volume 2 of the *Kosmos Trilogy* (published on the Internet), Wilber explained that the lower-right quadrant actually contains both artifacts and what he called "behavioral intersections:"

> Thus, when it comes to a social network (or system of its), those "it" items include both (1) the behavioral *intersections* of the members of the network and (2) the exterior *artifacts* that are the material components of the network. Both of those aspects are indeed "it" or "its." The exterior behavior of an organism and the exterior artifacts are both third-person dimensions of being-in-the-world.[3]

Although Wilber's latest writing now acknowledges the place of artifacts, none of the graphical expressions of his model have been altered to show this significant revision. Moreover, Wilber has not addressed the problems that this revision creates for his central and continuing assertion that "all holons have four quadrants."[4] Wilber has used a variety of examples from the realm of biology to illustrate his theory that every holon has four quadrants, with the example of a flock of geese being among the most recent. And if we consider the biological reality of geese (which can be located on his model's timeline somewhere between fulcrums 7 and 8), we can indeed clearly recognize the consciousness of each goose in the upper-left quadrant, the brain and body of each goose in the upper-right quadrant, the holon of the flock of geese in the lower-right quadrant (as evidenced by their distinctive V-shaped flight formation), and the internal holon of the flock's cultural community (literally the "pecking order") in the lower-left quadrant. In this example the inside and the outside of both the individual and the collective aspects of what it is to be a goose are all perfectly natural and holonic. Again, the quadrant model works well when we are looking at biological evolution. However, when we consider the evolutionary structures found in the model's timeline beyond fulcrum 10 (the approximate point of reflection), the external, visible, objective features of collective social organization become unmistakably artifactual. Even though Wilber has since tried to nuance his position in this area by claiming that at the level of human societies his interobjective quadrant of evolution consists of both holons (behavioral intersections) and man-made artifacts, it is difficult to see how these supposed "behavioral intersections" by themselves have enough "systemic weight" to be identified as semi-independent autopoietic holons. In our examination of the composition of human social systems, once we properly identify the *external artifacts and the internal intersubjective holons* which together comprise these systems, the additional postulation of self-organizing *external* holons becomes unnecessary.

In the upper half of Wilber's model, the semi-independent systemic reality of the body and the mind can be clearly seen in the way that each of these holonic systems exhibits a degree of autonomy. For example, if I am in a coma and my brain waves are virtually flat, my body may continue to function. And conversely, as has been recorded in numerous near-death experiences, if my body is biologically dead, my mind may continue to have experiences (this is well documented in a number of books, such as Jenny Wade's *Changes of Mind*). However, in the case of intersubjective cultural systems and the objective behaviors that evidence them, there is a lack of systemic independence on the part of the behaviors by themselves.

Recall that the right-hand side of Wilber's quadrant model is defined as that which can be actually seen with the senses or their extensions. The contents of the objective and interobjective quadrants are said to have "simple location." And when we look around us at the external society we live in, these outward manifestations of culture are indeed evident—they can be seen in language, architecture, technology, transportation systems, fashions, etc. These are the obvious exteriors of human culture, which Wilber originally and correctly identified in *Sex, Ecology, Spirituality* (as shown in the block quote on page 329). However, once we recognize that the exterior aspects of all these social structures are artifacts and not holons, once we have to prop up the idea of interobjectivity by retreating to "behavioral intersections" to try to locate the supposedly natural, self-organizing objective systems that the model requires, the "simple location" of these postulated self-organizing systems becomes difficult to find.

In fact, we can envision many social scenarios in which these "behavioral intersections" would be completely artifactual in themselves. In the example of the business corporation we discussed above, the actions and behaviors of the corporation's employees, when on the job, are largely dictated by their job descriptions and the functional design of the company. Even Wilber has acknowledged: "When an individual-I or a cultural-We produces artifacts … their exterior behavior is itself an artifact of their intentionality."[5] We can thus imagine many common situations in which intersubjective entities—human relationships—are connected to both external structures *and behaviors* that are all completely artifactual. And these kind of situations provide obvious examples of how nonholonic artifacts can supply all necessary exterior complexity.

Again, in the realm of biology, as we saw in the example of the flock of geese, there is indeed an inside/outside symmetry found in collective organizations that mirrors the inside/outside symmetry of the objective body and the subjective consciousness found in individuals. But as human civilization evolves beyond its biological roots, as the biosphere is transcended by the noosphere, this new kind of evolution actually *relies on the construction of human artifacts to supply the external and objective counterparts of its advancing intersubjective development.*

The crucial role of artifacts in the evolution of human conscious-

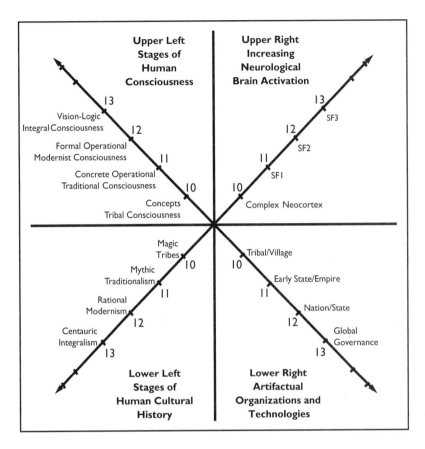

Figure B-3. Postreflection timelines of development.

ness and culture was well understood by Teilhard de Chardin, whose famous law of complexity-consciousness (discussed in chapters 7 and 10) recognized how artifacts serve to supply the additional physical complexity that is required for consciousness to evolve beyond the animal level. That is, according to Teilhard, whenever consciousness evolves, it always requires a corresponding evolution in the complexity of the external structures that contain it. And as human consciousness advances within the developing noosphere, the corresponding development of human social artifacts "stand in" for the lack of significant biological development, thereby supporting the growth of consciousness with *artificial complexity*. Teilhard showed how human cultural evolution is always accompanied by a corresponding development in artifacts, which are thus recognized as indispensable aspects of all human cultural evolution.

As we can see, the subjective complexity of human consciousness is intimately bound up with the marvelous physical complexity of the human body. The body's astounding material complexity is intensely evident and often painfully obvious. And similarly, the evident intersubjective complexity of human culture is also bound up with the physical complexity of human society. But this evident and astounding material complexity of our evolving society is not found in the rather obscure and intangible notion of "behavioral intersections" engaging in "social autopoiesis," it is found in the obvious societal constructions that surround and envelop us, artifacts such as clothing, furnishings, architecture, words and images, information systems, transportation systems, financial records, law codes, etc. The collective external structures of the biosphere are the products of genetic design; they have arisen autopoietically and through natural selection. But the physical complexity of the noosphere is the product of actual selection, not natural selection. Indeed, it is because humans are able to design and create artifacts that we have been able to intentionally extend the physical complexity of our society and evolve at a faster pace than biological evolution.

As another clear example of the fundamental interaction of holons and artifacts in the evolution of culture and society, consider the function of human language. The development of language is a key factor that allows human consciousness to grow beyond its biological roots. But the development of language relies upon the creation of words, which are unquestionably human-made artifacts. While the interior meanings and agreements that every word stands for (known as the *signifieds*) are indeed subjective and intersubjective holons, the "signs" or words themselves (known as the linguistic *signifiers*) are always artifactual. Language is a man-made construction, and the development of a society's language provides an excellent illustration of Teilhard's insight about how holons and artifacts emerge together in the advance of cultural evolution.

Let's summarize where we have come so far: Figure B-1 above

showed how, prior to the emergence of human consciousness, the quadrant model demonstrates the marvelous symmetry of the inside and outside of the individual and the collective dimensions of evolution. But once artifacts become an undeniably significant factor in the evolution of human culture beyond its biological roots, the elegant holonic symmetry of the quadrants begins to break down. As shown in Figure B-3, the timeline in the upper-right, exterior-individual quadrant tracks increasing electrical activity in the brain, which, as we noted, is not generally recognized as actual evolution. And similarly, the timeline in the lower-right, exterior-collective quadrant tracks a hierarchy of artifacts, which do roughly line up with internal cultural development, but which are not holonic and which do not have the symmetrical equivalent of the relationship between body and mind. Moreover, it is worth noting here that artifacts are both individual and collective, so they cannot be easily mapped or contained exclusively within the collective or plural quadrant of the model.

So why does this matter? What difference does it make whether the contents of the "exterior-collective" dimension of social evolution are holons or artifacts? Well, according to Wilber himself: "... the three words 'whole,' 'part,' and 'hierarchy' can apply to individual holons, social holons, artifacts, and heaps—but they mean something very different in each case, and we have to keep these differences in mind or we will commit all sorts of severe category errors, and these errors have grave and unfortunate consequences when pressed into social action and policy."[6] In other words, while human artifacts do develop and evolve as societies progress in the timeline of evolution, and while an understanding of artifacts is very important for any theory of cultural evolution, man-made structures play a different role in the process of development than do holons, and they need to be recognized as distinct from the holarchy of naturally arising holons that Wilber's model purports to map.

So why does Wilber continue to insist that the external aspects of collective human culture are interobjective systems of self-organizing "its"? The answer, I believe, is that he is trying to honor the work of systems scientists and their theories of "social action systems."

Social Action Systems

The idea of autonomous social action systems originated in the 1930s with the famous Harvard sociologist Talcott Parsons. Parsons maintained that the structure of a social system consisted of the acts of the individual participants. Social systems were postulated to consist of enduring patterns of social action directed by the desired ends and available means of the actors in the system, and constrained by the environmental conditions encountered by those actors. As systems science evolved, Parsons's theory of social action systems would be carried forward and refined by German sociologist Niklas Luhmann, whom Wilber calls "the world's greatest systems theorist."[7] According to Luhmann, all social systems are "independent autopoietic systems constituted by communication."[8] That is, unlike other systems scientists who had mistakenly assumed that a social system could be understood as a kind of higher-order organism, Luhmann correctly identified *exchanged communication* as the substance of the systems that make up human society.

However, although Luhmann did correctly identify the central and constituent role of communication in the formation of social systems, his materialistic worldview prevented him from also recognizing the *internal and intersubjective* component of all human social systems. And this blindness to interiors forced him to try to locate the self-organization of these systems in the external realm, which for him was the only realm in existence. Luhmann's theory accordingly required the existence of ontological, physical, and external—yet somehow also autopoietic—social systems. And now, following Luhmann, Wilber has carried forward this theoretical postulate in the construction of the interobjective quadrant of his model.

In other words, for scientifically minded social systems theorists such as Parsons and Luhmann, the distinction between an internal (nonphysical) system, such as a human relationship, and an external (physical) system, such as a biological organism or ecosystem, is not fully recognized. That is, in a materialist's worldview, all systems are essentially physical—the idea of an internal universe is not considered or even recognized. These theorists cannot see that the actual systems of the human relationships they are trying to describe are primarily nonphysical. Yet as we have shown throughout this book, the essence of a human relationship is essentially internal and intersubjective. But this key distinction is lost on these theorists who generally belong to the school of thought that similarly sees consciousness as merely an "epiphenomenon" of the material brain. The subtle distinction between intersubjective cultural holons and objective artifacts is not understood. So it is not that these systems theorists are all wrong, it is just that they have not had the benefit of integral theory in their analysis. They can recognize the authentic systemic behavior of human social systems, but they have not recognized that the systems they are trying to understand reside primarily in the internal universe. And they cannot recognize or acknowledge the intersubjective domain for the same reason they reject the subjective domain (which is considered to be a worn-out conception of Cartesian dualism). Thus, without an understanding of intersubjectivity, these systems theorists are left to construct theories of human society that can only recognize the external, objective manifestations of the underlying intersubjective structures. Because these theorists are unwilling to consider any kind of metaphysics in their understanding (such as the metaphysics of intersubjectivity), they find themselves resorting to a kind of "metabiology" under which they attempt to understand the internal intersubjective systems of human culture as though they were biological organisms or external ecosystems.

These theorists can point to external, objective behaviors and actions, but these "behavioral intersections" are not self-organizing dynamic systems in and of themselves—in the realm of human culture these objective acts merely clothe the underlying intersubjective cultural structures that are the real dynamic systems. We can see this process of physical behaviors clothing internal systems in the way a person's objective facial expression can mirror the state of that person's subjective consciousness. If I am happy, my face will behave in an objective way that reveals the subjective reality of my happiness. And similarly, if you and I have a relationship, we will both behave in an objective way that reveals this underlying intersubjective reality. However, just as my face's expression of my mood is not a self-organizing dynamic system by itself (the physical holonic counterpart of my happiness being in my brain and not my facial muscles), the physical behavior of two people in a relationship likewise does not constitute a self-organizing physical system by itself.

In any human social/cultural system, if the underlying human relationships become dissolved, there will no longer be an "action system." There may be an artifactual organization that serves as the residual objective container of intersubjective systems that once existed, but this objective structure will not be a natural self-organizing system with its own semi-independent holonic reality.

Systems science's misunderstanding of the intersubjective nature of cultural evolution has been well pointed out by Jürgen Habermas, who conducted a series of famous debates with Niklas Luhmann in which he objected to Luhmann's use of biological systems theory to try to understand society. According to Habermas, "Luhmann simply presupposes that the structures of intersubjectivity have collapsed..." Habermas continues: "Societies cannot be smoothly conceptualized as organic systems because their structural patterns are not accessible to observation; they have to be gotten at hermeneutically, that is, from the internal perspective of participants. The entities that are to be subsumed under system-theoretical concepts from the external perspective of the observer must be identified beforehand as the [intersubjective] lifeworlds of social groups. They must be understood in their symbolic structures."[9] In other words, according to Habermas, human social groups and societies are essentially intersubjective in nature and it is a mistake to try to see them as natural physical systems that engage in "social autopoiesis." Contrary to Luhmann's reductionistic theory, the artifactual systems of communication that form the exteriors of human culture do not arise autopoietically by themselves; they are always activated and sustained by the internal holons of human agreement.

In his writing Wilber has clearly shown why social holons cannot be seamlessly grafted on top of individual holons in a continuous holarchical line of development (i.e., ecosystems are not simply "higher-level organisms"), but he has not yet recognized how a similar problem arises when you try to stack the noosphere on top of the biosphere within the interobjective quadrant of development. Recognizing the difference between social holons and individual holons is crucial for integral theory, and it is just as crucial that we also clearly recognize the difference between interobjective biological holons and human-made artifacts.

A Simplified, Alternative Explanation

When we take a clear look at complex human cultural phenomena such as religious, political, or economic organizations, we can see that the evident structures of these institutions—the external manifestations of these cultural entities—are actually artifacts that have been designed by humans. And once we see the important role that artifacts play in the evolution of human culture, this requires that we no longer insist that the exteriors of human social evolution are "interobjective holons." An alternative explanation that better accounts for the artifactual exteriors of human cultural activity is simply that all internal holarchies are connected to the objective realm—all evolutionary activity is tied to physical reality of one sort or another. Subjective consciousness at every level is always connected to physical, objective structures, such as biological organisms. And intersubjective relationships and cultures are also always connected to objective structures. Prior to the appearance of humans, the intersubjective culture of animals is connected to self-organizing holonic ecosystems and natural physical groupings such as flocks and herds. But as the intersubjective culture of humans rises above its biological roots, it is increasingly connected to the accumulating structures of artifacts and man-made organizations. The point is that every inside has an outside, but the "outside," the external universe that can be seen with the senses, is simply objective. Within this objective realm of evolution we always find an external counterpart of internal evolution, both individual and social. We don't need to insist that all human culture must always be connected to a holonic system of "dynamic its"—we don't need the erroneous concept of a social action system to justify the existence of an internal intersubjective system; all we need are the artifacts of communication, such as language, art, or intentional action.

Using Ockham's razor (which favors the simplest explanation), in our understanding of human cultural evolution, we can effectively eliminate the interobjective quadrant while still accounting for the exteriors of intersubjective systems. This simplified explanation does a better job of helping us see how human-made artifacts serve as the exterior forms of evolving human culture and actually "stand in" for the lack of further biological development in the timeline of human history. And this explanation also allows for the recognition of individual artifacts as well as collective ones by not insisting that all the exteriors of culture be classified as "collective." Through this understanding, the whole interobjective quadrant can be easily reduced to simply the objective domain (as Wilber in fact often does in his writing, rendering the "quadrants" as "I, We, and It"). And as William of Ockham himself famously said: "What can be done with fewer is done in vain with more."

However, although the interobjective quadrant can be reduced to simply the objective domain, I hasten to add that the intersubjective domain cannot be reduced to the subjective realm. Although the evolution of consciousness and culture are intertwined, our understanding of intersubjectivity as a distinct realm of evolution is a critical component of the integral reality frame.

As we have shown throughout this book, integral philosophy is founded on the recognition of evolution within the clearly understandable and observable realms of nature, self, and culture. And these three essential kinds of evolutionary development are brought into focus through the philosophical categories of the objective, subjective, and intersubjective domains. These are the "Big Three" that have been recognized throughout history by a wide variety of prominent thinkers and visionaries. While we *can* recognize interobjective aspects of evolution in biology prior to the appearance of humans, and while our conception of this evolutionary category *can* be useful (especially when the role of artifacts is properly understood), the interobjective quadrant does not have a symmetrical ontological equivalence with the more fundamental and obvious categories of objective, subjective, and intersubjective evolution.

Nevertheless, it is easy to see how Wilber concluded that there is a distinct interobjective domain that does have a symmetrical equivalence with the objective, subjective, and intersubjective domains of evolution. However, when it comes to human sociocultural evolution, when we really examine Wilber's interobjective quadrant carefully, we find that it consists of a hierarchy of artifacts mixed together with the erroneous concept of social action systems. We can clearly see a biological body—its observation does not depend on the recognition of its internal consciousness. Yet if we try to observe a so-called "social system of action units," unless we also at the same time recognize the underlying values and relationships that activate these actions, the actions by themselves do not disclose a true non-artifactual system. Indeed, the heart of Parsons's original social action systems theory was the ends and values of the actors in the system. And as we have seen, values are not objective, but subjective and intersubjective structures. It thus bears repeating that by trying to honor and include the work of the social systems theorists, in his depiction of human social and cultural evolution Wilber has inadvertently committed the opposite of "subtle reductionism"; he has followed Luhmann in the mistake "subtle expansionism" by postulating a distinct interobjective realm of social action systems that were themselves the mistaken results of subtle reductionism in the first place.

Conclusion

Like any map, the quadrant model contains distortions and simplifications; but these problems do not render it completely invalid. Like just about every aspect of integral philosophy, Wilber's four-quadrant map is true but partial. Even after we have corrected the mistaken assertion that in the noosphere "all holons have four quadrants," the quadrant model remains an important conceptual framework for understanding the inside and the outside of the individual and collective aspects of evolution. However, as integral philosophy evolves and begins to occupy a larger position in the marketplace of ideas, we need to better understand the limitations and weaknesses of this important model, so that overreliance on it does not undermine the credibility of integral philosophy as a whole. This is why, throughout this book, I've corrected this oversight by Wilber and have described the integral reality frame as consisting of the "Big Three" (not four) domains of nature, self, and culture. As recognized by some of the world's greatest thinkers and theorists, these are the *three* evident and essential realms in which all evolutionary activity takes place.

Part 1 Quotation References

Chapter 2

"quasi-religious commitment to the metaphysical principles of scientific materialism" David Lorimer, in: "The Need for a Noetic Revolution," review of Alan Wallace's *The Taboo of Subjectivity*, in *Journal of Consciousness Studies* 9, No. 12, 2002, pp. 89–91; *"The being who is the object of his own reflection, in consequence of that very doubling back upon himself, ..."* Teilhard de Chardin, *The Phenomenon of Man*, page 165, combined quote from Barlow, *Evolution Extended*, p. 151; *"sat behind a million eyes and told them what they saw"* David Bowie, lyric from "Song for Bob Dylan," on the album *Hunky Dory* (Virgin Records 1971); *"Scientific evidence of the patterns traced by evolution in the physical universe ..."* Laszlo, *Evolution: The Grand Synthesis*, p. 5.

Chapter 3

"... tells a story of increase, or greater complexity ..." Kegan, *In Over Our Heads*, p. 229; *"Each successive stage, wave, or level of existence ..."* Graves, from the article: "Summary Statement: The Emergent, Cyclical, Double Helix Model of the Adult Biopsychosocial System," Boston, May 20, 1981; *"Belonging to a group and being identified with it are the benchmarks for achieving a conformist orientation ..."* Loevinger and Wessler, *Measuring Ego Development*, pp. 57–58; *"Achievement orientation allows a person to conceptualize plans from a vantage point ..."* Wade, *Changes of Mind*, p. 136; *"[T]ransforming our epistemologies, liberating ourselves from that in which we were embedded ..."* Kegan, *In Over Our Heads*, p. 34; *"Put bluntly, the I and the WE were colonized by the IT ..."* Wilber, *The Marriage of Sense and Soul*, p. 56; *"If we don't like capitalism or consumerism, which are expressions ..."* Don Beck, quoted from the interview in *What Is Enlightenment?* magazine (fall/winter 2002) pp. 116–17; *"The spiral is messy, not symmetrical, with multiple admixtures rather than pure types. These are mosaics, meshes and blends"* Don Beck, quoted in Wilber, *A Theory of Everything*, p. 7; *"the battle*

has to be fought anew with every birth" Wilber, *Sex, Ecology, Spirituality,* p. 168; *"there is no structure which lacks a development ..."* Gardner, *The Quest for Mind,* pp. 187–88, quoted in (with the word "development" substituted for Piaget's word "genesis"): Wilber, *Sex, Ecology, Spirituality,* p. 83.

Chapter 4

"... simply asserting that we should all learn a worldcentric ecology ..." Wilber, Excerpt D, Part IV, part 2 of *The Kosmos Trilogy,* published on: http://wilber.shambhala.com; *"Damn it all, a person has the right to be who he is!"* Graves, quoted in Beck and Cowan, *Spiral Dynamics,* p. 28; *"Where the formal-mind [modernist consciousness] establishes higher and creative relationships, vision-logic establishes networks of those relationships"* Wilber, *"Eye to Eye,"* p. 288, quoted in *Ken Wilber in Dialogue,* p. 287; *"the capacity to see conflict ..."* Kegan, *In Over Our Heads,* p. 351; *"the officially and legally sanctioned philosophy prevailing in universities and academies, and dominating philosophical and scientific discourse and textbooks"* Israel, *Radical Enlightenment,* p. 16; *"It was unquestionably the rise of powerful new philosophical systems ..."* Israel, *Radical Enlightenment,* p. 14; *"a senescent structure of pedagogical dogmatism that no longer spoke to the new spirit of the age. Little or nothing fresh was emerging from its confines"* Tarnas, *The Passion of the Western Mind,* p. 299; *"the Cartesian critical intellect has reached its furthest point of development, doubting all ..."* Tarnas, *The Passion of the Western Mind,* p. 400; *"new movement in the symphony of human history"* Clare Graves, in the article *"Human Nature Prepares for a Momentous Leap,"* in *The Futurist,* pp. 72-87 (World Futurist Society, April 1974).

Chapter 5

"To be effective, global markets demand global governance" Stewart, *Evolution's Arrow,* p. 284; *"Can it be believed that the democracy which has overthrown the feudal system and vanquished kings will retreat before tradesmen and capitalists?"* Alexis de Tocqueville, quoted by Marjorie Kelly in a 4/19/02 interview by Robert Hinkley on the Common Dreams website, http://www.commondreams.org/views02/0419-09.htm; *"Man's capacity for justice makes democracy possible; but man's inclination to injustice makes democracy necessary"* Niebuhr, *The Children of Light and the Children of Darkness,* p. xiii.

Chapter 6

"human beings must be known to be loved ..." Blaise Pascal; *"to turn our attention to the fruits of the religious condition, no matter in what way they have been produced"* James, *The Varieties of Religious Experience*, p. 218; *"making effective use of thought while at the same time discounting the spiritual serviceability of all thinking"* *The Urantia Book*, p. 1121; *"Truth, goodness, and beauty form a triad of terms which have been discussed together throughout the tradition of Western thought ..."* M. Adler *The Great Ideas: A Syntopicon of Great Books of the Western World* (Encyclopedia Britannica Publishers, 1980), vol. 2, p. 275; *"these three ways, combined and followed concurrently, have a most powerful effect"* Aurobindo, *The Future Evolution of Man*, p. 16; *"cosmic support for truth, beauty, and goodness"* and *"The eternal forms are the material of the divine persuasion ..."* Griffin, *Religion and Scientific Naturalism*, p. 293; *"the urge towards the realization of ideal perfection"* Whitehead, *Adventures of Ideas* p. 275; *"You take hydrogen gas, and you leave it alone, and it turns into rosebushes, giraffes, and humans.... The point is that if humans are spiritual, then hydrogen's spiritual"* Brian Swimme, from an interview with *What Is Enlightenment?* magazine, issue 19 (spring/summer 2001) p. 40; *"a meta-religious contribution that can enrich ... the full diversity of religious expression ... [an] over-arching narrative that includes and uplifts all sacred stories"* Thomas Berry, quoted on the website: http://www.thegreatstory. org/metareligious.html.

Part II Endnotes

Chapter 7

1.   Solomon & Higgins, *A Short History of Philosophy*, p. 217.

2.   Tarnas, *The Passion of the Western Mind*, p. 380.

3.   Ibid., p. 381.

4.   Ibid., pp. 382–83.

5.   From Charles Darwin's personal correspondence. Quoted at http://www.ucmp.berkeley.edu/history/lamarck.html.

6.   Spencer, *First Principles*, p. 216.

7.   Mullarkey, *Bergson and Philosophy*, p. 67.

8.   Copleston, *A History of Philosophy*, vol. IX, p. 214.

9.   Magee, *The Story of Thought*, p. 214.

10. Bergson, *Creative Evolution*, p. 186.

11. Solomon and Higgins, *A Short History of Philosophy*, p. 266.

12. Griffin, *Religion and Scientific Naturalism*, p. 9.

13. Ibid., p. 297.

14. Kane & Phillips, eds. *Hartshorne, Process Philosophy, and Theology*, p. 6.

15. Birx, *Pierre Teilhard de Chardin's Philosophy of Evolution*, p. 86.

16. Teilhard de Chardin, *The Vision of the Past*, p. 167.

17. Teilhard de Chardin, *The Future of Man*, p. 174.

18. Gebser, *The Ever-Present Origin*, p. 42.

19. Ibid., p. 409.

20. Combs, *The Radiance of Being*, p. 102.

21. Gebser, *The Ever-Present Origin*, p. xxix.

22. Pandit, *Sri Aurobindo*, p. 19.

23. See Johnston, *Pitirim A. Sorokin: An Intellectual Biography*.

24. Wilber, *Sex, Ecology, Spirituality*, p. 124.

25. Habermas, *The Philosophical Discourse of Modernity*, pp. 313–14.

26. Wilber, *A Theory of Everything*, p. 38.

Chapter 8

1. See Whitehead, *Science and the Modern World*, chapter 3, especially pp. 75 and 77. According to Whitehead scholar, A. H. Johnson, "In criticizing the work of previous thinkers, Whitehead points to a persistent tendency on the part of many to perpetrate the Fallacy of Misplaced Concreteness. This, as the title indicates, consists in mistaking the abstract for the concrete." Johnson, A. H., *Whitehead's Theory of Reality*, p. 150. This can be applied to materialism's regard for sensations of matter, which may seem to be concrete, but which are actually just as abstract as subjective thoughts themselves.

2. From Thomas McCarthy's introduction to Habermas, *The Philosophical Discourse of Modernity*, p. viii.

3. As an example of the connection between developments in postmodern philosophy and the rise of postmodern culture, Howard Gardner cites the famous student protests that occurred in Paris during 1968. According to Gardner, these uprisings were directly tied to a rejection of modernist social science. "'Structuralism is dead' cried the students: whether or not they had ever read a word of Lacan or Levi-Strauss, they sensed a tie between the philosophy of these men and the establishment that they had come to despise." See Gardner, *The Quest for Mind: Piaget, Levi-Strauss, and the Structuralist Movement*, pp. 213–15.

4. From Thomas McCarthy's introduction to Habermas, *The Philosophical Discourse of Modernity*, p. xvii.

5.　Tarnas, *The Passion of the Western Mind*, p. 353.

6.　From the article on "Metaphysics" in *The Encyclopædia Britannica*, 2005. Encyclopædia Britannica Premium Service: http://www.britannica.com/eb/article?tocId=15984.

7.　Wilber, *Sex, Ecology, Spirituality*, p. 6.

8.　Wilber, "Excerpt D," from vol. 2, part I, of *The Kosmos Trilogy*, published on: http://wilber.shambhala.com.

9.　This insight about the contrasting "myths" of "the Given" and "the Framework" is explored further in Jorge N. Ferrer's recent book *Revisioning Transpersonal Theory*.

10.　Wilber, *Integral Spirituality*, p. 238.

11.　Wilber, "*Excerpt A*," note 26, from vol. 2 of *The Kosmos Trilogy*, published on: http://wilber.shambhala.com.

12.　Wilber, *Sex, Ecology, Spirituality*, p. 125.

13.　Ibid., p. 197.

14.　Wilber, *A Theory of Everything*, p. xiii.

15.　Wilber, *The Marriage of Sense and Soul*, pp. 74–75.

16.　Wilber, *Integral Spirituality*, p. 33.

17.　This passage by Wilber is quoted in Daryl Paulson's book review of *Revisioning Transpersonal Theory*, by Jorge N. Ferrer, which is published on: http://wilber.shambhala.com. Curiously, in this book review Paulson uses quite a few quotes from Wilber, and he provides citations for all of them except this one. But given the fact that the review is published on Wilber's official website, I suppose we can rely on the accuracy of this quotation.

18.　Wilber, *Integral Spirituality*, p. 246.

19.　Barbour, *Religion and Science, Historical and Contemporary Issues*, p. 152.

Chapter 9

1.　Broughton and Freeman-Moir, eds, *The Cognitive Developmental Psychology of James Mark Baldwin*, p. 213.

2. Graves's references to Piaget can be found in *The Bibliography in Support of Existence of Qualitatively Different Neurological Systems* compiled by Clare Graves, and found on http://www.clarewgraves.com/source.html.

3. Kegan, *In Over Our Heads*, p. 35.

4. Gardner, *Intelligence Reframed*, p. 14.

5. Ibid., p. 44.

6. Ibid., p. 66.

7. Ibid., p. 77.

8. Wilber, "Excerpt D," Part II, p. 2., from vol. 2 of *The Kosmos Trilogy*, published on: http://wilber.shambhala.com.

9. Wilber, *Integral Spirituality*, p. 60.

10. Ibid., pp. 58–59.

11. Ibid., p. 64.

12. Wilber, "Excerpt D," part IV, p. 1., from vol. 2 of *The Kosmos Trilogy*, published on: http://wilber.shambhala.com.

13. Ibid.

14. Ibid., p. 2.

15. Wilber, *Integral Psychology*, p. 37.

16. Ibid., p. 38.

17. Wilber, *Sex, Ecology, Spirituality*, p. 40.

18. Ibid., p. 76.

19. Gardner, *Intelligence Reframed*, p. 32.

20. Ibid., p. 206.

21. Kegan, *In Over Our Heads*, p. 363.

22. Wilber, *Integral Spirituality*, p. 60.

23. Ibid, p. 66.

24. Goleman, *Emotional Intelligence*, pp. 8–9.

25. For example, Abraham Maslow is famous for his "hierarchy of needs"

theory. And in the seminal work in which he introduces this influential theory he writes: "The gratification of any such need is a 'value.'" Maslow, *Motivation and Personality*, p. 6.

26. Gardner, *Intelligence Reframed*, p. 77.

27. Goleman, *Emotional Intelligence*, p. 285.

28. Maslow, *Motivation and Personality*, p. 162.

29. One example of how the will develops as the spiral is ascended can be seen in the way that groups containing large degrees warrior consciousness are often more vulnerable to becoming addicted to alcohol and drugs than groups with less warrior consciousness. Warrior consciousness' egocentrism is often locked in the moment, unable to resist self-gratification or to consider the future consequences of the pleasures of the present. However, as will develops in the higher stages, the dangers of addiction become easier to resist for most.

30. Combs, *The Radiance of Being*, p. 8. With regard to his statements about mentality being strictly intentional, Combs adds that he does believe freedom from intention can be cultivated in consciousness through meditation.

31. Visser, *Ken Wilber: Thought as Passion*, p. 279.

32. Baldwin, *Genetic Theory of Reality*, p. 188. In connection with the notion of "modes of consciousness" introduced by Baldwin, I should point out that Wilber's writing has come close to the idea that feeling, thought, and will are the "modes of consciousness." On page 1 of *Integral Psychology*, Wilber states that "the modes of consciousness are aesthetics, science, and morality." This relates to his earlier writing about the value spheres of culture, wherein he approvingly discusses Max Weber's conception of the "value spheres" of aesthetics, science, and morality. Wilber, however, does not elaborate about what he means by "modes" as a term of art. Moreover, he certainly does not mention these modes as any kind of essential organizing structures in consciousness in his latest writing, which focuses on the explication of his psychograph model and its corollary in the sociograph discussed in note 34, below.

33. Figure 9-4 is presented for the limited purposes of suggesting how

the intersubjective structure of the spiral of development influences a variety of aspects, spheres, or lines of development within the overall sphere of human volition. This simplified diagram is not intended as an exhaustive chart of all possible subspheres or lines of development within human consciousness. Moreover, the positioning and relative relationships among the various subspheres represented in this diagram are not intended to be descriptions of how these subspheres relate to each other or otherwise overlap. Further, as with Wilber's psychograph model, the relative size of each line or sphere of development will vary with the profile of each individual. In other words, please do not take this diagram too literally, it is only intended to illustrate a single point, and is, of course, constrained by the need for graphical simplicity.

34.   In his discussion of the psychograph model in his recent writing, Wilber says that the independent lines of the psychograph find a parallel in a similar analysis of developmental lines within culture, which he calls a "sociograph." And as we will discuss in chapter 10, the model of consciousness that recognizes feeling, thought, and will as the primary spheres of development likewise has a social parallel that recognizes aesthetics, science, and morality as the primary spheres of cultural development.

35.   See Goleman, *Emotional Intelligence,* chapter 16, "Schooling the Emotions," pp. 261–87.

36.   Wilber, *Integral Psychology,* p. 34.

Chapter 10

1.   Wallace, *Darwinism: An Exposition of the Theory of Natural Selection with Some of its Applications,* pp. 476–77.

2.   Whitehead, *Process and Reality,* p. 21.

3.   Wilson, *Consilience, the Unity of Knowledge,* p. 107.

4.   Jantsch, *The Self-Organizing Universe,* p. 75.

5.   Laszlo, *The Systems View of the World,* p. 44.

6.   Whitehead, *Process and Reality,* P. 32.

7.   Evidence of Teilhard's recognition of the interpenetrating forces of unity and complexity can be found in his discussion of the "laws of evolution" found in *Science and Christ*, pp. 29–30, wherein he describes the "law on which reality is built up, an hierarchical law of increasing complexity in unity." Similarly, in *The Phenomenon of Man*, p. 262, he describes the "law of union": "In any domain—whether it be the cells of a body, the members of a society or the elements of a spiritual synthesis—*union differentiates*. ... the only fashion in which we could correctly express the final state of a world undergoing psychical concentration would be a system whose unity coincides with a paroxysm of harmonized complexity."

8.   Swimme and Berry, *The Universe Story*, p. 71.

9.   Here I need to acknowledge a discrepancy between Swimme and Berry's description of the threefold process of evolutionary development and the description of this process set out in our previous discussion of holonic *agency* and *communion* and holarchic *eros* and *agape* (and which I elaborate further in the upcoming section entitled "The Dialectical Quality of the Master Patterns of Evolution"). The difference between us is that, in my view, differentiation or complexification is best understood as a kind of "reaching out," a "pull on the circumference," that contrasts with the complementary yet antithetical trend of increasing integration, which can be seen as a kind of "pull from the center." The evolutionary process of complexification can thus be most directly associated with the reaching out of holonic communion and the reaching up of holarchic eros. Conversely, Swimme and Berry contrast their description of evolution's complexification with what they call "communion." Although their idea of evolutionary "communion" is said to be synonymous with "internal relatedness," it is also said to be synonymous with "interconnectivity and affiliation." Thus, in Swimme and Berry's description of evolution's master patterns, the essential process of unifying integration *from within* is not adequately accounted for. Nevertheless, we do agree that evolution evinces a threefold pattern, and we do agree that increasing differentiation, communion, and consciousness are indeed some of its most significant trends. I, however, see increasing unification as the third essential element (with differentiation and communion

seen as different aspects of the same "reaching out" process), and in this I have the support of most accepted definitions of evolution, which recognize that development proceeds through the interpenetration of the forces of differentiation and integration. Perhaps the discrepancy in our respective descriptions can be accounted for by the evident self-similarity of these patterns of development—as we noted earlier in this chapter, the patterns of development can be seen operating both "within the levels and across the levels." However, to their credit, Swimme and Berry do say that their description of the Cosmogenetic Principle will be "undoubtedly deepened and altered in the next era as future experience expands our present understanding." And this is exactly what I have attempted to do in this chapter.

10. Wright, *Non-Zero: The Logic of Human Destiny,* p. 17.

11. Stewart, *Evolution's Arrow,* back cover.

12. Whitehead, *The Aims of Education,* p. 39. As we consider these overlapping spheres that are being used to represent the Cosmogenetic Principle in each domain, it is worth recalling that just as the spheres of feeling, thought, and will contain multiple sublines, we can also recognize similar sublines of constituent elements within each of the spheres in the other quadrants.

13. Sorokin, "Integralism is My Philosophy," in Whit Burnett ed., *This Is My Philosophy,* (Harper and Brothers, 1957), p. 184; quoted in Johnston, *Pitirim A. Sorokin: An Intellectual Biography.*

14. Quoted from Hegel, *The Phenomenology of Spirit,* preface, pp. 1–45, in Kaufman, *Hegel: Reinterpretation, Texts and Commentary* (New York: Doubleday, 1965), p. 448. Quote originally found in Finocchiaro, *Gramsci and the History of Dialectical Thought* (Cambridge University Press, 1988), p. 198.

15. Whitehead, *Adventures of Ideas,* p. 11.

16. Griffin, *Religion and Scientific Naturalism,* p. 294.

17. I heard Dr. Margolis make this statement at a scholarly conference on evolution and religion held at the Claremont Graduate School of Theology, in October 2004. I do not know if this idea has been articulated in any of Dr. Margolis's many books, but the profundity

of this simple statement was not lost on the conference participants.

18. Darwin, *The Descent of Man*, p. 400. Quoted in Griffin, *Religion and Scientific Naturalism*, p. 268.

Appendix A

1. See, e.g., Glossop, *World Federation?*; Adler, *Haves without Have-Nots;* Tetalman and Belitsos, *One World Democracy;* Stewart, *Evolution's Arrow.*

2. See Joseph Preston Baratta's essay, "The World Federalist Movement: A Short History," in Tetalman and Belitsos, *One World Democracy*, pp. 224–38.

Appendix B

1. Wilber, *Sex, Ecology, Spirituality*, p. 197.

2. Kofman, *Holons, Heaps, and Artifacts*, 2001. Published at http://www.integralworld.net.

3. Wilber, "Excerpt D," part IV, page 3, vol. 2 of *The Kosmos Trilogy*. Quoted paragraph ends with note 52. Published at http://wilber.shambhala.com.

4. Wilber, *Integral Spirituality*, p. 172.

5. Wilber, "Excerpt D," part IV, page 3, vol. 2 of *The Kosmos Trilogy*. Published at http://wilber.shambhala.com.

6. Wilber, *On Critics, Integral Institute, My Recent Writing, and Other Matters of Little Consequence: A Shambhala Interview with Ken Wilber.* Published at http://wilber.shambhala.com.

7. Wilber, *Integral Spirituality*, p. 170.

8. Bausch, *Emerging Consensus in Social Systems Theory*, p. 336.

9. Ibid., p. 88.

Selected Bibliography

Adler, M. *Haves without Have-Nots* (Macmillian, 1991).

Aurobindo, G. *The Future Evolution of Man: The Divine Life upon Earth* (Quest Books, 1974).

———. *The Life Divine* (Lotus Press, 1985).

Baldwin, J. M. *Genetic Theory of Reality* (G. P. Putnam's Sons, 1915).

Barbour, I. *Religion and Science: Historical and Contemporary Issues* (HarperCollins, 1997).

Barlow, C., ed. *Evolution Extended: Biological Debates on the Meaning of Life* (MIT Press, 1994).

Bausch, K. C. *The Emerging Consensus in Social Systems Theory* (Kluwer Academic/Plenum Publishers, 2001).

Beck, D., and C. Cowan. *Spiral Dynamics: Mastering Values, Leadership and Change* (Blackwell, 1996).

Bergson, H. *Creative Evolution* (Macmillan, 1928).

Birx, J. *Pierre Teilhard de Chardin's Philosophy of Evolution* (Charles C. Thomas, 1971).

Broughton J., and D.J. Freeman-Moir, eds. *The Cognitive Developmental Psychology of James Mark Baldwin* (Ablex Publishing, 1982).

Combs, A. *The Radiance of Being* (Paragon House, 2002).

Copleston, F. *A History of Philosophy* (Newman Press, 1975).

Darwin, C. *The Descent of Man,* vol. II (London: John Murray, 1871).

Ferrer, J. *Revisioning Transpersonal Theory* (SUNY Press, 2002).

Feuerstein, G. *Structures of Consciousness: The Genius of Jean Gebser, an Introduction and Critique* (Integral Publishing, 1987).

Gardner, H. *The Quest for Mind: Piaget, Levi-Strauss, and the Structuralist Movement* (Alfred A. Knopf, 1973).

―――. *Intelligence Reframed* (Basic Books, 1999).

Gebser, J. *The Ever-Present Origin* (Ohio University Press, 1985).

Glossop, R. *World Federation?* (McFarland & Co, 1993).

Goleman, D. *Emotional Intelligence* (Bantam Books, 1995).

Griffin, D. R. *Religion and Scientific Naturalism: Overcoming the Conflicts* (SUNY Press, 2000).

Habermas, J. *The Philosophical Discourse of Modernity* (MIT Press, 1987).

Haught, J. *Deeper than Darwin: The Prospect for Religion in the Age of Evolution* (Westview Press, 2003).

Hegel, G. W. F. *The Phenomenology of Spirit* (Oxford University Press, 1979).

Hunter, J. D. and Wolfe, A. *Is There a Culture War?* (Pew Research Center, 2006).

Inglehart, R. *Human Values and Social Change* (Brill, 2003).

Israel, J. *Radical Enlightenment: Philosophy and the Making of Modernity, 1650–1750* (Oxford University Press, 2001).

James, W. *The Varieties of Religious Experience* (Adamant Media, 2000).

Jantsch, E. *The Self-Organizing Universe* (Pergamon Press, 1980).

Johnston, B. *Pitirim A. Sorokin: An Intellectual Biography* (University Press of Kansas, 1995).

Kane, R., and S. Phillips, eds. *Hartshorne, Process Philosophy, and Theology* (SUNY Press, 1989).

Kegan, R. *In Over Our Heads* (Harvard University Press, 1994).

Laszlo, E. *Evolution: The Grand Synthesis* (Shambhala, 1987).

———. *The Systems View of the World* (Hampton Press, 1996).

Loevinger, J., and R. Wessler, *Measuring Ego Development* (Jossey-Bass, 1970).

Magee, B. *The Story of Thought* (Dorling Kindersley, 1998).

Maslow, A. *Motivation and Personality* (Harper Collins, 1987).

Mullarkey, J. *Bergson and Philosophy* (University of Notre Dame Press, 1999).

Niebuhr, R. *The Children of Light and the Children of Darkness: A Vindication of Democracy and a Critique of Its Traditional Defense* (Scribner's Sons, 1960).

Norwine, J. and Smith, J. M., eds. *Worldview Flux* (Lexington, 2000).

Pandit, M. P. *Sri Aurobindo* (New Dehli: Munshiram Manoharlal Publishers, 1998).

Ray, P., and S. Anderson. *The Cultural Creatives: How 50 Million People are Changing the World* (Harmony Books, 2000).

Rothberg, D., and S. Kelly, eds. *Ken Wilber in Dialogue: Conversations with Leading Transpersonal Thinkers* (Quest Books, 1998).

Solomon, R., and K. Higgins, *A Short History of Philosophy* (Oxford University Press, 1996).

Spencer, H. *First Principles,* 1st ed. London: Williams and Norgate, 1863).

Stewart, J. *Evolution's Arrow* (Chapman Press, 2000).

Swimme, B., and T. Berry. *The Universe Story* (HarperSanFrancisco, 1992).

Tarnas, R. *The Passion of the Western Mind* (Ballantine, 1991).

Teilhard de Chardin, P. *The Phenomenon of Man* (Harper & Row, 1955).

———. *The Future of Man* (Harper & Row, 1964).

———. *Science and Christ* (Harper & Row, 1965).

———. *The Vision of the Past* (Harper & Row, 1966).

Tetalman, J., and B. Belitsos, *One World Democracy* (Origin Press, 2005).

Urantia Foundation. *The Urantia Book* (Urantia Foundation, 1955).

Visser, F. *Ken Wilber: Thought as Passion* (SUNY Press, 2003).

Wade, J. *Changes of Mind: A Holonomic Theory of the Evolution of Consciousness* (SUNY Press, 1996).

Wallace, A. R. *Darwinism: An Exposition of the Theory of Natural Selection with Some of Its Applications* (London: Macmillan, 1923).

Whitehead, A. N. *Science and the Modern World* (Macmillan, 1925).

———. *The Aims of Education* (Mentor Books, 1929).

———. *Adventures of Ideas* (Macmillan, 1933).

———. *Process and Reality* (Free Press, 1978).

Wilber, K. *Eye to Eye: The Quest for the New Paradigm,* rev. ed. (Shambhala, 1990).

———. *Sex, Ecology, Spirituality* (Shambhala, 1995).

———. *The Marriage of Sense and Soul* (Random House, 1998).

———. *Integral Psychology* (Shambhala, 1999).

———. *A Theory of Everything* (Shambhala, 2000).

———. *Integral Spirituality* (Integral Books/Shambhala, 2006).

Wilson, E. O. *Consilience: The Unity of Knowledge* (Vintage, 1998).

Wright, R. *Nonzero: The Logic of Human Destiny* (Pantheon, 2000).

Index